OXCART CATHOLICISM ON FIFTH AVENUE

Notre Dame Studies in American Catholicism

Sponsored by the
Charles and Margaret Hall Cushwa Center
for the Study of American Catholicism

The Brownson-Hecker Correspondence
Joseph Grower and Richard Leliaert, editors

The Survival of American Innocence:
Catholicism in an Era of Disillusionment, 1920–1940
William M. Halsey

Faith and Fatherland: The Polish Church War in Wisconsin, 1896–1918
Anthony J. Kuzniewski

Chicago's Catholics: The Evolution of an American Identity
Charles Shanabruch

A Priest in Public Service: Francis J. Haas and the New Deal
Thomas E. Blantz, C.S.C.

Corporation Sole: Cardinal Mundelein and Chicago Catholicism
Edward R. Kantowicz

The Household of Faith:
Roman Catholic Devotions in Mid-Nineteenth-Century America
Ann Taves

People, Priests, and Prelates:
Ecclesiastical Democracy and the Tensions of Trusteeism
Patrick W. Carey

The Grail Movement and American Catholicism, 1940–1975
Alden V. Brown

The Diocesan Seminary in the United States:
A History from the 1780s to the Present
Joseph M. White

Church and Age Unite:
The Modernist Impulse in American Catholicism
R. Scott Appleby

Oxcart Catholicism on Fifth Avenue

THE IMPACT OF THE PUERTO RICAN MIGRATION UPON THE ARCHDIOCESE OF NEW YORK

Ana María Díaz-Stevens

University of Notre Dame Press
Notre Dame London

Library of Congress Cataloging-in-Publication Data

Díaz-Stevens, Ana María, 1942–
Oxcart Catholicism on Fifth Avenue : the impact of the Puerto Rican migration upon the Archdiocese of New York / Ana María Díaz-Stevens.
p. cm.—(Notre Dame studies in American Catholicism)
Includes bibliographical references and index.
ISBN 0–268–01509–0 (alk. paper)
1. Puerto Rican Catholics—New York Region—History—20th century. 2. Catholic Church. Archdiocese of New York (N.Y.)—History—20th century. 3. Puerto Ricans—New York Region—Religion. 4. Immigrants—New York Region—Religious life. 5. New York Region— Church history. I. Title. II. Series.
BX1417.N4D53 1993
282′.7471′089687295—dc20 92–53747
CIP

∞ *The paper used in this publication meets the minimum requirements of the American National Standard for Information Sciences—Permanence of Paper for Printed Library Materials, ANSI Z39.48-1984*

ACKNOWLEDGEMENTS

No literary, artistic or scientific work is ever done in isolation. In the process of carrying out his or her creation, many are the persons to whom the writer, artist or scientist becomes indebted. This book is the product of many years of lived experiences and scientific endeavor, not only on my part but on that of many others who preceded me or who were my companions as it took form. I have dedicated my work to the many Puerto Rican migrants who since the beginning of this century have sought to make a place for themselves in the United States, far from their homeland and culture. To them my respect and appreciation as subject of my scholarly interest and object of my fraternal affection.

I must acknowledge the commitment of the Roman Catholic Archdiocese of New York, most especially in the dedicated work of so many local parish priests and religious personnel who ministered to the Puerto Rican community. I remember with appreciation the contributions of Robert L. Stern and Robert Fox as archdiocesan directors of the Spanish-speaking apostolate and I am also thankful to them for the personal help they gave me. Besides encouragement, Robert L. Stern made available to me first-hand information and primary documentation without which the task of completing this book would have been impossible. Robert Fox, despite his ill health, received me with kindness and openness, answering my many questions and giving me insights into his vision and accomplishments on behalf of the Spanish-speaking apostolate and the urban poor in the 1960s.

I want also to acknowledge the legacy of those intellectuals who have preceded me and who have tried to put our needs and the need for a response into perspective. To my friends at Fordham University and New York University who taught me the "tricks of the trade" and to those in the Puerto Rican community who encouraged me to write "our own story in the church of New York;" to Philip Gleason, who having seen the chapter on the historical background of the archdiocese, gave sound advice and criticism and the initial encouragement to enter the entire manuscript in the Cushwa competition; to Jay P. Dolan, Jaime Vidal and Dolores Fain at the Cushwa Center for all the information and help in the process of submitting the final version; and those unknown others—members of the evaluation committee—who read the manuscript and recommended my work for the Annual Cushwa Award on the Study of American Catholicism (1991), a heartfelt thank you.

Most of all I am grateful to the members of my extended and immediate family. To each and every one of you, my deep appreciation and gratitude, as to all the oxcart Catholics in my life. To Antonio, my husband, who spent sleepless nights helping me type and edit the final manuscript, and Adán Esteban, our Brooklynite *jibarito,* who has been so patient and loving during this whole process, my very special *gracias.*

Throughout this work the memory of two very special persons has been my faithful companion and has served as guiding light and constant reminder that something worth doing is worth doing well—my two beloved *jíbaros,* who in their wisdom gave me three precious gifts: life, a nurtured faith in the Creator and enduring love for the *Patria* God gave us as inheritance. To you *papá* Benito and *mamá* Felipa in deepest love and gratiutde I pledge my undying devotion and to your blessed memory I dedicate these pages.

CONTENTS

Con filial amor y veneración a aquellos que en su paso por la vida llevaron en las manos, callos; en la memoria, el aroma de las flores de su tierra tropical; en el corazón, la fe y el amor de Dios. A mis queridos padres, Felipa y Benito.

INTRODUCTION

As a little girl growing up in Puerto Rico the idea of ever leaving the mountains for the city seemed unnatural and unappealing. To leave Puerto Rico for another land was unthinkable; that was something other people did. By 1948, when I went to the first grade in a one-room schoolhouse three miles away from our farm, the exodus of the mountain people to the urban *barriadas* and to the great northern metropolis was well underway. Members of my extended and immediate family were caught in the exodus. By 1952, when Puerto Rican governor Luis Muñoz Marín proclaimed his Commonwealth constitution, two of my sisters—barely eighteen and seventeen years of age—had migrated to far off Brooklyn, to work in factories. Though distant, I was told they were still in the family, under the care of a maternal uncle who lived in the Northern city.

This was the destiny of many, despite the promises of Don Luis and his new political party, the Partido Popular Democrático. Among many *jíbaros* the much celebrated Operation Bootstrap had scant meaning: strapping up a boot meant little when many of the mountain dwellers went barefoot! During political campaigns, however, the marvelous deeds of the *populares,* along with the benevolence of the United States, were exalted in political slogans, poetry, and music heard everywhere in Puerto Rico. These sounds drowned the soft sobs and tears of thousands upon thousands of Puerto Ricans who made their way from the countryside to the airport in San Juan and from there to the Northeastern United States.

Despite my innocence and youth I remember noticing how houses were clamped up and farms abandoned as heavy machinery was brought in to clear out the wooded land. Our uncle's one-hundred acre farm, next to ours, which had produced quality coffee, was sold overnight to some sugar interest for three thousand dollars. Eventually our own small eighteen-acre plot was encircled by large tracts of land owned and operated by one or two influential families from out of town. Ours was one of the few remnants of large holdings belonging to the so-called old rural bourgeoisie. But the days were numbered; we had to make way for "progress and development."

"Mamá, en la finca que era de tío Gil ví una máquina de esas grandotas que llaman puercas y ya han tirado la mitad del monte" ("Mom, I saw heavy equipment in what used to be Uncle Gil's farm and already half of the wooded land has disappeared") was the exiting yet alarming news that one of my brothers brought back when he came from school one day. My mother, true to her enduring love for nature and her wise folk ways, responded: "¡Pobre tierra! El mundo está patas arriba, mi hijo. Esta gente no sabe lo que hace. Es bueno progresar pero esos aparatos nos van a comer el vivir. Nos tragan a nosotros y la tierra se nos va a morir" ("Poor land! The world is upside down, my son. These people do not know what they do. Progress is good but this type of machinery is going to do away with our very existence. They will swallow us alive and the land will refuse to go on living for us").

Soon there was more news about the neighboring farm, which had belonged to my grandfather and to his father before him. An army of workers was coming in to take down *el cafetal* and begin the planting of a new crop, sugarcane. In all the excitement most people failed to realize that the best lands of the *barrio* were owned by outside interests and that they were taking on a distinctive but unattractive new appearance.

When I was about eight years old, I remember one of my mother's *comadres* running sobbing to my mother. The woman told her that her eighteen-year-old-son, who had refused to work in the family's small farm, had just had an accident in the nearby sugarcane plantation. "He wanted to make money to go to *El Norte,*" she said. "He would not listen to his father and said that we should get rid of our land because all it is producing are headaches. We should do as Don Fulano, who took the family out of this hell hole. He says we should move to a civilized place. Look what his dream brought him, his index finger gone. Lame forever!" Days later I heard this woman speak again to my mother, but this time she was smiling. "Comadre," she said, "Dios según da la llaga da el remedio" ("The God that inflicts pain is also responsible for a cure"). It seemed as if the owner of the plantation had some minimal insurance for his workers and her son was going to be able to cash in on his unfortunate accident. Furthermore, he was planning to use the money to emigrate to the United States.

As time went on I remember a fear taking hold of me. Sucking on a sweet and refreshing piece of sugarcane was a favorite treat among Puerto Rican schoolchildren after a long day of school, especially when the road was long and water was not accessible. But the thought of inadvertently stepping over some poor worker's finger left on the ground after one of these no-longer-occasional accidents kept me thirsty. Part of my fear was also that somehow we would lose our eighteen acres to the sugar companies, become hired hands, and run the risk of physical dismemberment. Today I wonder how many of my compatriots made their trek North at the cost of a finger or other bodily injury.

Years later, when I was a college student in New York, a friend handed me a copy of *The Oxcart*, a play by René Marqués about the Puerto Rican migration. I will never forget that first impression. I was transported back to the eighteen acres my family had left unsold because, with the Puerto Rican poet Virgilio Dávila, my mother believed that "they who sell their land also sell their patrimony."

The fictional Doña Gabriela was my *mamá*, pure and simple. They shared the hope of a better future for their children and a secret dream of one day returning to their mountain home. But while Doña Gabriela ultimately held the promise of returning to her mountain town, my own mother's life-long dream of returning to that small corner of Puerto Rico where she was born and seen the birth of her nine children was not to be realized. Doña Gabriela's return is presaged by the death of her adopted son, who is mangled by the treacherous *máquina* in the great metropolis. Destiny's price is very high: his blood for her safe passage back to her roots. Unattainable for herself, my mother shared in the happiness of two of her children's return to Puerto Rico, and she nurtured in all of us the realization that *La Patria* is never too far away because it encompasses much more than a geographic boundary.

As to the other characters of Marqués's drama, I have seen them incarnated in the many people I have met and among whom

I have had the privilege of working in both islands, Puerto Rico and Manhattan. I have talked to them, listened to their stories, befriended, comforted, and cried with them. Every time I read *The Oxcart,* and every time I encounter persons like those portrayed there, my heart is wounded. I realize that just as the *comadre's* son was physically wounded in the sugar cane fields we, as a people, have been wounded even more deeply by a colonial situation. But in spite of the scars of our political reality, I am also renewed in the hope that one day, like Doña Gabriela, the profound realization of who we truly are and the promise of all that we can become will be ours. Like her, we will stand erect as the *asubo* tree of our native land, proud and strong among the other members of the human family and the peoples of this world, humble before God, who has given us the strength to endure so many struggles.

I have chosen *The Oxcart* to introduce the present socio-historical interpretation of the Puerto Rican migration vís-à-vís the Roman Catholic Church of New York. I have done so because despite the sociological and literary criticisms that may be leveled at the author of *The Oxcart,* I believe he captured the spirit of the mountain dweller. Among these people, like many of the migrants of the Great Migration, I also find my roots. Ours is a humble yet honorable origin.

The experiences of the three-stage migration portrayed in *The Oxcart* has been repeated time and time again, in part or whole, among our people. There are those who, like Don Chago, the grandfather, refuse to come no matter how dire the economic circumstances of the island home. Others, like Chaguito, lose their way en route. There are those who come seeking marvelous things, lured by technology and the promise of a better life, like Luis. And like Luis, they find themselves engulfed, swallowed, broken by the relentless *maquinaria* of the monstrous city. Like Paco, some attain a measure of socio-economic success and become upwardly mobile, but may in the process lose their *criollismo,* that flavor that made them uniquely Puerto Rican. Theirs is an insipid and isolated existence in the margins of two worlds, the one from which they are fleeing and the one that has as yet to embrace them. Others, like Juanita, leave the hinterland candid and innocent. They find pain and degradation, but ultimately gather strength from life's experiences and achieve transformation into better persons.

The oxcart that gives the play its title symbolizes a return to our cultural roots, to the values of the earth, and a holding on and nurturing of the faith our ancestors passed down to us. In my own personal life the oxcart has the singular significance of being a ray of hope on the horizon, a place of rest and unburdening. As a child, on those long journeys from school to my house, it was a welcome sight. It meant a ride back, at least part of the way.

I suppose the oxcart means many things to many people. It was a way of life. It carried goods and merchandise to and from *la carretera,* the paved road leading into town. On special days it carried the about-to-be married couple on their way to the church to receive the blessing from the parish priest; the child to be baptized or confirmed; the sick who needed more than a *curandera;* or one who had departed to a better life to the final resting place in the *camposanto.* At one time the oxcart had also brought the old priest who once a year preached a mission and extended the sacraments to those who ordinarily could not make it Sunday after Sunday to the church in the big town.

By the time I was of the age of reason, the old priest was too old to ride in the oxcart. Knowing my father had a *paso fino,* which only he rode, Padre Sambrano thought nothing of asking my father to meet him with his horse at the bridge Don Luis had constructed on behalf of the *populares* in my *barrio.* From there they would make their way up and down the mountain pathways, the priest on Rubio, as triumphant as Jesus entering Jerusalem on Palm Sunday, and my father by his side on foot making sure the horse behaved properly. Afterward the grateful priest would bless Rubio for being such a noble beast. I suppose he also thanked my father for having the good sense to own such a fine animal.

On one occasion of the priest's yearly visit, Maruca, the toothless midwife, who had been awaiting my father's return with my mother, exclaimed: "There comes *compadre* Benito Díaz, *el santo catequista,* and *el cura,* cassock up to his waist, riding the *paso fino.* One has to be a priest to ride that horse. Truth is we have made much progress. A few years back, religion used to come to us by oxcart; now in the finest of horses. Pity for Rubio, the way we are going. With so much progress, soon he too will be put to pasture. The *predicadores* and religion will then come to us motorized as will everything else." This Cassandra-like prophecy caught us unawares. Still, Maruca was as old as the hills, and age was venerated.

Indeed, Maruca's authority in certain matters was not to be questioned. Her success in midwifery had earned her the respect of many. Though her loyalty and love were with our little *barrio,* her good reputation had carried her name well beyond its boundaries. Her counsel was sought by neighboring midwives. From the municipality came requests for her to address nurses and interns on "the art of midwifery." And there she was always eager to give a helping hand, to share her skills and wisdom, to help bring forth new life and new hope. Knowing scarcely how to read and write, she was nonetheless consulted by the medical profession in cases of risk pregnancies and difficult childbirths. And in time, she was officially recognized and rewarded for her efforts and her generosity. On one of the thatched walls of her dirt-floor hut, two treasures were proudly displayed: a set of *Santos Reyes* (carved wood statues of the Magi) and the celebrated "*ploma*" (official diploma or certification as nurse and midwife) of which she was so proud.

This poor, toothless, wrinkled peasant woman inspired reverence and confidence. Besides, by reason of her profession she was every parent's *comadre* and every child's *madrina.* It was said that she was responsible for more baptisms than all of the priests who had served that municipality, as the custom was to baptize a child immediately after birth. Maruca claimed that since she was responsible for bringing them safely into this life, she also had the privilege of initiating their life as Christians. In fact, every child in our mountain town and many a parent as well bowed in her presence and asked for her blessing as she approached. Maruca Hernández, the humble midwife of Barrio Cerro Gordo in Moca, Puerto Rico, had the wisdom that only comes from seeing life and death at a very close range; no one disputed her claims. Indeed, in terms of our horse, Rubio, being replaced by technological advancement she was prophetic. He was put to pasture shortly thereafter when the rest of our family joined the migration trek of the 1950s to New York.

Religion in that mountain town of my childhood was part of daily life despite the fact that some of us saw the priest and visited the town church sparingly. The day would always begin with my mother opening up the windows and doors and proclaiming: "May God's grace enter upon this house and those therein and may it remain with us always." When we left home to help in the fields or to go to school, we always asked for a blessing from our parents.

The same was done upon returning. Passing a place marked with a cross, we knew someone had met an untimely death there; we said a quick prayer for the repose of that person's soul. And, upon entering a crossway, we remembered the agony of Jesus on the cross and the souls in purgatory. A statue or an icon of the Blessed Mother made the rounds to the dwellings of the mountain town, where it was kept overnight. There was a prayer to greet the statue and a prayer to take leave of it. We prayed the holy rosary promptly after sunset every night, and no one in the family was excused from this obligation. On special feast days like *la Candelaria,* or Candlemas day, each family prepared bonfires, which were set ablaze at sunset. The families got together to recite the rosary, sing hymns, and tell stories of bygone days. All Souls' Day was a time for pranks but also for prayer for the departed souls of relatives, friends, and neighbors. On the feast of St. John the Baptist, the patron saint of the island, everyone made a special effort to go to church and then to the closest town near the ocean to take the ritual baths. Oftentimes modesty only allowed walking, fully dressed, knee-high into the water and sprinkling the face and arms. People believed that because on that day Jesus was baptized in the River Jordan, all the waters, especially ocean waters, were blessed. There was a prayer for every hour of need: when you left the house, when you returned, when it rained too much, when it would not rain enough, for the living, for the dying, for the dead, to find a good husband, to straighten out the one you already had, to be blessed with a child, to stop having so many, and so on.

Holy Week was a time of penance. No one was allowed to sing, dance, shout, do unnecessary work, or make noise. It was a time of prayer and recollection. My father would bring out one of our most precious possessions, the old *Camino recto y seguro para subir al cielo,* an old prayer book yellowed with age and the tropical weather. He would read aloud to us all kinds of mysterious prayers about the passion of Jesus before our humble home altar of *santos de palos* and the imported Santa Teresita, which my grandmother had secured after her youngest son, missing in action in World War II, was found, wounded but alive.

My father had a reputation for being a good *rezador.* That coupled to the fact that he had a magnificent voice made him the most sought-after *cantador* as well. For Christmas *parrandas,* for the *rosarios de cruz* in May, for *bakinés* and *velorios* (child and adult wakes), my father was always present. People from neighboring towns would seek his services. He brought this reputation to the United States; it carried him into many Puerto Rican households on both sides of the Hudson River until age and cancer no longer allowed him to move his aching body. Perhaps that was the one thing he regretted most. In an interview in his eightieth birthday, he told a priest he missed being able to provide this service and that he hoped one day he would be well enough to continue his mission among his people.

Back in our hometown my father had inherited, by public acclamation, the post of catechist after my uncle's departure. He and my mother instilled in us the belief that we should pray at home when we could not go to church on Sundays and that each member of the family should at least go the one Sunday a month assigned to the sodality to which each one belonged. For the girls in the family, it meant inviting all the girls from the neighboring farms to sleep over (in a house barely big enough for an ten-member family). It also meant getting up before the crack of dawn, getting dressed in the white uniform of the *Congregación de Hijas de María,* walking miles to the paved road (crossing two streams of water on the way), and then boarding a *público,* in which we literally felt like we were packed in a can like sardines. This was a three to four hour expedition. If we were lucky some gallant young fellow would give up his only day of rest to take us in an oxcart to the public transportation. Our pale, youthful faces, were a perfect match for the white uniforms (the venerable curate frowned and even prohibited the use of "that worldly, almost satanical use of *esencias y colorines,*" that is, perfumes and make-up!). Upon arriving at church, everyone had to go to confession. The lines were interminable, and since church law at that time prohibited the consumption of water or any other food from the previous midnight on, many became dizzy and suffered fainting spells.

To be a churchgoer was indeed a very hard task. To be religious, however, was something else. This was expected; it was as natural as being a Puerto Rican mountain dweller. Everyone we knew was a Catholic. In my town there was no other religion practiced or believed, except for the exceptional occasion when someone consulted a *curandera* in case of emergency or when the doctor's medicine did not have the expected results. No one asked if a person was Catholic, only if he or she was religious. This meant, were you and your children baptized? If so, did you truly believe in the Creator and live as if your life depended on him? Did you pray and meet your obligations as a parent, a son, a neighbor?

As an employee of the Roman Catholic Archdiocese of New York, after my tenure with the Maryknoll Sisters of St. Dominic at Ossining, New York, and *La Congregación Dominica de Hermanas de Fátima* in Puerto Rico, I would pass by St. Patrick's Cathedral on my way to work. To this day I cannot make up my mind if I find the Cathedral on Fifth Avenue beautiful or simply awesome. I do know that more often than not I felt lost in its vastness. I also often wondered if the feeling would some day go away forever, but I can honestly say that it has not. The imposing St. Patrick's on New York's Fifth Avenue is a far cry from my village's *Nuestra Señora de la Monserrate,* just as downtown Manhattan, with its magnificent skyscrapers, its sophistication, and its hurried existence, is a far cry from my hometown of Moca in the northwestern plateau of Puerto Rico. And although at times I could almost hear the irreverent whisper, "You've come a long way, baby," deep in my heart I knew (and still know) that I cannot help preferring the hills to the skyscrapers, or the church of my youth to the cathedral of my adult life, or my native tongue, in which my most fervent prayers are always said, to the language of the metropolis, which is mostly reserved for professional purposes.

In *The Oxcart,* Juanita and Doña Gabriela went back to Puerto Rico and probably took with them the little model of the oxcart that Miguel, Juanita's boyfriend, had made for her, even if it had been knocked down a couple of times and was in need of repair. Juanita, no longer innocent but much wiser and stronger, had vowed that henceforth she would guide the oxcart of her life, taking charge of it at all times, returning to the land where she would give birth to a new and stronger generation. For the two million of us who have had to make a u-turn, however, the oxcart remains symbolic of our longing and our heritage. Our quest for empowerment and identity can no longer be limited by geographic constraints. Just as religion in the Puerto Rican highlands was lived fully in the absence of the institution, we have proven beyond the shadow of a doubt that *La Patria* can be lived outside of the island, for it is a way of life, not a place.

When masses of Puerto Rican left our mountain towns, especially during the period following the Second World War and ending with the end of the Muñoz era in 1964, we brought with us this *oxcart Catholicism.* What impact it had upon the New York Catholic church and what changes it itself encountered in the process of adaptation is the subject of the following study.

Despite some similarity in title, my book takes a different track than Robert Orsi's *The Madonna of 115th Street.* I did not set out to describe how Puerto Ricans adapted to life in New York City, a task Orsi addresses in his analysis of Italian-American Catholics. Instead, I focus upon the adaptations of the institutional church—Fifth Avenue—as it was encountered and challenged by the Puerto Rican way of practicing and projecting its own faith—oxcart Catholicism.

The first chapter of the book is dedicated to a brief demographic review of three periods of Puerto Rican migration from the beginning of century. The church as institution is defined and various analytical approaches are presented. Chapter 2 defines and traces the historical development of the religion of the Puerto Rican people. The concept of social distance is introduced as a means toward understanding the relationship of people to institution. In order to set the tone for the encounter of Puerto Rican Catholicism with that of New York, chapter 3 offers a historical summary of the growth and development of the Roman Catholic Church in New York from the level of village parishes to that of a centralized cosmopolitan entity. Chapter 4 gives details regarding the rise of the basement churches among Puerto Ricans, as well as the concept of the integrated parish and an archdiocesan office to coordinate the apostolate toward this group from an institutional perspective. The attempts of intellectuals to analyze the situation and offer guidelines for an appropriate response are presented in chapter 5, along with a summary of key persons responsible for this analysis. Chapter 6 outlines the work of Robert Fox, one of the coordinators of the archdiocesan office. The program "Summer in the City" is summarized as the office changes its focus from a chancery-based response to community-oriented programs. Chapters 7 and 8 describe the process of "deroutinization" of archdiocesan-sponsored programs under the leadership of Robert L. Stern and the ensuing conflictive situation leading to a fragmentation of the apostolate. Finally, in chapter 9, the concluding remarks include the presentation of a new sociological construct for an analysis of the processes detailed in the study.

I have attempted in the present volume to cast some light upon the encounter of Puerto Rican Catholicism with New York Catholicism through a sociological analysis that includes both sociology of religion and that of institutions and processes. Although a participant myself in some of these processes, I have tried to present the material and conduct the analysis in as objective a manner as the situation warrants. If inadvertently, in the process, I offend, this has not been my intention. I am grateful, as I know other Puerto Rican Catholics are, to the Archdiocese of New York and to the many priests, religious, and laity who at the archdiocesan, local parish, or the community level have spent personal and material resources to respond to our needs.

1. *The Stone and the Pitcher: Gospel Reality* vs. *Institutional Self-Interest*

Si el cántaro da en la piedra, ¿es malo para el cántaro o para la piedra?

If the pitcher is struck upon the stone, is it bad for the pitcher or the stone?

—Sancho to Quixote

More than a half-million Puerto Ricans left their tiny Caribbean island to come to New York City from 1946 until 1964. When one adds the children born to these migrants, which is what demographers do in such calculations, this means that nearly 40 percent of all Puerto Ricans in the world have come to New York and the northeastern United States (Bonilla and Campos, 133).

The eighteen-year period from 1946 to 1964 represents the Great Puerto Rican Migration, which has forever transformed the life of Puerto Rico's people. Few nations in the twentieth century have lost such a great percentage of their citizenry to the United States. Equal or larger numbers of European immigrants have come to the United States, but these do not represent the same high proportion of total population as the Puerto Rican experience (Jones, 12–13; Ehrlich et al., 8–13). For an island scarcely one hundred miles long and thirty-five miles wide to send away so many of the two million inhabitants of the period is a demographic wonder. The largest comparable migration was the exodus of 40 percent of Ireland's population during the potato famines of the nineteenth century. But Ireland lost its population at a time of natural disaster; Puerto Rico's migration was planned by its government as a part of a development plan called "Operation Bootstrap."

The transformation of the island witnessed not only the loss of a high percentage of its native population but rapid urbanization and industrialization. By 1960 Puerto Rico had become a mostly industrial society, although it had been largely rural and agricultural scarcely two decades before (Deitz, 240–81). Such rapid development has brought a series of problems to traditional culture and its values (Seda Bonilla) as well as attendant political tensions regarding the island's unique commonwealth status. Neither a state of the union nor an independent Latin American country, Puerto Rico is on that account generally considered a colony of the United States (see Bloomfield, 97–161). Yet if Puerto Rico is the poorest region under the Stars and Stripes (Bloomfield, 29–58 et passim; see Deitz, 297–310), it is nonetheless the most materially developed region of Latin America.

Puerto Rico's unique political relationship with the United States has meant that Puerto Ricans have been United States citizens since 1917, but without the right to vote in federal elections unless they leave Puerto Rico to reside in one of the fifty states. The Great Migration is peculiar in that Puerto Ricans were not foreigners upon their arrival, although few of them spoke English. Already possessing citizenship since 1917, they did not need passports to enter the United States, nor have their numbers been limited by quotas or other kinds of immigration laws. Moreover, migration to the United States is not permanent, because Puerto Ricans travel freely and frequently between the island and northern cities (Hernández Alvarez).

Figure 1 (Stevens-Arroyo and Díaz-Ramírez 1982, 201) shows the numbers of Puerto Ricans entering the United States in ten-year periods and interprets these cumulative numbers for yearly averages.[1] Migration to the United States did not begin with 1946, of course. Figure 1 suggests that migration to the United States steadily rose each decade in the twentieth century from a tiny trickle of a couple of hundred to a yearly average of 4,200 before the Great Depression. The troubled years of the 1930s witnessed a drop to fewer than 2,000 Puerto Ricans annually, but with the outbreak of the Second World War the average again rose to approximate the 4,200 yearly norm.

The Great Migration exploded this pattern. The yearly average increased nearly eight times over, to 34,165 persons a year for eighteen years. The ten years after the conclusion of the Great

Figure 1

Average Annual Net Migration Between Puerto Rico and the United States for the Great Migration (1946–1964) and Selected Periods

Years	Total Net Migration	Average per Year
1900–1909	2,000	200
1910–1919	11,000	1,100
1920–1929	42,000	4,200
1930–1939	18,000	1,800
1940–1945	24,129	4,121[1]
1946–1964	614,940	34,165
1965–1974	17,239	1,724
	to U.S.: 109,842	to U.S.: 21,968
	to Puerto Rico: 92,603	to Puerto Rico: 18,520

[1]The average net annual migration to the United States from 1900 to 1945 was 2,111.

Source: Harvey Perloff, *Puerto Rico's Economic Future* (Chicago: University of Chicago Press, 1950) and the Puerto Rico Planning Board. The averages and periodization are from Antonio M. Stevens-Arroyo.

Migration showed a pattern of back-and-forth migration (see Figure 1). There were five years of net migration into the United States, and five years of net return migration back to Puerto Rico. The numbers of people changing residence was five times higher than the pre-War norm. But as Figure 1 shows, the total net migration to the United States at the end of the period 1965–1974 (18,000) was at the same level as during the period 1930–39 (17,239), the peak years of United States economic depression.

These averages are helpful in comparing one period with another, but an examination of the yearly flow discloses that the Great Migration began by doubling the rate of 1945, peaked in 1953 at 74,603, and returned to approximately the 4,200 annual norm in 1964 (Figure 2). This pattern forms something very close to a bell curve. Figure 3 reproduces the annual numbers in graph form, including numbers since 1974.

Other scholars have produced excellent analyses of the migration phenomena—its causes and its demographic implications. I would like to focus upon the way such migratory patterns affected Puerto Ricans and the church of New York. The periodization I have offered elsewhere (Stevens-Arroyo and Díaz-Ramírez 1982) has also been repeated in the work of Dr. Clara Rodríguez (1989, 3–4), largely because it offers an opportunity to examine the interactive social patterns that accompanied the phases of Puerto Rican migration.

The period before 1946 may be called the Pioneer Migration. It is characterized by relatively absorbable numbers of migrants. Their associations included labor unions and self-help "brother hoods," which provided typical services to newcomers such as credit-unions, civic and neighborhood activities, and meeting places that provided both continuity with the homeland and orientation for city life (Sánchez-Korrol 1983; Vega). As will be seen, New York society, including the Catholic church, treated Puerto Ricans more or less as if they were European immigrants. Although there was a discernible racial perception of Puerto Ricans that forced many to live in East Harlem on the borders of the segregated African-American ghetto (see chapter 3), on the whole Puerto Ricans were treated as an ethnic group. Not surprisingly, they usually reacted socially in the same way.[2]

With the rapid entry of Puerto Ricans into New York City during the Great Migration, the previously existing associations and scattered Puerto Rican neighborhoods could no longer absorb the newcomers. Puerto Ricans overflowed from East Harlem eastward into the South Bronx, and—skipping over Black Harlem, which was also growing—expanded on to the Upper West Side of Manhattan. The inhabitants of the Lower East Side crossed over the Williamsburg Bridge into Brooklyn and from there into East New York, while the original Brooklyn population of the Red Hook section moved south and east into Sunset Park.[3]

Moreover, power-brokers like Robert Moses decided against building more low-cost housing, preferring to allow the Puerto Ricans to inhabit older apartment buildings (Caro; Jackson, 240–53 et passim). The overflow of Puerto Ricans into neighborhoods that previously belonged to middle-class ethnic Catholics meant that parishes that had been largely Irish or Italian were now rapidly losing their old line congregations. Hence, the Puerto Rican

Figure 2

Migration between Puerto Rico and the United States Mainland

Fiscal Year	Traveled to U.S. Mainland	Traveled to Puerto Rico	Net Migration to U.S. Mainland[1]
1920	19,142	15,003	4,139
1921	17,137	17,749	−612
1922	13,521	14,154	−633
1923	14,950	13,194	1,756
1924	17,777	14,057	3,720
1925	17,493	15,356	2,137
1926	22,010	16,389	5,621
1927	27,355	18,626	8,729
1928	27,916	21,772	6,144
1929	25,428	20,791	4,637
1930	26,010	20,434	5,576
1931	18,524	20,462	−1,938
1932	16,224	18,932	−2,708
1933	15,133	16,215	−1,082
1934	13,721	16,687	−2,966
1935	19,944	18,927	1,017
1936	24,145	20,697	3,448
1937	27,311	22,793	4,518
1938	25,884	23,522	2,362
1939	26,653	21,165	4,488
1940	24,932	23,924	1,008
1941	30,916	30,416	500
1942	29,480	28,552	928
1943	19,367	16,766	2,601
1944	27,586	19,498	8,088
1945	33,740	22,737	11,003
1946	70,618	45,997	24,621
1947	136,259	101,115	35,144
1948	132,523	104,492	28,031
1949	157,338	124,252	33,086
1950	170,727	136,572	34,155
1951	188,898	146,978	41,920
1952	258,884	197,226	61,658
1953	304,910	230,307	74,603
1954	303,007	258,798	44,209
1955	315,491	284,309	31,182
1956	380,950	319,303	61,647

1957	439,656	391,372	48,284
1958	467,987	442,031	25,956
1959	557,701	520,489	37,212
1960	666,756	643,014	23,742
1961	681,982	668,182	13,800
1962	807,549	796,186	11,363
1963	930,666	925,868	4,798
1964	1,076,403	1,072,037	4,366
1965	1,265,096	1,254,338	10,758
1966	1,475,228	1,445,139	30,089
1967	1,628,909	1,594,735	34,174
1968	1,858,151	1,839,470	18,681
1969	2,105,217	2,112,264	−7,047
1970	1,495,587	1,479,447	16,140
1971	1,566,723	1,605,414	−38,691
1972	—	—	−19,462
1973	1,780,192	1,799,071	−18,879
1974	1,622,001	1,630,525	−8,524

[1]A minus sign (−) denotes return migration.

Note: Figures from 1920 through 1969 are for total passenger traffic between Puerto Rico and all other destinations (U.S. mainland, Virgin Islands, and foreign nations), but the net migration figures accurately reflect migratory trends between Puerto Rico and the U.S. mainland.

Source: Data from Commonwealth of Puerto Rico Planning Board, published by Migration Division, Commonwealth of Puerto Rico, Department of Labor (Nov. 4, 1975).

Great Migration generated a negative meaning for some Catholics and spawned a sharper, less tolerant attitude toward the newcomers, who were perceived as the cause of the decline of the neighborhoods. The notion of an assimilable ethnic group gave way to that of an inassimilable racial group (Handlin; Padilla 1958, 61–81; Fitzpatrick 1971, 101–14). The drama of these changes inspired Leonard Bernstein and Stephen Sondheim in their musical *West Side Story,* which cast these racial antagonisms in the setting of the Romeo and Juliet tale circa 1950.

Secular Puerto Rican organizations during the Great Migration were largely voluntary, consisting of hometown social clubs

Figure 3

Migration from Puerto Rico, 1920–86

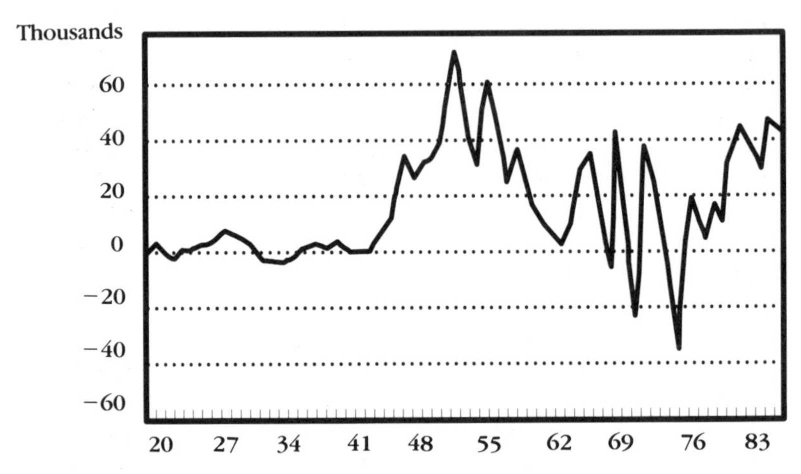

Sources: For data from 1920 to 1940: U.S. Commission on Civil Rights (1976). For data from 1940 to 1986: Junta de Planificación de Puerto Rico, Negociado de Análisis Econoómico, 1940–86.

(Stevens-Arroyo and Díaz-Ramírez 1982, 212–15). These clubs performed the social function of alleviating anomie, replacing the town and kinship structures that had characterized island society (Alers-Montalvo, 85–103). Religion also served a similar function, although there is a paucity of studies on its importance as a component of community stability.[4] Moreover, Catholicism had competition for Puerto Rican allegiance (Poblete). Protestantism and Pentecostalism drew converts from the Puerto Ricans in the city.[5] The chief social services agency for Puerto Ricans was the New York Office of the Commonwealth of Puerto Rico, which utilized the island government's funds to facilitate the settlement of Puerto Ricans in New York (Fitzpatrick 1971, 63–65). By the end of the period, however, a small number of Puerto Rican professionals, some of them children of the Pioneer Migration, had begun some instrumental organizations, dedicated to specific tasks of assisting Puerto Ricans in education and employment and responding to an agenda of cultural affirmation in the United States (Fitzpatrick 1971, 65–72; Stevens-Arroyo and Díaz-Ramírez 1982, 215–16; *infra* chapter 6).

Since 1964 migration has been characterized by an increasing preference for cities other than New York. In 1950 82 percent of Puerto Ricans lived in New York, but by 1982 the majority resided outside New York City (Rodríguez 1989, 4). The educational level of the migrant has steadily risen, so that a good proportion of migration from Puerto Rico today classifies as part of a "brain drain," taking highly qualified individuals away from their homeland (Bonilla and Campos, 151–55; Rodríguez 1989, 6, 97–98). Most striking has been the volatility of in-and-out migration, resulting in significant shifts toward and away from the United States in alternating patterns. I call this the Revolving Door Migration.[6] This period has been characterized by militancy, empowerment of Puerto Ricans in electoral politics, and a growing consciousness of a Latino identity. Unfortunately, these positive developments have been paralleled by a drastic disintegration of the city's industrial base and a general deterioration in the quality of life in New York (Rodríguez 1989, 110–15; Lankevich and Furer, 287–311).

Today, Puerto Ricans rank as the poorest and the most depressed of the major Latino groups in the United States. They rank below the Cubans and Mexican-Americans in virtually every category, despite the fact that they speak English better than either of the other two groups (Rodríguez 1989, 30–31). Given the success of Puerto Ricans in other areas of the country, this lack of progress seems attributable to the decline of New York and the northeastern United States, rather than to some cultural defect of Puerto Ricans (Rodríguez 1989, 42–45). Moreover, Puerto Ricans also rank below African-Americans in New York, so that if racism is an explanation for underachievement, Puerto Ricans would appear to suffer more from racism than blacks (Rodríguez 1989, 31–48). In sum, Puerto Ricans have not "made it" in the United States.

The Great Migration then, marks not only the failure of Puerto Ricans to achieve the so-called American dream, but also of the American dream to deliver its promise to Puerto Ricans. In search of the qualities that differentiate this migration from previous ones, an examination of the significance of the period is in order.

The year 1946 marked the first regularly scheduled commercial air flights between New York and San Juan. The short hours of travel at relatively little cost encouraged Puerto Ricans to migrate.

Psychologically, Puerto Ricans do not feel themselves as far from their homeland as the European immigrants, who took a long boat ride across the ocean, watching the homeland grow faint on the horizon and then awaiting the image of the Statue of Liberty near Ellis Island. Europeans returned home, of course, but this option was not as available to them as it was to the Puerto Ricans in the second half of the twentieth century (Saloutos in Greer). Puerto Ricans came to the New York in a matter of hours and could return as easily (Hernández Alvarez, 111–17). Once in New York the availability of a cultural tie through radio, cinema, phonograph records, and eventually, television also lessened the psychological perception of isolation of the immigrant in a foreign land. Thus, Puerto Ricans anticipated the contemporary immigration, which comes by airplane from all parts of the world to New York (Ehrlich et al., 311–61).

The year 1946 was also an important date in Puerto Rican political history. In that year Luis Muñoz Marín achieved the concession from Washington of the appointment of the first native Puerto Rican to govern his own land since the brief tenure of his father under the autonomy Charter of 1897 granted by Spain. Muñoz quickly engineered an election for the island's governorship, which took place in 1948. He occupied this post in four consecutive terms, until 1964. He secured the promulgation of Public Law 600 in 1950, and by 1952 had achieved the commonwealth status for his homeland by agreement with the government of the United States (Wells, 317–38).

Along with Muñoz's political hegemony, came his program for economic development: Operation Bootstrap (Dietz, 182–239). Centered upon attracting investment from the United States by way of exemption from federal income tax and a large labor force willing to work at low wages, the development plan was nonetheless unable to fulfill all the expectations for industrial jobs for the mountain peasants who abandoned agriculture (Centro, 58–90). This was the scenario for the massive immigration to New York. The wages in the big city were superior to those of the island, and the supremacy of the United States manufacturing economy in the years immediately after the Second World War meant that the factory production of New York could still find world markets. But as has been pointed out by other scholars, this opportunity was only temporary. Industrial manufacturing increasingly left the United States for places such as the Pacific Basin and Puerto Rico. The attractiveness of New York gradually diminished as manufacturing waned. This is the principal reason for the end of the Great Migration in 1964 (Centro, 133–44).

The end of the Great Migration saw the retirement of Muñoz Marín from the governorship and the emergence on the island of a new generation of technocrats. Thus the political scene, which had long held Muñoz at center stage, began to change. The migrants in New York were unlikely to be as familiar with the island's new leaders as they had been with the founder of the Popular Democratic Party.

In the United States President Lyndon B. Johnson launched the War on Poverty in 1964. One of its aims was to give political strength to the residents of urban ghettos by developing agencies of self-help. The amount of funding available for these programs was contingent upon representation of the underprivileged group in the administration of government money (Haveman, 241–83, passim). Thus, in the very year that the political landscape of Puerto Rico became unfamiliar to the Puerto Ricans in New York, new opportunities opened up in the city for greater political involvement. A new era had begun.

The next year, 1965, brought sweeping civil rights legislation. An amendment by New York's Senator Robert Kennedy to the Voting Rights Act eliminated the English language requirement for the registration of voters. This was to benefit greatly Puerto Rican political power. The twin effects of the War on Poverty, with its funding of neighborhood agencies, and the civil rights legislation identified the Puerto Ricans with African-Americans as minorities. Legislation favorable to minorities alleviated the racial stigma that had prevailed for Puerto Ricans during the Great Migration and substituted a sense of empowerment. In the process the categories of ethnicity and race were fused, so that Puerto Ricans were classified with blacks and whites as different races (Rodríguez 1989, 59–69). Subsequently, an era of militant racial affirmation was to transform the political structures of New York.

Finally, also in 1965, the revision of immigration laws tilted the influx of newcomers away from Europe. From the end of the Open Door Policy until 1965, immigration had been limited to a quota established on the basis of maintaining a proportion of ethnic distribution measured by the 1910 census (Ehrlich et al.,

65–70). President Johnson's promulgation of a new law altered this provision to allow immigration irrespective of established numbers. The result in New York was an increased Caribbean immigration (Sutton and Chaney, 56–83). The unrest in the Dominican Republic at the end of the dictatorship of Rafael Trujillo and the subsequent invasion by the United States in 1965 produced conditions for a substantial immigration from the Dominican Republic (Doyle et al., 2:106–8).

Together with the dispersion of Puerto Ricans to other cities of the northeastern region and other parts of the country, this Latin American migration lessened the Puerto Rican percentage of the total Spanish-speaking population in New York City. Nonetheless, although Puerto Ricans became only approximately 65 percent of the city's Spanish-speaking population in the 1980s (they had been 80 percent in the 1950s), the subsequent influx of Dominicans and other Spanish-speaking groups with lower educational attainment increased Puerto Rican political power. Because they were already citizens, Puerto Ricans acquired a role as spokespersons for a rapidly growing Spanish-speaking population.

These factors, with others that will be discussed below, combined to make the Puerto Rican Great Migration quite unlike most of the migrations New York City had experienced before 1946. The question examined in this book is how such a massive migration affected the Roman Catholic Church of New York. The majority of Catholics in the United States are descendants of previous immigrants, who came to this country from European homelands, and the Catholic church played a major role in the socio-cultural adaptations to life in the new homeland. Nonetheless, the role of the church in these adaptations varied from one group to another and from one diocese to the next. Although there are continuities in the migrations to the city, new dimensions of social, economic, and cultural changes have altered the structure of New York's institutions.

> Thus, the coming of the Puerto Ricans is not just a repetition of the past, because the past no longer exists, and no people exactly like the Puerto Ricans have ever come before. Any interpretation of the meaning of the migration in the perspective of earlier migrations must be related to the unique characteristics of the Puerto Rican people and of New York City in the third quarter of the twentieth century (Fitzpatrick 1971, 1).

While the role of the church in the integration of the immigrant has traditionally held center stage in socio-religious studies, I also have become increasingly more interested in what the Puerto Rican migration has meant to the church. The Office of Pastoral Research for the Archdiocese of New York reported that there were 1,693,335 Catholics in the archdiocese in 1980, with 1,326,946 of these living in Manhattan, the Bronx, and Staten Island. Hispanics, according to these statistics, constituted 47 percent of the Catholic residents in these three boroughs and 41 percent in the total archdiocese. Puerto Ricans constitute 63 percent of the Hispanic population of the three aforementioned boroughs and over 64 percent of all Hispanics in the geographical area corresponding to the Catholic Archdiocese of New York.[7] By these numbers, Puerto Ricans now comprise the largest single ethnic group in the city boroughs of the Archdiocese of New York. They are, in other words, the core of the city's "Catholic vote" today.

It seems to be in the institutional self-interest of the Catholic church to hold the loyalty of Puerto Ricans. Already in the 1960s this was readily accepted by students of the Puerto Rican reality.

> In a way, this left the Catholic Church with one of the most serious problems it had yet faced. . . . If the Puerto Rican mass should abandon Catholicism, or split on the issue, Catholics would shortly become a numerical as well as a political and cultural minority in the city (Glazer and Moynihan, lxix).

But although the need for New York Catholicism to include Puerto Ricans is simply stated, it is not so easily accomplished. Like most religions, the Catholic church is a combination of beliefs and practices based on faith and a social organization instituted to foster these beliefs and practices. Faith represents the spiritual or divine element in religion, while its social organization and leaders are the human components. What makes the sociology of religion such a demanding study is the recourse within religion to faith as the legitimation for action. By definition, faith does not derive from reason, while human institutions depend upon rational organization for their effectiveness. Hence, religious institutions ultimately function upon non-rational premises, that is, faith. These faith premises are expounded by religious leadership that earns its legitimation from fidelity to the beliefs, yet serves the institution by rational policies. It is this contradiction within religion that so fascinates sociologists (Nisbet, 77–82).

This reliance on faith, however, does not prevent the church from following rational administrative decisions in day-to-day operations. Indeed, as the institution becomes more complex, more bureaucratic, and more tied to the infrastructure of staff, personnel, management, budget, and so on, it becomes more efficient. Reliable administrative performance thereby forestalls crisis and the need to resort to faith as the ultimate criterion for policy. Therefore, the maintenance of routine in the administration of religious activities, resources, and policy becomes the self-interest of the institutionalized church. Avoidance of crisis preserves its power in the rational sphere and prevents the interruption of faith decisions.

This then, in general terms, is the religious system: a faith legitimation for organizational leadership that depends upon nonrational cognition for legitimation but relies on rational policy as well in deciding a course of collective action. I like to think of the process of decision-making within a religion in terms of Quixote's squire's saying about the stone and the pitcher. When the two forces of faith and rational organizational behavior collide, the weaker one is shattered. But which is the weaker one, faith or institutional self-interest? It would be comforting to religious believers to decide that faith is the stone, shattering human organization. But as Dostoevsky eloquently expressed in his portrait of the Grand Inquisitor rejecting a returning Christ, the institutional church sometimes becomes the stone and religious belief suffers in the exchange.

I have chosen to focus upon the social organization of the Catholic church in New York in this book. Clearly, I cannot divorce my considerations from the faith premises of Catholicism, premises I share. But although I hope to explain the interaction of faith cognition and institutional self-interest, I wish to do so scientifically and objectively, insofar as that is possible. Consequently, I will examine the behavior of the institutional church with the sociological methodology appropriate to the analysis of any such organization.

The church's institutionalized expectations may be seen to "include definitions of statuses and roles, goals, and prescribed and permitted means, [as] they articulate with the culture of the society and with the personality structure that the socialization processes have produced in a given society" (O'Dea 1974, 271–72). Catholicism has a generally conservative trend, as do most churches; it tends to uphold the "statuses and roles, goals, and prescribed and permitted means" of the society. But as recent events in Latin America have proven, there is a revolutionary dimension to religion that can make it a source of delegitimation for social authority (Leroux).

The church as an institution has a variety of components to carry out its tasks at various levels. Among these one finds diocesan units, canon law, parochial life, corporate worship, pastoral activities, national divisions (episcopal conferences and the office of the apostolic delegate or papal nuncio). Within the diocesan units, one of the most important components is the chancery, the bureaucratic extension of the bishop's administration. The chancery is entrusted with implementing policies of church authority within a diocese for the bishop, the designated leader of the Catholics in a determined territory, according to a hierarchical protocol that situates bishops, archbishops and cardinals under the pope. Policy formulation, the pace and manner of change, are institutional functions for the local bishop's or archbishop's leadership. In this book I limit my analysis to the Archdiocese of New York and its chancery, which has jurisdiction over Manhattan, Staten Island, and the Bronx of New York City's five boroughs.

The archbishop (or bishop) is not the only leader within a diocese. His leadership is shared with other members of the clergy and occasionally with influential lay persons. Access to and influence with the bishop represents power within the chancery, considered sociologically as a human institution. Moreover, this access and influence are subject not only to the protocol of rank but also to the interplay of personalities. Those who exercise leadership and influence in the church at the level of policy formulation and promulgation function sociologically as elites.

The concept of "clerical or religious elite" is crucial in the analysis of authority, conflict, policy formulation for problem-solving, and legitimation of new strategies for the Catholic church. Underlying the religious control system is the organizational dimension of authority in religion, which was first systematically explored by Weber. In an effort to refute determinism in its various forms, Weber undertook to study religion in its institutions and leadership as a cause for the diversity in social behavior and economic structures in the world. Insisting that only humans make decisions to guide their actions, rather than merely reacting to instinct and class determinism, Weber constructed a method based upon explanation of action in terms of meaning attached to it by the actor (See Weber 1947, 1958, 1963).

> In social theory our main task is to explain observable social phenomena by reducing them to the individual plans (their elements, their shape and design) that typically give rise to them (Lachmann, 31–32).

While not all of Weber's methodology has withstood the test of time, his contributions to the sociology of religion and the study of institutions and processes are formidable. Of particular relevance to this book is Weber's notion of the interpenetration of religious ideas and social forces. Leadership influences religious institutions at critical moments. And as Parsons points out, in Weber's view of institutions and social forces, history could be described as

> . . . a relatively delicate balance between the forces working in radically opposed directions, so that the *difference* made by a war, a political movement, or even the influence of a single man may be of very far-reaching consequences. It is not that such a factor "creates" the result. It is rather that, in addition to the other forces working in that direction, it is sufficient to throw the total balance in favor of the one possible outcome rather than the other (Parsons, 1942, 168–69).

As I will show in chapter 5, however, the notion of leadership is not limited to a Weberian methodology.

The concept of the control system involves all those mechanisms by which religious leadership defends, controls, and organizes the thrust of the institution among the followers and the overall society. It is widely recognized that usually the purpose is twofold: to secure firsthand a sound position of influence (or at the very least acceptability and respectability) in the overall society, and to secure a strong position among the followers through their loyal adherence to existing norms and structures so that change can be proposed. Ultimately, through the everyday activity of the followers, the church's influence is expected to "overflow" into the secular realm. In addition, there is always the probability of direct influence-building and a support process being initiated and maintained by the followers (laity), who act as pressure groups, voting blocs, and participants in social history.

The religious elites are ultimately responsible for keeping the religious control system in place. To this purpose the religious elites are "continually defining new strategies and trying to improve the effectiveness of their various programs. These modifications may be geared to building insulative barriers against nonreligious influences or reaching new status groups. They may also be focused on acquiring new bases of religious association and cultural legitimacy" (Vallier 1970, 161).

Institutions may fail because they do not adapt to changing social circumstances, but they may also change institutionally so rapidly as to lose the legitimacy derived from faithfulness to belief. Thus there is no easy solution to the dilemma of the stone and the pitcher, of faith and institutional self-interest. During the period under study, the Second Vatican Council (1963–65) took place. The Council precipitated a challenge of its own to the internal structures of authority in Catholicism, requiring ecclesiastical authorities to alter their instruments of religious influence. Along with considerable changes in the traditional goals and organizational patterns of Catholic institutions, the Council also brought a certain freedom for variation in the interpretation and adaptation of these reforms at national and diocesan levels.

With the Council, New York Catholicism had not only to continue its response to the Puerto Ricans as a new group with unprecedented characteristics, but had also to begin to institutionalize, in relationship to this ministry, a response to the Council's mandates. The Council redefined the link of culture and religion. With the document *Gaudium et Spes,* which examined the role of the church in the modern world, this link between culture and religion required a pluralistic acceptance of different cultural values:

> Because it flows immediately from man's spiritual and social nature, culture has constant need of a just freedom if it is to develop. It also needs the legitimate possibility of exercising its independence according to its own principles. Rightly, therefore, it demands respect and enjoys a certain inviolability, at least as long as

the right of the individual and the community, whether particular or universal, are preserved within the context of the common good. (*Gaudium et Spes,* no. 59)

With this faith mandate to readjust its perception of cultural diversity, the Archdiocese of New York had to redefine its rational organizational plan for ministry to the Puerto Ricans. The encounter with a different culture allows for various strategies by institutions, and the church tends to reflect the general society in considering its options.

The editors of *The Minority Report,* Rosalind and Gary Dworkin, set sociological functions for the cohesiveness of a minority group (15–21). Group members have to be identifiable to themselves and to members of other groups; they must be aware and accepting of the common bonds and goals that unite members of the group; and they must recognize that their limited level of power at present is not something they have brought upon themselves but that it has been imposed from without. When these conditions are present, the minority group members realize that any differential or pejorative treatment they receive is not merited. In such a situation, reason the Dworkins, chances are that the minority will bring pressure to bear upon the majority, thus demanding in whatever measure possible that a positive response be made to it.

Dworkin and Dworkin also propose a schematic construct outlining the response that the majority is apt to give the minority group. They begin by cautioning that a majority-minority construct is not dependent upon the numerical quantity but upon the degree of actual power—the availability of resources and the capacity to mobilize these. They give the following six techniques that majorities (or those in power) use in order to maintain their dominance over minorities: tokenism, coercion, co-optation, gerrymandering of districts, divide and conquer, and socialization (Dworkin and Dworkin, 36–38). In the United States, the last one would be tantamount to Anglo Conformity, Americanization, or what many sociologists have called assimilation (Dworkin and Dworkin, 105–16).

The first of the techniques, *tokenism,* is defined by an attempt on the majority's part to give positions devoid of decision-making power to members of the minority group. In order to further limit the power of the minority, such positions often are given to persons who can "speak for" more than one minority, for example, a Hispanic-black women. *Coercion,* the second technique, is still widely used in our modern world. Coercion is the threat or reality of violence, imprisonment, and even death itself in order to make minorities comply with majorities' demands. *Cooptation* is a third technique the majority may use to control those less powerful. Here the intent is to avert the threats that the minority may make to the control of power of the majority. In this case particularly dynamic and active members of the minority group may be appointed to majority-controlled organizations, but the only power given is geared to control the minority. In this way not only are these co-opted individuals controlled as members of the majority organization, but their effectiveness in leading the minority for the minority's sake is minimized or totally destroyed.

To keep minorities from claiming and working toward their empowerment, the majority may resort to the fourth and fifth techniques: *gerrymandering*, or redistributing voting districts, and polarizing and *dividing* the groups. In the first instance political power is diluted because members of the minority are not able to speak with one voice. In the second instance the diverse minorities are kept busy fighting one another, while the majority goes on its merry way maintaining the status quo. One technique, which has become not only legitimate but respectable, is that of controlling through *socialization.* The minority's children are educated so that the role models and legitimacy of the majority are not only acknowledged but accepted, while the minority issues, contributions, achievements, and aspirations are downplayed or even ridiculed. This deprives the individual of self-awareness and maximizes the desire to emulate the power group. It is believed that if minority members learn to desire the language, beliefs, values, and customs of the majority, they may be less likely to question majority control. As they begin to identify more with the majority than with the minority, their aspirations and desire for upward mobility become personal and individualistic, not group oriented.

The minority has two options open to it: legal and extralegal power (Dworkin and Dworkin, 33–37). Either it plays by the rule of the majority, or it resorts to civil disobedience ranging from sit-ins to riots (in some cases guerrilla warfare) to call attention to the abuses of the majority, to shame majority members into granting concessions, to gain independence from the majority's domination, and to gain control over its own destiny.

In this book's description of archdiocesan policy toward Puerto Ricans, and toward the religious elites that represented them before the chancery, most of these responses were employed. I have included these notions, if not this precise terminology, in the analysis provided in this book.

Before concluding this chapter, it will be useful to summarize three key studies of clerical elites that have been of great service to the field. The first in terms of appearance was "Bishops, Priests and Prophecy: A Study of the Sociology of Religious Protest," the doctoral dissertation of Patrick Hayes McNamara in 1968. This was followed by his research on clerical elites among Mexican-Americans in Los Angeles, California, and San Antonio, Texas; it was included in the important study of Leo Grebler, Joan Moore, and Ralph Guzmán, published in 1970.

The dissertation is a very straightforward typology based on Weber's ideal types of priest and prophet. Interpreting these Weberian types, McNamara states:

> The priest is considered to be rooted in a service of a sacred tradition, and tends to uphold the status quo in the larger institutional world supporting the cultic enterprise. The prophet comes from outside the ranks of the priesthood, a charismatic figure, and the recipient of a personal revelation which urges him to protest against abuses both within the practice of the cult and in the larger society, i.e., social injustices. The prophet comes from the ranks of the laity and recruits supporters from this stratum (McNamara 1968, vi).

When Weber posited this initial typology, he did so as a theoretical classification, with mutually exclusive properties. McNamara demonstrates that Catholic priests have functioned as prophets and cites examples from the ministry to Mexican-Americans to prove it. In the 1970 article he develops the notions of pastoral care and social action (I prefer to use the phrase *social concerns*). The definition of pastoral care comes from Jesuit sociologist Joseph Fichter.

> Certain truths must be believed by all members of the Church. These constitute the Christian creed. There are also certain pat-

> terns of conduct, called "the Christian code of behavior," as outlined basically in the Ten Commandments, the counsels of Christ, and the precepts of the Church. Third, the Christian cult, or form of worship, comprises the sacramental, liturgical, and devotional system of the Church. Finally, the Christian communion of all members with one another idealizes the essential social nature of the Church (Fichter, cited by McNamara in Grebler et al., 453 n. 26).

These functions support the faith dimension of the religion. Social concerns, on the other hand, address the material needs of the people. The expenditure of financial resources, the attention of personnel, and the use of buildings to remedy human needs constitute this sphere of church activity.

McNamara (1970) establishes a rough identification of pastoral care with conservative (that is, "priestly" clergy) and of social concerns with liberal (that is, "prophetic" clergy). All Catholics more or less accept that both pastoral care and social concerns are parts of the gospel message, but the priority placed on each in relation to the other sets the degree of conservatism or liberalism. In demonstrating that the priest can also be a prophet, McNamara (1968, 17 n. 39) cites Stark to explain that in analyzing the charismatic prophet and the routinizing priest, Weber failed to understand "that one man can start a charismatic movement and another revivify it—that a successor can fan again the flames, burning low, which his predecessor had first lit and fanned" (Stark, 206).

The institutional church's response to the needs of the Mexican-Americans was an interplay between those who stressed pastoral care at the expense of social concerns and those who saw a more important role for direct aid to the material needs of the people without direct connection to pastoral care. This analysis is highly relevant to my study of a similar process at the same time in New York within the ministry to the Puerto Ricans. McNamara stresses that these functions are not mutually exclusive if the episcopal authority in the diocese legitimates the simultaneous exercise of these functions. If episcopal sanction is lost, however, McNamara finds it likely that the priest who also seeks to exercise a prophetic function will lose legitimacy. Hence the chancery exercises a key role in integrating a new focus upon social concerns with pastoral care. There is even a role for a priest within the bureaucracy of the chancery to introduce charismatic goals and thus deroutinize the pastoral care operations of the institution. He offers St. Charles Borromeo as an example of Stark's "de-routinizer of the first order" (McNamara 1968, 18 n. 42).

A New York archdiocesan priest, Philip Murnion, has offered a second analysis of clerical elites based upon the ideal types of Max Weber. In his study *The Catholic Priest and the Changing Structure of Pastoral Ministry, New York, 1920–1970* (1978) Murnion acknowledges the mutual dependence of social relations and social theory. He states:

> One can see in the organizational life of the church forces that promote its own development. We can see in the role of the priest elements that lead to some new styles of ministry. And we can locate in the relationship between the church and society its own dynamic. But the dynamic in one area or at one level is also conditioned by the dynamic inherent in the other (Murnion, 383).

According to Murnion, whether the development is one of growth and progress or of decline, it is always a dynamic of change, and change is seldom harmonious. Members of the church have intervened at points of history either to appropriate the dynamic occurring in some field of experience or understanding, or to block such a dynamic.

> Change is rarely harmonious or unilinear. . . . We find that the changing structure of pastoral ministry is a function of multiple trends that are conditioned by each other (Murnion, 384–86).

Murnion attempted to analyze and interpret the changes that occurred in the structure of Catholic pastoral ministry within the Archdiocese of New York during the past half-century. His focus, then, was upon the priests ordained for the archdiocese in the decades 1920–29 and 1960–69 and upon the differences between these two groups in terms of social origins and recruitment of the priests; patterns of training for the priesthood; the practice of pastoral ministry; and the conceptualization of central aspects of religion, life, church, and ministry. Against this background he tried to give an explanation of the dialectical relationship among conceptualization (theology), organization (ecclesiology), and role (pastoral ministry, that is, the balance between pastoral care and social concerns). Murnion touched upon the link between the modernization of the church and the elaboration of a new theodicy for pastoral ministry. He reconstructed Weber's typology of theodicies and included the constitutive process of modernization.

Basically, his model presents three main ways of looking at reality: the transcendent, the theopolitan, and the immanent. He cross-tabulates each with three interpretative modes: immediate/experience, symbolic/sacrament, and instrumental/sign. The nine types that emerge from this cross-tabulation are identified as follows:

	Transcendent	Theopolitan	Immanent
Immediate	Type I, equated with other-worldly mystical meaning systems	Type II, where secular experience is found immediately to contain religious significance	Type III, equated with this-worldly mystical systems
Symbolic	Type IV, where myth is the basis for religious cosmogonies	Type V, where the integration of the secular and the sacred occurs, rendering the Christian a "mystical citizen of the world"	Type VI, where myth is the basis for national legends
Instrumental	Type VII, equated with a religious ascetical system	Type VIII, where the relationship between religious and secular experiences is reduced to an organizational or religio-political one	Type IX, equated with a secular ascetical system

Murnion details the social variables at work in seminary education, social class, and general education during the period he examines. With this information he makes a valuable contribution toward linking pastoral attitudes with a changing theology. He has done what McNamara did not, and he has provided a perspective to view the activity of priests active in the Spanish-speaking apostolate not merely as individuals but as members of a new generation of clerics able to respond to new challenges presented by society.

Murnion suggests that the theopolitan/symbolic type has a paradoxical nature in its fusion of goals:

> It seems, in other words, that the Catholic Church is being pulled toward the center again, toward a new form of integration, the symbolic theopolitical, in a specifically modern social situation. This means that it is being pulled toward an essentially unstable and complex existence. The priest and the parish priest especially is at the center of this shift because he stands at the juncture of these centrifugal tendencies and is being asked to both exemplify and instruct others in the way of integrating sacred and profane. In a sense, this is like asking him to be a mystical citizen of the world, which is to suggest paradox, if not contradiction.... The convergence of theological and social development issues is a demand for one who is able to mediate the sacred-secular relationship from a position that is deeply involved and respectful of secular processes but discerns a larger meaning in these processes which he can so formulate that the formulation will indeed serve to interpret human experience and to enable the expression of his human experience in rites that raise it to the level of religious experience (Murnion, 402).

This abstract theorization by Murnion has proven to have great applicability to the case of the Office of the Spanish-speaking Apostolate in the Chancery of New York, and strikingly, also to Murnion's tenure as director of an office in the same institution.

Although Murnion's categories are more satisfactory than those of McNamara in demonstrating a greater play of variables in the perception of the options open for church action, Murnion's paradigm, nonetheless, lacks a clear linkage between the historical process of social change and its impact upon clerical training and modes of conceptualization within the institution. For example, while he shows that the spiritual reading at the seminary shifted from the monastic conception of spirituality to a more parish-oriented one, he does not explain how this is related to urbanization and the modernizing trends of the general society. Thus, while Murnion's typology is excellent for showing the connections between theological attitudes and pastoral activity, it does not show how social forces modify both. Nor does Murnion's study consider the possibility of lay leadership becoming part of the religious elite.

The third work key to my analysis studies both Mexican-Americans and Puerto Ricans in the Catholic church in the United States. The book *Prophets Denied Honor,* by Antonio M. Stevens-

Arroyo, portrays the typology shown in Figure 4. This typology, modified from one first developed by Ivan Vallier (in Lipset and Solari), explains the role and diversity of an emerging "indigenous" leadership in post-Conciliar Catholicism.

Figure 4

Stevens-Arroyo's Typology of Hispano Catholic Leadership

		Structural Principle of Catholic Activity	
		Hierarchical	Cooperative
Sphere from Which Church Influence Is Drawn	Internal to Church	Cursillistas	Pastoralists
	External to Church	Politicians	Liberationists

Source: Antonio M. Stevens-Arroyo, ed., *Prophets Denied Honor* (Maryknoll, New York: Orbis Books, 1980), p. 176.

The typology is based upon structural principles of activity and sphere for influence. Within that conceptual framework Stevens-Arroyo, following Vallier, develops four basic types. Vallier argues that, although these groups do not exhaust the kinds of elite differentiation to be found in contemporary Latin American Catholicism, the differences that set these groups apart involve two major dimensions of analytical importance: 1) the choice of sphere from which the church is to gain its major source of influence (*internal*—its organizations and rituals, that is, pastoral care; or *external*—involvement with secular issues, that is, social concerns); and 2) the organizing principle of religious-social relationship, which he terms "hierarchical" and "cooperative" (Stevens-Arroyo 1980, 175ff.; Vallier, in Lipset and Solari, 206).

Stevens-Arroyo describes two groups that view the church as a hierarchical structure: *cursillistas* (papists for Vallier) and politicians. Pastoralists and liberationists (Vallier's pluralists) stress the cooperative nature of church activity. The politicians and the liberationists are extremely interested in church political action, although from different ends of the ideological spectrum. The former are ultra conservatives, who would subordinate even pastoral care to maintenance of the status quo in secular terms. The latter are radicals, who would place social concerns over pastoral care, even if it subverted the social system. The *cursillistas* and pastoralists, on the other hand, are equally concerned with the internal affairs of the church, although with different conceptions as to how that activity is structured. The liberationists are likely to agree with the pastoralists about the form and style liturgy ought to take, but do not see such matters as central to their concerns. Stevens-Arroyo relates how the two concepts of church activity and sphere of influence produced shifting alliances within Hispanic Catholicism in the United States.

The traditional Catholic upper class, or *politicians,* are oriented to the power structure of secular society and look to outside groups for support, protection, and legitimation. To achieve influence through skillful maneuvering, short-run coalitions, and the maximization of ad hoc situations as they arise is their task. The hierarchy within the church is important because it represents a set, formal, recognized position from which the clergy or bishops can establish themselves as influentials in the wider community. The reference group is the upper classes, while the poor are ignored except as objects of charity. Rituals are perfunctory; the sacraments are dispensed to those who can pay; lay involvement and ecumenical movements are resisted; and social evils are accepted as implicit in the human situation. Indispensable for their existence are interconnections with the polity and manipulation of public opinion and power groups, thus the label *politician.*

The *cursillistas,* or papists, are those who aim toward "re-Christianizing the world." First they must "penetrate" the social milieu and then become involved with rising status groups, especially the urban proletariat, in order to find avenues that will give the church internal strength and organizational power. They rely, however, on the church's own authority and resources to achieve influence and visibility viewing themselves as a missionary elite whose main task is to expand the frontiers of Christian-Catholic values. Lay participation must be in "collaboration with the hierarchy" and under its supervision. Rome is the ultimate ecclesiastical authority, and tradition is sacrosanct.

The *pastoralists,* or pastors, are the bishops and clergy who see their main role as building up strong, worship-centered congregations where the priest is not only spiritual leader and teacher but *compañero* as well, where social distance between clerics and laypersons is at a minimum, and where solidarity is emphasized as the "meaning of the sacraments," "cooperation," "pastoral care," and "community" are sought (Vallier, in Lipset and Solari, 203, 204).

The fourth and last elite group in this typology, the *liberationists* or *pluralists,* is defined as a very mixed and changing group. Vallier points out its central premise, "that Catholicism in Latin America is a minority faith—one religion among many other religions (Vallier, in Lipset and Solari, 205). Stevens-Arroyo identifies the group with the theology of liberation (1980, 269–82). The liberationists or pluralists have a major objective: to develop policies and programs of a nature such that the church may be able to take an active part in the institutionalization process of social justice on all fronts. Important here are the grass-roots ethical action in the world, the efforts at community integration, and attention to the poor—and ecumenical ties but also long-range planning for all of these.

Interested in the institutionalization process of social justice on all fronts, this group holds that in the social revolution Latin America is undergoing the church "must find her place" and "play an important role therein." This is not to be undertaken as a "political party" or as "an anxious guardian of established privilege." The church must act as a "differentiated, grass-roots agency of moral and social influence" (Vallier, in Lipset and Solari, 206). Stevens-Arroyo (1980, 295–302) suggests that many Puerto Ricans who are in favor of the total independence of their island from United States rule are liberationists.

But Stevens-Arroyo's typology, like that of Vallier from which it was derived, is focused primarily upon the religious elites, without consideration of the dynamism inherent in the institution as a whole. While the terminology and his documented examples ring true to the history of the ministry to Puerto Ricans, it focuses upon the leaders themselves rather than upon their functions within the institution.

Hence, while each of these typologies adds important fullness to the subject, none of them permits an institutional analysis of the process of decision-making within the Archdiocese of New York in its attempt to adapt to the Puerto Rican Great Migration and its aftermath. In the following chapters I will try to tell the tale of the stone and the pitcher as Oxcart Catholicism came to Fifth Avenue. Before concluding, I will return again to this theoretical discussion of how best to understand sociologically such an encounter.

2. Island within the Island: Faith and Institution in Puerto Rico

En mi tiempo no había que buhcalo. El cura ehtaba metío en tó, jahta en el plato de marota. Me acueldo de Don Hilario. Cuando uno menoh lo ehperaba se aparesía montao en su burro... trabajaba duro el Don Hilario peleando con er demonio... Aquel cura era un hombre de trabajo. Hoy disen que loh cura modernos se perfuman y jahta usan calsonsillo e sea.

In my time you didn't have to fetch the priest. He was always into everything, even your plate of grits. I remember Don Hilario. When you least expected him, there he was, riding on his old donkey... but he worked hard that Don Hilario, fighting with the devil.... That priest was a hard worker. They say that today's priests use perfume and even wear silk underwear.

—Don Chago, Act I, *The Oxcart*

Before beginning an analysis of Puerto Rican Catholics in the United States, it is important to provide an overview of the nature of the religious attitudes formed on the island over nearly four centuries.[1] In what ways, some may ask, do Puerto Ricans differ from the Irish, Italian, Polish, or other Catholic groups that came to New York?[2] Are there significant differences between Puerto Ricans and Mexican-Americans or other Latinos in the way they practice their Catholic faith? An exploration of the history of Catholicism in Puerto Rico will provide the background to frame such questions with precision.

I do not intend to argue that Puerto Rican Catholicism is doctrinally different or unorthodox from the faith. What seems relevant is a summary profile of the historical and social forces that have lent the practice of religion in Puerto Rico certain attitudes and traditions. It may well be that scholars more familiar with comparative studies can draw parallels with other experiences. I do not so much seek to claim some uniqueness for Puerto Rican Catholicism as to offer an interpretative summary of those characteristics most likely to explain what happened when Puerto Ricans came in large numbers to New York in the twentieth century and the archdiocese began a pastoral outreach.

The institution of the Roman Catholic Church was first established in the Western Hemisphere on the island of San Juan Bautista of Puerto Rico when the newly appointed bishop, Alonso Manso, arrived in 1511. The Spanish colonization of the sixteenth century was focused upon establishing urban coastal centers so that the island colony could maintain communication with Spain and the rest of the empire. Although the church was one of the strongest and most cohesive Spanish institutions of the time, scarcity of resources, the geographic distance from Spain, and the lack of adequate avenues of communication made it virtually impossible for Holy Mother Church in Spain to exercise complete control over its young daughter in the New World.

For instance, the dissatisfaction of Alonso Manso's successor, Rodrigo de Bastidas, with the "poor little church" he inherited, together with his frustration over ongoing conflict over resources with the Dominican friars, led him to seek fortune and a new post in the neighboring island of Hispaniola. This left the Puerto Rican see vacant for a period of three years and the clergy and faithful to fend for themselves (Figueroa 1972, 79, 144, passim).

Travel between the empire and the small colony was sporadic. In some years ten or twenty vessels would arrive from the Peninsula, the Canary Islands, or neighboring possessions, while other years no vessel would arrive (Silvestrini and Sánchez, 170 ff.). Royal money was spent almost exclusively for fortification of the city. These policies neglected the countryside and produced a society of deep contrasts, where differences between urban and rural life styles ran deep (Silvestrini and Sánchez, 174 ff.).

Spain's restrictions on Puerto Rico's trade throughout the seventeenth and the first half of the eighteenth century unintentionally set the basis for contraband trade. But while the illicit trade solved the personal need of the inhabitants by providing basic commodities, the lack of revenues left "the royal treasury in arrears, to the detriment of public works such as roads, ports, schools and hospitals, and [*in general*] public services" (Figueroa 1972, 101). These factors, and others better explained by historians, resulted in the Puerto Rican colony becoming little more than a military outpost for Spain, valuable only for its strategic position against pirates and privateers (Figueroa, 79ff., 144ff.; Silvestrini and Sánchez, 170ff.; Lewis, 34–41). While there were backwater regions in virtually every colony under royal Spain, the Caribbean islands were so neglected that other European countries were virtually invited to prey upon these Spanish possessions, and eventually only Cuba and Puerto Rico remained under the Spanish flag. This historical isolation is the first element in the profile I wish to trace of Puerto Rican society.

The economic underdevelopment and isolation resulted in a paucity of colonists from Europe willing to endure the harsh conditions of insular society. Puerto Rico was left with a relatively small number of European colonists, whose numbers were not significantly expanded by new immigration from the Iberian peninsula for much of two and a half centuries. During this century and a half (1508–1765), Puerto Ricans begin to set the foundations for a society that was remote from Spain (Figueroa, 106). The erosion of the Taíno culture and the virtual disappearance of the native population through continuous biological intermixing, war, or natural causes made the Caribbean different from much of Latin America. Morse (1960) points to limited resources, inadequate communication, and rigidly established class boundaries and asserts that the resulting fragmentation, dependency, and isolation created an identity crisis and were detrimental to the Spanish colonization of Puerto Rico. In fact, he believes there was no real colonization and, on that account, views the island as culturally distinct from Latin America. Whatever one's evaluation of Morse's theory, it is sufficient here to underscore that isolation from the outside world on the island of Puerto Rico had significant effects on society and culture.

The biological mixture of races in Puerto Rico has been measured scientifically as well as through the characterizations of numerous census taking since the sixteenth century (Figueroa, 74, 83, 103; Silvestrini and Sánchez; Fernández Méndez). Also important is the cultural mixture or transhumanization that took place.

The early settlers, whatever their race, had to learn from the Taíno inhabitants how to live on a tropical island. Place names, plant cultivation, and local customs show the effects of cultural borrowing.

The Spanish crown made attempts, and even laws, to minimize, regularize, or even prevent racial intermarriage (Gross and Bingham, 40, 41). However, miscegenation among the lower classes was the norm in Puerto Rico, not the exception (Figueroa, 247–56). As in other parts of the Spanish-speaking Caribbean, the racial mixture of the population had a much higher percentage of African blood than in Mexico and most other parts of the Spanish possessions. Correspondingly, the native Indian culture is significantly less than in other parts of continental Latin America (Mörner, 127–33, passim). Demographically, then, Puerto Rico is different from much of Latin America and forms part of the Caribbean, where African influence is significant. However, Puerto Rico never developed the number of sugar plantations that characterized the non-Hispanic Caribbean or Cuba, and always had fewer African slaves than Cuba or Hispaniola (Figueroa, 249ff.; Díaz Soler, 77ff.). While Puerto Rico's culture is African, like its Caribbean counterparts, it cannot be lumped together with cultural traditions from Cuba or the Dominican Republic, where Africanisms were more influential (Mintz, 28ff. See Gónzalez for a different view).

Until the reforms of the Enlightenment in the middle of the eighteenth century, official policy was usually sporadic, ill-planned, and dictated by the needs of the empire and not by those of the island. The absence of imperial attention forced the insular inhabitants to develop a way of life in isolation from urban life and the strictures of civil laws; this produced a cultural phenomenon of skepticism toward others and toward institutions on the part of the peasant population (Mintz, 28–33. See also Landy 1959; Brown 1964). Colonial administrators concentrated scant resources in urban areas, and the countryside was abandoned to its own devices. As a result, the rural areas of the mountainous interior produced social forms independent of civil codes. If they were not taken seriously by the city and the Spanish lords, why should they observe city laws, institutions, and restrictions? Rather than seeing this isolation as a negative thing, the peasants were content in a world of their own social norms. Although they had few commodities and luxuries, they enjoyed freedom from taxes and the laws of city life (Brau, in Manrique Cabrera, 173, 174. Cf. Bergard, 60ff.).

Some have compared the ordinary Puerto Rican peasants to the hillbillies of Appalachia in the United States (Wagenheim, 218). Sidney Mintz calls the Puerto Rican peasants "unlettered, laconic, shrewd." (28), while Brau (in Manrique Cabrera, 173, 174) perceives marked differences in attitudes and personal qualities depending on the set of social agents with whom they were asked to interact. To peasants may be attributed such qualities as joviality and resoluteness within their close circle of family and friends and circumspection or even lack of taste in public matters. Brau thus describes individuals who have the highest respect for authority but seek to avoid it and other social conventions at all costs. And this they would do even if they had to forego certain benefits. Only the threat of losing individual freedom, which for centuries had been safeguarded by the isolation in which they had lived, could not be sacrificed. Whether the peasants and their world view is described in laudatory or negative terms, what is important to this discussion is the interaction of historical isolation, demographic composition, and cultural attitudes toward social institutions.

For instance, when combined with the historical isolation of the entire island, the demographics of Puerto Rico made the urban-rural dichotomy a racial segregation as well. Those who lived in the city were mostly white and *criollos,* if not actually born in Spain, while those in the countryside were generally of mixed racial origins (Mintz, in Cordasco and Bucchioni, 28). It seems safe to say that skepticism toward authority dominated the culture of the peasant and the racially mixed population, while whites and city dwellers had more establishment attitudes. The Puerto Rican culture, therefore, is a composite of both sets of attitudes as they interact on each other.

One may consider the historical isolation, the special demographics, and cultural values to have created a "social idiom," which

> rests on the known need for members of different social groups within a single society to interact meaningfully with each other. To do so, they must present images of themselves that are consistent with the social usages and expectations of others. The relational process—or more simply put, the way people carry on behavior

in emotionally and symbolically comprehensible ways—requires some basic conventional understanding (Mintz, 76).

Mintz utilized Kluckhohn's binary value categories in an attempt to characterize Puerto Rican culture for a Congressional panel in 1967. Using classifications derived from general anthropology, he profiled contemporary Puerto Rican culture. He found the same pattern of "withdrawal for autonomy" (50) and skepticism toward institutions described above. While the Puerto Rican perceives society as a determinate social order of class and color, human society is perceived as basically flawed and therefore to be guarded against (37–41).

This skepticism toward authority appears to be used only against those of higher prestige (Brameld, cited by Mintz, in Cordasco and Bucchioni, 75). The various anthropological and sociological studies during this century, as well as the historical accounts dating back to colonial times, give credence to the notion that the urban population has one set of cultural norms while the rural has another. Both, however, are held together by Catholic values, "less expressed as an aspect of religiosity than as an aspect of national culture" (Mintz, in Cordasco and Bucchioni, 78–79). In defense of "social idiom," Mintz argues that sexual mores, social censure, gender role expectations, and customs like *compadrazgo*[3] require a tradition of Catholicism (78).

A survey of Puerto Ricans on the island and some residents in Chicago was taken by psychologists Albizu and Marty-Torres (1958). This survey underscored the foregoing categorizations and pointed out that they are important because they rely on what the people say of themselves and not on the descriptions of professionals, who are nonetheless "outsiders" (cited by Mintz, in Cordasco and Bucchioni, 76). Skepticism toward authority was found to be about the same in both populations and extends not only to previous mountain dwellers, *jíbaros,* but also to black Puerto Ricans from other parts of the island. This attitude, called *la peleita monga* by the respondents, is described as "circumventive aggression" by the psychologists.

I would like to summarize all this data with the sociological concept of social distance, that is, "the degree of intimacy that prevails between groups and individuals" (Coser, 360). In Puerto Rico this distance historically has produced an urban-rural dichotomy with racial and cultural characteristics. Social distance implies all these dimensions and sets the framework for the social idiom of inter- and intra-class relations.

This view of the island as a dichotomized reality persists. When a traveler arrives at the island's main airport today the first question put to him or her is: "¿Para San Juan y área metropolitana o para la Isla?" ("Going to San Juan and the metropolitan area or to the island?"). The city with its hastened way of life, the maze of urban bureaucratic apparatus, only serves to make life a bit more uncomfortable than it already is. Its laws do not offer counsel or meaningful guidelines. At best they are a point of departure, a testing ground indicating what is punishable or not permissible, setting limits rather than guiding social behavior. From the example of their officials the common people have seen that *el que hace la ley, hace la trampa.* (he who is responsible for making laws, is also capable of setting traps). Laws are meant to be used, circumvented, bent to serve one's purposes. Moreover, for the poor black as well as for the *jíbaro,* law is a racial phenomenon. "Allá ellos que son blancos," (roughly translated as "Let white people take care of white people's affairs") is said time and time again in reference to law and government. "*Blanquitos*" (white people) is a category of distancing (Mintz, 59), while its obverse "*negrito*" is a term of trustworthiness (Pietri, 11).

Naturally this cultural complex has its repercussions in religious expression; it is to these characteristics that the rest of this chapter is devoted. The period from 1640–1765 has been described as the formative epoch for Puerto Rican popular Catholicism (Stevens-Arroyo 1981, 4). At the beginning of this period of formation the settlers lived in almost total isolation, lacking access to one another and to the urban centers. There were no churches, schools, or the trappings of any other ecclesiastical or governmental institution among them. Religion was expressed in pious prayers, often recited before home altars adorned with flowers, offerings, and homemade statues of wood or *santos* (Steward, 86, 128). In the countryside *ermitas* or shrines for group devotional prayer were sometimes visited by clergy, although lay people maintained them. The custom was not unlike that of Spain in the late Middle Ages (see Christian, 105–25; Rivera Bermúdez, 55–69).

Midway through the formative period the interior of Puerto Rico had become dotted with towns, and Puerto Ricans had ceased to be solely coastal dwellers identified with the ocean, fishing, and cattle raising. In the mountain habitat they became *jíbaros*—intimately tied to the cycles of nature and to the land. At first woodsmen and charcoal producers, they ultimately became small farmers of tobacco, banana, and coffee (Picó 1981, 179). In this new situation, beliefs and practices were recast to respond to the environment and corresponding needs. God's power and wondrous deeds were constantly manifested in daily occurrences, in the forces of nature, in the seeming ease with which, season after season, the once dormant seeds woke up to warmth and sunlight. Amid these miracles and their many needs and suffering, *jíbaros* forged a distinctive mode of existence.

Their religious expression arose, then, both out of a need to believe in a Supreme Being and to live in harmony with nature as they responded to its many challenges. When the fit between the liturgical and the agricultural cycle clashed, material needs were often pushed aside and preference given to the socio-religious festivities. Picó notes the difference in religious expression between an ecclesiastical cycle and a popular or community-oriented one. The first, encompassing both Advent and Lent, extends from November to the procession of Corpus Christi in June; this is the Christological cycle. The second, from Corpus Christi to November, coincides with the dry season and is called the sanctoral cycle. During these months many important feast days are celebrated, including many dedicated to the Blessed Mother and the patron saint of the island, St. John the Baptist, on June 24.[4]

This sanctoral cycle, coinciding as it does with a period of low agricultural activity, the *tiempo muerto,* provided ample time for the *jíbaros* to take stock of their condition of dependence both upon the *hacendados* and the forces of nature. The cult to the Virgin and the saints, according to Picó, were based on this awareness: "Therefore, the Virgin and the Saints—and not Christ—came to be the arbiters of climatic changes as well as those called upon to soften the hearts of the *hacendados*" (Picó, 141, 144ff.). Noting the difference between adherence to church-based practices and popular religiosity, he explains:

> Events in the liturgical year, especially during the sanctoral cycle were less likely to be marked by Mass attendance—which was impeded by bad roads and traveling difficulties—than by devotional

> observances. . . . The burden of daily needs for the workers were made more acute when resources were scarce. Then there is a saint for each moment of need: for tooth aches, for a happy delivery, to keep away the plague, to bring good luck, and so that the transplanted tobacco take root properly. The rural dweller is not so much a prayerful man as he is a keen observer. He knows how to distinguish the various signs and to take the necessary precautions. God and his saints are always busy. The world is full of supernatural forces, but there are also the Evil Spirit and his companions; and there are the souls of those who have expired by hanging roaming about along the roads at midnight. All of this cannot be controlled. But one can prevent some unfortunate events (Picó 1981, 145, my translation).

This description of popular religiosity calls to mind folk religion. Certainly, the mixture of orthodox Catholic beliefs with pre-Colombian religion is common in all Latin American countries. Yet, in the Caribbean, where much of the native Taíno population disappeared and Africans were imported as a work force, there are significant differences from the continent. The likelihood of African beliefs as part of the non-European admixture is higher in the Caribbean than in most other parts of Latin America.

In Puerto Rico, when one speaks of the Black Madonna, the image that is invoked is that of Our Lady of Monserrate. Although the title of Monserrate comes from medieval Spain, there is a unique Puerto Rican devotion that originated in Hormigueros, a mountain town in Puerto Rico. Tradition has it that in 1640 an eight-year old peasant girl named Monserrate González reported a vision of the Madonna. The event encouraged a local devotion to the Madonna. Some years later a farmer saw his own daughter in danger of being killed by a bull; he vowed to build a chapel in honor of Our Lady of Monserrate if the child was spared. The frescos on the walls of the chapel today depict this episode. Many cures have been reported there. Beneficiaries have left a number of crutches, walking-sticks, or gold and silver *ex-votos* or charms representing the part of the body cured, such as a leg or an arm. By the eighteenth century popular devotion had made this into a uniquely Puerto Rican devotion. In fact, Alejo de Arizmendi (1804–16), the first and only native Puerto Rican bishop during Spanish colonial times, asked to be buried at this shrine (see Díaz-Ramírez 1978, 24, 25, 83, 99). From the collections of *santos* it is evident that Monserrate is the most common theme of all the *santos* or native carved wooden images of all times (Curbelo, 13). In this popular art Our Lady of Monserrate is often depicted as a black woman with a child and is referred to as *la virgen negra.*[5] In Mexico, on the other hand, *la morenita* is an Indian princess. Moreover, Our Lady of Guadalupe provides for a "national cult of identity" (Elizondo 1978, 119–85), something that has not happened in Puerto Rico, which remains today without its independence as a nation.

Far-reaching social and political reforms began in Puerto Rico during the reign of Bourbon king Carlos III (1759–88). With a notable increase in population due to natural growth and immigration after 1765, both civil and ecclesiastical authorities sought to bring the isolated rural dwellers into an economic system centered on export production (Silvestrini and Sánchez, 194–201). Nonetheless, the *jíbaros* proved stubborn in their resistance (see Figueroa, 121). The impressive study of the Puerto Rican reality by the Spanish cleric Iñigo Abbad y Lasierra in 1788 offers a snapshot description of popular piety, including the rural-urban dichotomy:

> The islanders are very devoted to Our Lady: they all wear the rosary on their necks, and recite it at least two times a day; every family begins the day with this holy exercise, some repeat it at noon, none omits it at night. But the isolation in which they live, the lack of instruction and of schools for the youths occasion a great deal of ignorance in all, since the majority do not know Christian doctrine precisely. Not living in village clusters begets this and other grave evils (Abbad y Lasierra, 193, my translation).

This citation should not be interpreted to indicate a lack of priests. As Salvador Perea indicates, already in the sixteenth century Puerto Rico had enough native vocations to export clergy to other parts of the Spanish colonial world (Ferrée et al., 4/26). Perea goes on to say that in 1765 there was one priest for every 660 inhabitants (Ferrée et al., 4/27), which is a better ratio than in the New York Archdiocese in 1955, where the ratio was one priest for every 750 inhabitants (Glazer and Moynihan, 88). It was lack of communication between the institutional church, largely urban, and the rural population, scattered through the countryside, rather than a paucity of native priests that characterized this separation of the people from institutionalized religion.

By the beginning of the eighteenth century interior towns were planned, and the church was essential to the establishment of a municipality. But initiation of institutions gave no guarantee of their continuity. In Utuado, for example, from 1744, when the church first opened its doors, to the beginning of the nineteenth century, temporary pastors predominated, some remaining for scarcely two months. Fernando Picó states that even in the nineteenth century, with the assignment of more permanent priests, the situation changed little in terms of pastoral care and commitment to the parish.

Picó places the blame for the ignorance of the inhabitants on the church hierarchy, which failed to provide adequate personnel with apostolic zeal. The ecclesiastical leaders, like the civil authorities, looked down on the rural way of life so separated from theirs. This pattern set the tone for Puerto Rican social interaction for nearly two hundred years, until it was fractured by the creation of a middle class in the second half of the twentieth century (Mintz, in Cordasco and Bucchioni, 33).

After Spain lost most of its continental colonies in the Wars of Latin American independence (1810–21), immigration from Spain, especially from the Canary Islands, increased markedly. These new immigrants moved into an island that, although underdeveloped in economic and social terms, already had a cultural and social identity. With each new immigration, however, the social role of the Puerto Rican–born white population (that is, urban *criollos*) was redefined by comparison with the social distance of the *jíbaros.*

The new immigrants from Spain, other European countries, and neighboring colonies were closer to Spanish culture than the colonists who had come during the formative centuries. The upper class *criollos,* accustomed to preeminence in the tiny island, began to suffer a slippage in social prestige as Puerto Rico received more colonists from Spain. They were now victims of social distance from the seat of Spanish power. When thus displaced by Spanish newcomers, the Puerto Rican upper-class *criollos* felt relegated to a social role analogous with the *jíbaros.* Eventually these conditions nurtured a sense of nationalism and produced efforts for political separation from Spain (Bergard, 49, 134–44).

It is the man of the mountains and his way of life that the urban *criollo* Manuel Alonso described and celebrated in his book *El gíbaro,* which was published in 1849. One must understand that if upper-class medical student Alonso bemoans the possibility of losing the values, customs, and traditions that are the foundation for a uniquely Puerto Rican experience, it is because such a way of life had existed for a relatively long period of time. One must also take into account that the *criollismo* he describes, far from excluding the mountain dweller's experience, dwells upon it and exalts it. When Alonso describes the *jíbaros* of the 1840s he describes a people with particular linguistic and cultural expressions, values, and world view. If there is any criticism, it is focused upon the urban institutions for their inability to cope with pressing needs and the infiltration of foreign elements. When an amplified second edition of his book was published in 1884, it became more than just a description of quaint inland traditions; it was a charter for political and social identity of a people (see Brau's introduction to Alonso 1884, ix-xxvi; Manrique Cabrera, 101–3).

One should not equate the romantic view of the *jíbaros* with a socio-economic description of reality. The mountain dwellers suffered from ignorance, endemic illnesses, and poverty in personal and family relations (Dietz, 127–32; Bergard, 60ff.). The remedies for these conditions, such as schools and hospitals, however, were stubbornly shunned. Spanish authorities resorted to extreme anti-vagrancy measures such as the workbook or *libreta*. This was hung around the neck and carried a record of the last job. An improperly filled *libreta* could place a *jíbaro* into forced labor (Bergard, 61, 96, 116). Such policies, of course, proved to the *jíbaros* that society was not to be trusted; at the same time, the *jíbaros'* resistance was sufficient proof to the authorities that they were dealing with a lazy and immoral lot.

The institutional Catholic church had always been tied to the values of the urban elite. Very briefly, before the Napoleonic wars, the *criollos* were allowed some participation in the privileges of the ruling class. This led to the appointment of the first native Puerto Rican as bishop in his homeland, Juan Alejo Arizmendi (1803–14). However, Arizmendi showed great sympathy with the *criollo* movements for independence in Spanish colonies on the continent, inclining the governor to threaten him with exclusion from burial in the cathedral crypt with previous Spanish-born prelates because his conduct was unworthy of his predecessors. Arizmendi replied that when the time came, he preferred to be buried in the Puerto Rican shrine at Hormigueros with his people (Gutiérrez del Arroyo, 37). Unlike Arizmendi, both his predecessors and those who followed him preferred to award parishes and vicariates to Spanish clergy (Perea, citing Coll y Toste, Ferrée, et al., 4/27). Spain never again named a native Puerto Rican to the hierarchy of the island. Since Catholicism was identified with Spanish rule, the official church lost the support of the Puerto Rican *criollos*. Separation of church and state, destruction of Catholic privileges, and permission for religious freedom were among the goals of the separatist movement. In rejecting these aims of the separatist movement, the Catholic hierarchy also opposed the abolition of slavery on the island. This negative and pro-Spanish stance of the official Catholic church also brought it to disapprove generally of more moderate efforts at political self-rule for Puerto Rico until the end of Spanish rule.

The role of Catholicism among the rural peoples, however, had a different trajectory. Religion, unlike party politics, fulfills the basic need that humans have to believe in something beyond earthly existence and to celebrate rites of passage and important events in the lives of the individual, the family unit, and the community. While the pronouncements of government and hierarchy were relevant to general policy, the notion of social distance helped the *jíbaros* escape the entanglements of both religion and politics. Confident of their personal relationship with the divine and with nature, the peasants sacrificed little of this interior piety while living in the countryside. Generally, this piety was characterized by fidelity to certain Spanish norms but with some incorporation of Taíno and African beliefs. It always preserved a propensity to divorce itself from the institutional church.

The *jíbaros* of the mountains, like the black of the coast, had been drawn into the economy of nineteenth century Puerto Rico. But this participation was peripheral and disadvantageous to the lower class and certainly not a reason to abandon the protections of social distance. The rural people had to visit the town or *pueblo*, just as they had to have either title to land or an employer (Dietz, 42–53; Bergard, 45–48, 109, 110; Brau, in Manrique Cabrera, 174), but they sought to maintain a separate economy of subsistence farming for their own needs. Thus the peasants worked in two parallel economies: the official one of the city or town, and their own in isolation. The peasants used the money or credits from the official economy to buy items that could not be made on the farms.

As upper-class leaders, the clergy dealt with the *jíbaros* in the same manner as many of the secular authorities. They used sermons to admonish the faithful and denounce the vices found among the poor, such as drinking and gambling. But their personal conduct sometimes contradicted such pronouncements, destroying credibility among the people (Figueroa, 81). In essence, both *criollos* and the Spanish clergy were part of two social classes that, despite antagonism toward each other, were usually united against the poor (Moore, 1/3).

The key to understanding the power of the rural culture is tied to the deinstitutionalized nature of folk Catholicism. The customs, devotions, reliance upon and familiarity with the spirit world, the mode of speech, the sympathy with the land—these were not bits and pieces of *jíbaro* life. They were essential to a world view that was held together with the legitimizing force of Catholicism. Yet the social distance built into this religion of the common people meant that it was responsive to the values of the *jíbaro* rather than to the clergy. In a sense, the people in the hinterland came to the church in the plaza as consumers of sacraments—those elements of Catholicism they could not manufacture themselves. In their mountain *bohíos,* however, they assumed the roles of clergy in organizing the prayers, devotions, processions, and multiple local customs, including familial baptism of the newborn.

The perpetuation of these customs was taken as a religious duty, because in fact virtually all of the folk traditions had some connection to the religious feeling of the people toward themselves, the land, and their values. Unspoiled by civic and ecclesiastical politics, the folk Catholicism of Puerto Rico preserved its core identity as an island creation. It was a cultural template that wove together culture, economics, and religion.

When Puerto Rico passed to United States rule in 1898 as a result of the Spanish-American War, the Spanish legacy of a state-supported Catholicism was abolished almost immediately (Fernández Méndez, 327; Stevens-Arroyo, in Sandoval 1983, 269, 270). The Washington-appointed governors responded to the tenor of the times and perceived Catholicism and the Spanish language as elements alien to the Americanization of Puerto Rico and its people. Alongside the military-political endeavor to Americanize was a religious impulse to Protestantize.

United States' Protestant churches united in an effort to snatch the inhabitants of the small island from "superstition" and Catholic obscurantism and lead them into the light of the gospel (Pantojas, 13–20; Moore, 2/1ff.) The full resources of the government—education, government agencies, social services—cooperated with Protestant ministers and their wives, who descended on the island as missionaries and school teachers and who were among the few to speak the official language of Puerto Rico, which was decreed as English in 1911.

The new rulers from the North drew few distinctions between the institutionalized Catholicism of the displaced Puerto Rican elite and the folk Catholicism that survived in the countryside, distant from city and cathedral alike. In its scarcely disguised disdain for Catholicism, United States rule minimized the differences between church as institution and as popular religion, thus often failing to perceive the social distance between urban and rural Catholics that had been part of pre-1898 Puerto Rico.

The penchant to treat Catholicism as a lower-class religion had its first impact on the Catholic elite, which had enjoyed a privileged status under Spanish rule. Members of the elite now found themselves lumped together with the country folk because of a shared Catholicism. These urban elites often reacted by becoming Hispanophiles, extolling Spanish culture for its humanist values and Catholicism for its superiority over Protestantism. Stevens-Arroyo (1980, 272, 273) has shown how certain Puerto Rican thinkers, such as José de Diego and Pedro Albizu Campos, sought to emphasize the validity of Catholicism in Puerto Rico and to prove its incompatibility with a United States brand of Catholicism as well as United States social and political agendas. Language, culture, and religion became the "blessed trinity" of the proponents of Puerto Rican independence, especially with the Nationalist Party from 1930 to 1954. Others, as in the case of the writers of *El ideal católico,* a weekly publication founded by a Spanish Vincentian, appealed to the United States as guardian against liberal free-thinkers (Julián de Nieves, 27–40). Fearful of the anti-church bias of the Puerto Rican *criollos* who had advocated separation from Spain in the nineteenth century, these conservative Catholics acquiesced to the Protestantization of the peasants in the countryside in exchange for privileges within the urban context (Silva Gotay 1985, 30).

In effect, religion became a part of the effort of members of the upper class to reverse the process that had removed them from power. Religion had been politicized, and Catholicism became a form of anti-Yankeeism for some and a protection against Puerto Rican liberal politics for others (Silva Gotay 1985, 27–29). These two sets of leaders—one liberal and nationalist, the other conservative and politically pro-American—complicated administration of the Puerto Rican Catholic church by an imported United States hierarchy from 1898 to 1964.

The North American Catholic hierarchy, still attempting to prove itself as pro-American and supportive of the 1898 war, advised Rome against placing a native Puerto Rican in the see of San Juan once the Spaniards withdrew (Hennesey, 204–5; Silva Gotay 1985, 9; Julián de Nieves, 63). It remained unclear until the Foraker Act of 1900 whether or not the United States would allow Puerto Rico to follow Cuba to gradual independence. The United States hierarchy generally advocated treating Puerto Rico as another California or New Mexico—a territory on its way to becoming a state in the Union. The Vatican was less decided. As a precautionary measure the Holy See placed Puerto Rico directly under the Propaganda Fidei in Rome and named a Bavarian-born bishop, James Humbert Blenck, a member of the Marist Congregation and naturalized American citizen (Julián de Nieves, 5–6, 40; Berbusse 1966, 204–8).

Blenck and his first four episcopal successors sought to discourage the Catholic elite from politicizing Catholicism as a form of anti-Americanism. This would have stoked the fires of bigotry in those in the United States who sought to paint Catholicism as anti-American (Julián de Nieves, 130–31). Until the Puerto Rican Aponte Martínez was ordained a bishop in the mid 1960s, all bishops appointed for the island were not only North Americans but "energetic Americanizers" as well (Julián de Nieves, 124).[6] For instance, the Catholic school system brought to Puerto Rico by the new missionaries was fashioned after that of the United States, with English as the language of instruction (Julián de Nieves, 191; Silva Gotay 1985, 16 n. 24; cf. Bierne, 99–116), treating Puerto Ricans in their own homeland as if they were the Catholic immigrants to the United States (Julián de Nieves, 193–94). The bishop suppressed the Christmas Eve midnight mass (*misa de gallo*) in 1898 in agreement with the military authorities for reasons of security (Julián de Nieves, 233). The *Catholic Standard and Times,* an official publication of the Philadelphia Archdiocese, joined the Protestant Yankee voice in abusing the Catholicism of Puerto Rico and extolling the invasion:

> [It] has been said . . . that Puerto Rico is a Catholic country without a religion. Talleyrand located that virtue in the female temperament; and this cynicism of the French author could have some validity in countries like Puerto Rico, where conditions of climate and circumstance exert an influence in religious practice, although religion is not all practice. . . . Perhaps it was fitting that Puerto Rico should come into contact with our robust American environment at a time least expected, thus placing her in our area of defense (cited in Julián de Nieves, 113).

With the preconceived notion that Catholicism in Puerto Rico was worthless, and with the contradictory advice of liberal Puerto Ricans on the one hand and conservative pro-Americanists on the other, the bishops after 1898 set about building a new Catholicism upon values imported from the experience of the North American Catholic church. In 1897 there were twenty-nine native Puerto Rican priests among more than one hundred practicing the ministry in Puerto Rico. The trauma of the invasion produced several notable apostates from this slim number (Moore, 2:17–78), and Bishop Blenck disbanded the native seminary, sending all candidates to the United States for priestly formation (Julián de Nieves, 73). By 1925 there were only twelve native priests left on the island, and the first newly ordained diocesan priest since American rule in 1898 came in 1926 (Julián de Nieves, 75–77). Even the conservatives of *El ideal católico* criticized the bishop in 1909 for giving virtually every city parish to North Americans instead of native Puerto Ricans (Julián de Nieves, 76). The religious orders fared even worse, so that by 1960 there were only four native Puerto Rican priests from among all of the North American–based orders that had come to Puerto Rico for missionary work. Thus, far from alleviating the discouragement of native vocations that had characterized the nineteenth century under Spanish rule, the bishops from the United States exacerbated the situation. Given the differences not only of class, but also of culture and language of these clergy from the people they served, social distance between rural Catholics in Puerto Rico and the clergy increased. The most vital native Catholic movement came from ordinary rural lay men, who were organized into a missionary institute called *Hermanos Cheos* to combat the Protestantization of the countryside (McCarrick, in Bates, 62; Ferrée et al., 4/73; 2/3).

However contradictory it may seem, the bishops appointed to the see of San Juan saw their task as building up Catholicism in a country that had practiced the religion some two hundred and seventy years before the founding of the United States. In order to compete with the Americanizing trend of Protestantism in Puerto Rico, the Catholic church undertook the Americanizing role for itself as well. The Knights of Columbus, for instance, were suggested as an antidote to Freemasons in Puerto Rico, just as they had been in the United States (Julián de Nieves, 128–29). Such upper-class Catholic organizations, says Elisa Julián de Nieves, had a "subversive role," and were "utilized for covert, political ends" (130). In 1924 the Knights asked the Holy See to place Puerto Rico under the Catholic hierarchy of the United States, and in 1928 they asked President Calvin Coolidge to make Puerto Rico a state of the union (Julián de Nieves, 130–31).

Within the typical rural parish on the other hand, pious groups rather than politicized ones were organized with regularity. Chief among these were societies that had been successful among the immigrants to New York City. Thus Puerto Ricans were asked to join the Holy Name Society, the Holy Rosary Society, and the Sodality of the Blessed Virgin Mary, renamed *Las Hijas de María* (Ferrée et al., 2/5; 2/46–49). These were voluntary organizations that provided a Catholic substitute for the sect organization of Protestantism in Puerto Rico. Lay organizations in Puerto Rico were primarily intended not for "conversion" but to affirm Catholic identity as the island's chief religious group.

The Synod of 1917 was held by Bishop Ambrose Jones (1907–21), noted for "his sledge-hammer diligence in pursuit of his Church image refurbishing objective" (Julián de Nieves, 87). This synod abolished the local canons of the cathedral (*cabildo*) in favor of total power for the ordinary (Silva Gotay 1985, 26; Julián de Nieves, 90, see 64). All parish finances were centralized in what was called *Fondos de Fábrica*, in imitation of some North

American dioceses. The synod set fixed "prices" on services, so that a high mass "cost" more than a low mass, not just on the personal discretion of the cleric, but as an institutional rule. Parochial schools, usually entrusted only to a North American order of religious women, acquired a distinct class orientation, targeting the children of the upper class (Silva Gotay 1985, 30; Julián de Nieves, 190–91). To its credit, the synod recognized the validity of traditions in the countryside, setting up regulations to govern objectionable abuses (Torres Díaz; Stevens-Arroyo, in Sandoval, 270). However, these concessions were granted in the nature of exception and as temporary submission to lack of more thorough Catholic education.

Cardinal Farley, archbishop of New York, was invited to preside at the Synod of 1917. Bishop Jones had the specific objective of encouraging more New York–based religious order to adopt Puerto Rico as a missionary territory. As a result of Jones's cultivation of Cardinal Farley's attention, and of his own Philadelphia-based contacts, the majority of the religious communities in Puerto Rico have come from the northeastern United States.[7] They began to arrive on the island, however, nineteen years after the Protestant missionaries, who had arrived in considerable numbers immediately after its occupation in 1898.

Moreover, when it came to the people of the countryside—those outside the reach of Catholic schools and the claim of partisan politics—the bishops called in missionaries from New York, Boston, and Philadelphia to bolster the practice of Catholicism on the island (Julián de Nieves, 82–84). Anxious on the one hand to distance themselves from the Spanish institution, and on the other fearful of losing important numbers of the faithful to their competitors, the North American missionaries emphasized the public practices that had always drawn the *jíbaros* to the church building—processions, rosaries, fiestas, novenas, and the like. Such devotions noticeably lacked the incorporation of Puerto Rican natives as clergy and perpetuated the marginal role as consumer of ecclesiastically produced sacramentalism that had developed under Spanish rule.

Of the mainland missionary groups the Redemptorists emerged as the most important. Not only were they more numerous among the priests, but they also had some of their clergymen named to the episcopacy in Puerto Rico.[8] The missionary approach of the Redemptorists placed emphasis upon personal piety and popular religion (Van Delft; Dolan 1978, 13, 19–50). The Redemptorists utilized the parish mission, a special form of intensive preaching at the grass-roots level, as a means of restoring a sense of vitality to the island's Catholicism. However, most of the pious practices utilized came from the Mediterranean traditions of Catholicism rather than from specifically Puerto Rican devotions. For instance, Marian processions, novenas, and festivals were encouraged, but devotion to Our Lady of Hormigueros was neglected and belief in direct contact and familiarity with the spirit world was condemned (Steward, 88).[9] Thus United States missionary practices set up a distinction between traditional piety, that is, Mediterranean devotions, and those features of popular religion the missionaries saw as superstitious (Stevens-Arroyo 1981, 20–29).

In the new Catholic institution initiated by the 1898 invasion, only educated Catholic leadership in urban centers suffered a loss in social prestige; the people who practiced the Puerto Rican form of folk Catholicism remained safe within the normal social distance from institutional religion. They were relatively unaffected by the shift from distant Spanish clergy to distant North American missionaries.

The change in this state of affairs in Puerto Rico began with Operation Bootstrap in 1948, when the secular, liberal political leader Luis Muñoz Marín initiated a massive industrialization program. The polices of Muñoz attracted large numbers of United States–owned factories to the country towns, but unlike previous political regimes, this one was populist and had earned the respect of many of the *jíbaros*.

The industrialization dislodged large numbers of peasants from the hinterland and thrust them into a new urban reality on the island. As an adaptive social mechanism, religion played a significant role in shaping Puerto Rico in the 1960s, as the birth control controversy and the foundation of a "Catholic" political party suggest (Silva Gotay 1988). Finding folk religious expression to be out of step with urban exigencies, many uprooted *campesinos* found in Pentecostalism a closer fit for a work ethic oriented to the needs of capitalism and urban life (Besalga, 89ff.; Rivera Pagán, 60–65). Those who stayed within Catholicism in the mushrooming towns or in the big city had to adapt. They were often left with a religion both Americanizing and distant from the traditional Puerto Rican folk Catholicism. Thus, as former *jíbaros* adjusted to the change of social distance in the modernizing Puerto Rican society, the old "fit" of rural folk Catholicism was eroded.

The conflicts between the American bishops and Muñoz Marín on the question of birth control and the Catholic vote in the 1960 elections help demonstrate that Catholicism had been politicized and that the erosion of social distance had altered a core folk culture that had endured for nearly three centuries (see chapter 5). Silva Gotay is of the opinion that the controversies of 1960 broke the back of the nationalist Catholic sentiment, and that subsequently the majority of urban Catholics were pro-statehood and pro-Americanizers (Silva Gotay 1985, 34; 1988, 174–76).

In the meanwhile, massive numbers of *jíbaros* were leaving the countryside and coming directly to the northeastern urban centers of the mainland, bypassing in the process the experience of urban reality in Puerto Rico and the ensuing conflict within Catholicism there. The journey of Oxcart Catholicism to Fifth Avenue had begun. Ironically, the *jíbaros'* core value was transferred to the greatest urban center of the United States. Its social distance from institutionalized Catholicism, however, remained as its principal characteristic within a new *isla* that begins in Manhattan.

3. From Village Parishes to Cosmopolitan Archdiocese

Enanteh se podía ser probe y tenel dignidá. ¿Y tú sabeh polqué? Polque el probe tenía argo en qué creer. Unoh creían en Dióh, otroh creían en la tierra, otroh creían en loh hombreh. Hoy no noh dejan creer en ná. Hoy a tuh sijoh sólo leh senseñan a creel en loh chavoh... y en eso que ñaman cencia... Pero del corasón, ná. Del corasón naide se acuelda. Y el corasón se seca como una habichuela vieja. ¡Ay mija, naide pué tenel dignidá ni velgüensa con el corasón seco como una habichuela!

Before, you could be poor and still have dignity. And you know why? 'Cause the poor had somethin' to believe in. Some believed in God, others believed in the land, others believed in men. Today they don't let us believe in anythin'. Today they just teach your kids to believe in money... and what they call science... But never anythin' about the heart. Nobody remembers the heart. And the heart dries up like an old bean. Oh, my child, you can't have dignity or pride with your heart shriveled up like a bean!

—Don Chago, in *The Oxcart,* Act I

In order to understand the ways in which the Puerto Rican migration influenced the policies of the Archdiocese of New York, it is necessary to profile the nature of the apostolate toward all newcomers to the city. The Puerto Ricans, after all, were not the first non-English-speaking Catholic group to arrive in significant numbers in New York.

In a sense, the Puerto Ricans inherited a role that had been defined over nearly a century and a half as both the city of New York and the institution of the archdiocese had evolved together. The pattern of resolving conflicts and fostering interests had established a set of expectations about what the archdiocese should do and how the newcomers should respond. These form the background for understanding the attitudes of the New York Catholic church towards Puerto Ricans. And while much of this institutional baggage was brought by the bishops to the island of Puerto Rico after 1898, the experiences in New York itself merits special treatment. Since a complete historical account of the Catholic church in New York is beyond the scope of this chapter, I can hope only to summarize a complex history in describing the essential pattern of administering to non–English-speaking Catholics within the New York Archdiocese in institutional terms.

The first point that requires emphasis is the defensiveness of Catholicism toward American nationalism. The view of Catholicism on the part of most American intellectuals has not been very different from the opinion of Protestant theologian H. Richard Niebuhr: "Doubtless Roman Catholicism has made important contributions to American life, yet both history and religious census support the statement that Protestantism is America's only national religion and to ignore that fact is to view the country from a false angle" (Niebuhr, 17).

One need not agree with this verdict to recognize that it sets the stage for understanding why American Catholicism has always professed a strong dose of nationalism in its religious production. Catholicism inherited a hierarchical structure from the Middle Ages, and during much of the modern era, the European church generally opposed social, cultural, political, and economic forms that Protestants identified as modern. Consequently, loyalty to the pope and the Catholic faith was often equated in the early North America with an obscurantism barely compatible with democracy. The disparate Catholic nationalities and non–English-language groups that migrated to the United States were often more familiar with authoritarianism than with electoral politics. A socioeconomic status inferior to that of the Protestant majority only complicated the Catholic dilemma of trying to adapt to society and culture in the United States (Gleason 1978, 5–7). It was often difficult to escape the accusation that the Catholic church was an institution foreign to the United States and the American democratic ideal. Catholic intellectuals of the nineteenth century, like Orestes Brownson and Father Isaac Hecker, both American-born converts from Protestantism, developed philosophical and historical arguments to defend Catholicism against these accusations. Sadly, such pro-American polemics sometimes demonstrated a prejudice of their own against immigrants, particularly the Irish (Hennesey 1981a, 103–15; O'Brien, 144).

The bias of the Protestant majority was not only an intellectualized premise, it also was a rallying cry for active persecution of Catholics, especially in the antebellum movement of Nativism. The Reverend Lyman Beecher denounced Catholicism in 1834 with notions that were to be repeated when the United States annexed Puerto Rico after the 1898 war with Spain: "The Catholic Church now holds in darkness and bondage nearly half the civilized world. . . . It is the most skillful, powerful, dreadful system of corruption of those who wield it, and of slavery and debasement to those who live under it" (cited in Hennesey 1981a, 119). Fanned by economic recession and political scapegoating, violent attacks against Catholics and their churches erupted in the spring of 1844, leaving permanent scars even after the demise of the Whig Party (Hennesey 1981a, 116–37; Ellis, 60–81).

As a result, Catholicism in the United States evolved institutional forms with accompanying political, ecclesiastical, and theological attitudes that can be traced to this immigrant experience. Philip Gleason suggests that the Catholic church in the United States is itself "an institutional immigrant" undergoing a process of adaptation and acculturation not unlike that experienced by the faithful at an individual level (Gleason 1969, 3–32). But even if one counts upon the Anglo-Catholic model as the starting point rather than the immigrant experience (O'Brien, 88–89), it is not a novel hypothesis to say that the immigration of ethnic peoples changed the institutions of the church in New York (Curran, in Alvarez, 26–50). Moreover, the Archdiocese of New York can be considered a representative of trends at work in the United States Catholic church. Because of its size and importance throughout both Catholic and general United States history down to the present, the New York Catholic archdiocese was often a protagonist in the policy decisions that have shaped the Catholic church in the United States. The words of convert-priest Isaac Hecker, first written in 1864, continue to have meaning: "The Archdiocese of New York is the largest and in every respect, the most influential in this country," he wrote to a friend in the Vatican. And New

York City "[is] the heart of this country, the Rome of our modern Republic" (quoted in Dolan 1975, 9 n. 18).

The institutions of the early American church in New York reflected the minority status that was a heritage from colonial times. Catholics lived in the tradition of the "gentility" of English Catholicism, quietly accepting an inferior status and social role (Dolan 1975, 3). Most decisions on pastoral practice were made at the level of the parish and not in an archdiocesan chancery. Moreover, mirroring the democratic participation of Protestant laity in church decisions, Catholic parishes usually had a board of trustees to manage church funds and set priorities for local ministry. But this apparently innocent adaptation of institutional organization to American practice led to bitter contests between bishop and trustees over the naming of pastors (Ellis, 44–46). New York's trustees, for instance, dismissed one pastor because they did not like his manners and named another because of his oratorical ability (Hennesey 1981a, 76–77).

The "Rome of our modern Republic" was built upon these humble foundations. For instance, it was not until 1784 that New York repealed its anti-resident priest statute (Hennesey 1981a, 75), and the first bishop to arrive in the city in 1815 "found only three churches, four priests, a substantial debt, and a far from quiescent board of lay trustees controlling the . . . property" (Hennesey 1981a, 91). Although the number of Catholics was rapidly increasing with the immigration of peasant Irish and Germans, and the number of churches increased to eight by 1836, the ministry was largely directed from the parish level.

The foundation of parishes was a haphazard affair, often without fixed boundaries and depending almost entirely on the generosity of the parishioners. The central authority of the church in New York was generally too poor to provide any more that the barest minimum to establish new churches and lacked the infrastructure to plan or control growth. Since parish limits were generally identical to those of the neighborhood, the parish churches were neighborhood institutions and formed part of what Dolan characterizes as "the ethnic village" (1975, 20, 27–44). Conflict among different Catholic ethnic groups was at a minimum among New York lay parishioners, usually because they were in different parishes (Dolan 1975, 20 n. 36).

The expansion of Catholicism in the New York City of the early nineteenth century depended upon service to the basic social needs of the immigrant. As a newcomer taking up life in a strange and often hostile environment, the immigrant needed social supports. The traditional solution to poverty of almsgiving was ineffective; there were so many immigrants and so few rich Catholics in the New York of 1820 that new means of self-help had to be found. Moreover, the role of government in early nineteenth-century New York did not include remedies of social work (Feagin, 29–57). Thus, Catholicism in New York had a commitment to social concern by attending to the compelling needs of the immigrants.

The apostolate was virtually directed at a local level in the parishes under the leadership of the pastor without much assistance from an archdiocesan-dictated policy. Parishes, not the diocese, sponsored education, charitable works, and often published their own journals (Dolan 1975, 100, 102–11). Representative of the parish apostolate of the time was the Cuban-born priest Félix Varela, who had come to New York in 1823 seeking political refuge from Spanish rule. He was founder and first pastor of Transfiguration Parish on Mott Street and was named vicar-general of the diocese. Varela administered to his mostly Irish immigrant parishioners with whatever clergy he could find—priests from Austria, Poland, Portugal, Italy, Ireland, and Cuba (Benedi, 11, 9). He was noted for his liberal ideas concerning democracy and abolition of slavery—the cause of his exile—and frequently wrote on these subjects in English-language newspapers. He founded the Temperance Movement in his parish, initiated works of charity by establishing a parish center for orphans and widows, and earned a reputation in his lifetime as the central figure in the social apostolate of New York (Dolan 1975, 126 n. 23). Yet, despite Varela's distinguished career, Dolan notes that after his death in St. Augustine, Florida, in 1853, the Cuban-born priest was "forgotten" by historians of the archdiocese (Dolan 1975, 47, 65 nn.123–24).[1]

This grievous omission is attributable to profound social changes in New York City and organizational changes in the church. During the period 1815–65, that is, from the end of the War of 1812 until the conclusion of the Civil War, New York City surpassed Philadelphia as the most populous United States city and established commercial and industrial leadership in the nation (Lankevich and Furer, 87–114). With the opening of the Erie Canal transatlantic commerce increased significantly, so that by 1860, two-thirds of all the nation's imports and one-third of its exports passed through the port of New York (Albion, 386).

The Catholic population in New York also increased dramatically. From a total of about 15,000 in 1815, New York's Catholic population soared to 400,000 in 1865, forming one-half of New York's population (Dolan 1975, 15 n. 10). The migrations of the famine years swelled the Irish population in the United States so that by 1860 foreign-born Irish living in New York numbered 203,740—about one out of every four New Yorkers (Dolan 1975, 22 n. 42). The Germans, for their part, had grown in number to nearly 120,000, and German was the language in eight of the thirty-two parishes in the city, although about half of the Catholic Germans were enrolled in non–German-speaking parishes (Dolan 1975, 22 n. 48). The French, Italians, and blacks formed the other major ethnic groups in New York City in 1860 (Dolan 1975, 23–24). While the Hispanic presence in New York was limited to a few merchants and political exiles from Spain, Portugal, and various Latin American countries (see Hennesey 1981, 75), this group was influential enough to secure a Spanish parish dedicated to Our Lady of Pilar in 1859 (Stevens-Arroyo, in Sandoval, 274). But this church was located in Brooklyn, which has a different ecclesiastical history and lies outside the immediate scope of this study.

The social and demographic changes were accompanied by a shift in the organization of the church in New York under the forceful leadership of Bishop John Hughes. Hughes came to New York as co-adjutor bishop in 1838, succeeded to the archdiocese in 1842, and remained the principal figure of New York Catholicism until his death in 1864. As ordinary, John Hughes centralized the authority of the archdiocese around himself. He transformed the cluster of neighborhood parishes—with their attendant schools, charitable institutions, and dedicated clergy—into a network of interrelated agencies for a single institution. He founded a school system and made New York the model for a similar process throughout the United States (Dolan 1975, 104 n. 26).

Hughes convoked the first diocesan synod in 1842, strengthening his own position as supreme ruler of Catholicism in New

York by a series of regulations that solidified the quasi-monarchical powers of the hierarchy over clergy and laity alike. Synods in 1850 and 1861 further strengthened his power (Dolan 1975, 163 n. 20). Hughes also founded the Chancery Office in 1852, which subsequently became the sole access to Rome for marriage dispensations and a host of other administrative aspects of church life.

Inasmuch as Hughes's style of church authority accompanied the emergence of "boss rule" and "machine politics" in the bustling city of New York, it is not erroneous to describe these changes as interrelated. According to T. J. Curran, by the 1850s Archbishop Hughes had certainly became "the most powerful bishop in America. As his power grew, so did his autocratic behavior" (Curran, in Alvarez, 130). Both church and city were undergoing a process of adaptation to the demands of the metropolis. Moreover, the cultural predisposition of the host of immigrants, most of whom came from Ireland, was for authoritarianism. According to Dolan, "Hughes ruled like an Irish chieftain, and the Irish respect for the hierarchy of power made his task all the easier" (Dolan 1975, 165).

The ability to speak English on the part of the Irish, who had already endured more than two hundred years of British rule in their homeland, was an advantage in America. The deprivation of the native Gaelic language, which had been intended as a tool of subjugation, ironically became a staff for liberation across the Atlantic (Greeley 1972, 26, 59–60). Moreover, laws for citizenship and voting residency were not as complicated as today. One Protestant politician in Boston complained: "Irishmen fresh from the bogs of Ireland are led up to vote like dumb brutes . . . to vote down intelligent, honest, native Americans" (Hennesey 1981, 119). The numbers of Irish and their acquired skills for collective action brought them considerable political power and patronage in antebellum New York. The visibility of the Catholic archbishop and the role of the parish organizations had contributed to this success in America, with the result that the archdiocese had become an urban institution that wielded considerable political influence. Hughes wrote "Among public men from the President down, there are few who are not under the impression that a spoken word of mine, or even a hint is sufficient to vibrate especially among Catholics, from one extremity of the United States to the other" (cited in Ana María Díaz Ramírez 1983, 111 n. 63).

Hughes utilized the Catholic position of majority population in New York City as a tool for collective power. Confrontation seems to have been his principal strategy. He used confrontation in the face of the Know-Nothing riots of 1844 (Ellis, 67); he used it to challenge the monopoly that the public schools claimed over all formal education (Ellis, 66); he employed it in disputes with his own clergy and in his dealings with dissenting ethnic groups. He is quoted as affirming that anti-Catholicism and religious bigotry were useful tools in fomenting the cohesiveness of the Catholic people (Dolan 1975, 54 n. 51, 162 n. 19).

Hughes observation finds some support in conflict theory, which states that a group's cohesiveness is strengthened when a perceived or actual threat from the outside is felt (Coser). Whatever the merits or defects of Archbishop Hughes's style of governance, it produced a profound change in the institutional organization of New York Catholicism. The social factors influencing the times in New York City were the huge demographic increase by mass migration from one specific group (Irish) and that group's ability to turn to its own advantage the urban Democratic Party machine of Tammany Hall (Glazer and Moynihan, 222–29). In the case of antebellum New York, the leadership of the archbishop reformed the institutional organization of the church in accord with these social changes. In so doing, he maximized Catholic political and economic power. This remarkable institutional leadership by the Archdiocese of New York on behalf of the Irish frames my analysis of how other Catholic groups have had an impact upon the institutional church in New York.

The financial advantage to the nineteenth-century institutional church presented by these changes is very clear. Hughes founded the Debt Association in 1841 in order to rescue bankrupt parishes. Eventually the collection of small sums of money from many of the faithful provided funds for investment and enterprise, leading to the foundation of the Emigrant Savings Bank (Dolan 1975, 47). Through these and other policies Hughes virtually eliminated the trustee system in New York. And with the repeal in 1863 of the Putnam Act, which technically prohibited the archbishop from holding property in his own name, his transformation of the organization of the New York church was complete. From a defensive, ill-coordinated and amorphous cluster of parishes populated by poor immigrants of polyglot origins, the church in New

York had become a powerful urban institution, directed by an authoritarian bishop who was not hesitant to use his power to veto unwanted policies.

The power brought by centralization enlarged Catholicism's ambitions. The church buildings in New York were considered to rival the classic cathedrals of Europe. Hughes did not live to see the opening of St. Patrick's on Fifth Avenue in 1879, but the event symbolized the acceptance among New York's officialdom that the Catholic cathedral, like Catholicism, was a landmark on the New York skyline (Dolan 1975, 166, 167). The prestige of the archdiocese increased worldwide when the successor to Hughes, Archbishop John McCloskey, became the first United States prelate ever named to the Sacred College of Cardinals.

The need to be an urban institution was rooted so deeply in the notion of advancement for the Catholic church that, even while he recognized the bucolic allure of the countryside (Dolan 1975, 132–36), Archbishop Hughes and his successors opposed the effort to disperse Irish immigrants into the American farmland (Brown 1950).[2] Hughes argued that "scattering Catholics throughout the West would leave them easy prey to Protestant ministers," and that in the urban situation clergy were more accessible than on the farm (O'Brien, 91). Similar opposition was shown two decades later by Hughes's successors toward the dispersal of the Italians (Tomasi, 84 n. 88).

David O'Brien suggests that this resettlement debate was not a fight between liberals, who wanted to Americanize the immigrant, and conservatives, who wished to preserve ethnic roots. The controversies were based on different notions of American nationalism (O'Brien, 63). Certainly, there is substance to O'Brien's explanation that Turner's "frontier thesis" played a large role in the thinking of the so-called liberals such as Ireland, Hecker, Brownson, Spalding, and Keane. Following Turner, they suggested that the frontier experience was a necessary element in the making of an "American" and the catalyst in breaking loose from European ways (O'Brien, 44, 56 n. 11). For Turner, the city represented an "artificial and parasitic growth permeated by European remnants and populated by alien Catholics and Jews, where the assimilating power of the American environment could be felt only indirectly if at all" (O'Brien, 55). On the other hand, for the urban prelates—and the archbishop of New York, in particular—the city was the one battleground in the United States where Catholicism had achieved a measure of success. The reluctance of these prelates to abandon Catholic schools, the Democratic Party machine, opulent urban church buildings, and power politics was neither a theological nor ideological issue; it was a structural necessity that brought upon Catholics a long-lasting criticism (Hennesey 1981a, 118).

From a sociologist's point of view, I think that the so-called conservative bishops demonstrated the soundness of the axiom that a group assimilates from a position of strength (see Fitzpatrick 1971, 42–43). Life in the city gave Catholics a group identity that helped them force the general society of New York to make accommodations itself, even as the Catholics were expected to assimilate to New York. Assimilation as individuals in a rural setting would have resulted in the loss of a Catholic identity and a complete absorption into a Protestant United States with even more frequency than that which did occur (Dolan 1978, 6–10).

But the acquired powers of an urban institution affected the nature of pastoral practice of the church. Hennesey says: "The hierarchical church had become an administrative church, where 'the most valued gifts [in episcopal candidates—and the same was true of pastors] were properly those of a banker and not of a pastor of souls' " (Hennesey 1981b, 26). Instead of a spiritual leader in works of asceticism and public charity, like Varela, there was a shift to pastors judged successful on the basis of their business and financial administration, the so-called brick-and-mortar priests (see Dolan 1973; Curran, in Alvarez, 130ff.)

As part of the city establishment, New York Catholicism considerably lessened its direct commitment to social concerns (Dolan 1975, 121–26). Archbishop Hughes urged upon the rich "moderation in enjoyment," and to the poor "patience under their trials and affection toward their wealthier brothers" (cited in Dolan 1975, 124). Orestes Brownson, once an advocate of utopian socialism at Brook Farm, advised the church to leave social concern to the government and concentrate on the moral rectitude implicit in pastoral care (cited in Dolan 1975, 122 n. 3). This is not to imply that there were no charitable institutions in the archdiocese under John Hughes; indeed, he founded hospices and homes for the indigent and the wayward (Dolan 1975, 132–33). Still, the dispensation of charity was now an institutionalized exchange, and the appearance of a form of Catholic philanthropy was itself a proof of the assimilation of Catholics to the norms of the dominant Protestant majority (Dolan 1975, 139–40). Thus, the first fruit of church institutionalization was political power and social prestige.

This rise in power and affluence for the New York church was accompanied by a strong display of nationalistic support for the United States. Catholics of an earlier period had been no less patriotic, but in general, bishops, pastors, and laity of that era adopted low visibility in political matters in order to avoid controversy. Archbishop Hughes, however, took vigorous steps to align the church with nationalistic issues, such as support for the War with México (Ellis, 68). Despite his dislike of abolitionists and African-Americans (Ellis, 87–90; Dohen, 98), he urged Catholics to support the Union in the War Between the States by enlisting in the army. Moreover, in a departure from the nonpartisan character of the episcopal role of previous decades, Hughes accepted a year-long commission by President Abraham Lincoln and Secretary of State William H. Seward to go to France in order to dissuade Napoleon III from supporting the Confederacy (Ellis, 95).

It has been suggested that active support of war on the part of Hughes and other American bishops was compensation for potentially anti-American theological positions. For instance, Hughes's support for the Mexican War coincided with the accusations of anti-Americanism from Whig Nativists; participation in the Civil War distracted from the embarrassing condemnation of religious tolerance and republican government in the aftermath of the loss of the Papal States and Pius IX's eventual 1864 *Syllabus of Errors* (Stevens-Arroyo 1990; see Hennesey 1981a, 124, 150–57). Most American bishops championed the war against Spain in 1898, and only John Lancaster Spalding opposed the acquisition of Puerto Rico and other colonial territories (Hennesey 1981a, 205). The identification of United States Catholicism with a crusade against "all that is old and vile and mean and rotten and cruel and false in Europe" was a factor in Rome's condemnation of an heretical Americanism in *Testem Benevolentiae* in 1899 (citing Fogarty, in Hennesey 1981a, 205 n. 5; see Stevens-Arroyo 1990). But whatever the motivation for the prominent and visible support by the episcopacy for war against Spain, it has already been shown above that the identification with imperialist motives complicated the apostolate of the North American church among Puerto Ricans from the outset. While the context of this support can be explained in terms of the dynamics of institutional needs in the United States, it presented Puerto Rican Catholics with reason to suspect that North American Catholicism was North American first and Catholic second.

The Archdiocese of New York was not alone in its American nationalism. In a sense, the nineteenth-century liberals, among them Spalding, Ireland, and Gibbons, gained this title because they often sided with the Republican Party, which at that time represented an aggressive role for federal government (Barger, in Alvarez, 53–62; Dohen, 59–63). The reason for New York's reputation for conservatism came from its imitation of the autocratic style of church government and ready cooperation with the urban political machine of the Democratic Party. Both "liberals" and "conservatives" however, advocated assimilation to American society for Catholics. The difference lay only in whether the assimilation was to be focused on individuals or the collectivity.

The identification of the church in New York with American patriotism was so complete that it generally excluded support for Irish nationalism. For instance, the New York–based Fenian Brotherhood, which subsequently evolved into the Irish Republican Army, was repudiated by the hierarchy, and Hughes's successor, Cardinal McCloskey, expressly forbade Catholics to attend a public rally for the Fenian movement (Dolan 1975, 92 n. 24; T. Brown, 40, 41). The fine-line distinction between cultural pride in one's ancestry and political nationalism was vigorously pursued by New York's bishops (see Hennesey 1981a, 188 n. 22). And ever since the flush of patriotism for the establishment of the Irish Free State in the twentieth century, the official stand of New York's cardinal has generally been cool to nationalist Irish movements (see Greeley 1972b, 23).

Catholic loyalty was not to any particular nation, even if largely Catholic. Hughes took the lead in rallying support for Pius IX against Italian Nationalists, and frictions frequently appeared between Germans who had supported the socialist movements of 1848 and those who had arrived previously in the United States (Dolan 1975, 91, 92). Hughes utilized loyalty to the Holy See as a supranational bond among the various ethnic immigrant groups. It became a custom to fly the papal flag at public occasions and frequently to place it alongside the high altar in churches (Dolan 1975, 161; Dohen, 139, 161; Grasso, 252, 253). This devotion to the papacy intensified after the declaration of the dogma of papal infallibility in 1870. Moreover, the centralization of the universal church offices in the Vatican, coupled with the cult of the pope as the single infallible voice of God on earth, coincided with the monarchical style of New York's episcopal authority.

Besides power and affluence, and United States nationalism, the third factor that characterized the archdiocese in the nineteenth century was its Irishness. Because of the institutional dominance of the Irish and Irish-descent members, a paradigm was established for New York Catholicism. Parish life and behavior were expected to conform to an Irish Catholic core (Novak, 55–57). Because the Irish were numerically the largest ethnic group in New York, as well as the most powerful in leadership within the church, they considered themselves the most successful of immigrant Catholic groups in adaptation to life in the United States (Gleason 1978, 14). The Irish usually attributed this success to their own efforts and expected that imitation of their behavior would lead other Catholics to similar success (Greeley 1972b, 93–94; Gleason 1978, 16–17).

Thus, the pattern for church organization that had been established during the years of Archbishop Hughes's administration came to be the form which governed archdiocesan policy toward the influx of immigrants from Poland, Eastern Europe, and Italy. In this process a sense of inferiority was imparted to the non-Irish groups who had not yet assimilated into United States society in the way the Irish had done, producing an edge of competition and conflict between the Irish and other Catholic ethnic groups (Greeley 1977, 32–38).

To power, prestige, nationalism, and an Irish paradigm must be added yet another characteristic: the national parish. An archdiocesan decree of 1841 had legislated the existence of non-territorial parishes whose membership was determined by language groups. Legally, the bishop could divide his jurisdiction over Catholics residing in a designated area as he wished. While most often this was done with the parish level consisting of smaller territorial blocks within the larger diocese, the national parishes were the exception (see Gleason 1978, 13–14).

Much has been written in current sociology about the positive functions of the national parishes for non-English speakers, especially in New York. Fitzpatrick (1988, 103–18) makes this church institution of the mid-nineteenth century a paradigm of secular America's search for cultural pluralism. The independence of the national parish, initially intended as a stigma, was often transformed into a tool for Italian Catholic consciousness in New York (Tomasi, 182–84). Indeed, some contemporary Hispanics have called for its restoration on a national level (Deck 1990; Vidal, 344; Stevens-Arroyo 1980, 154–57).

But however ingenious the non–English-speaking Catholics proved to be in transforming the national parish into a positive institution of cultural preservation, at the time of its establishment in New York it was intended to separate the pastoral care of the English-speaking Irish and German majority from other Catholics (Dolan 1975, 25–26). The practical effect of the legislation was to keep archdiocesan financial resources at the service of the English-speaking parishes—overwhelmingly Irish. Henceforth, a national parish was virtually orphaned by the archdiocese, left to the financial resources of a religious order or the immigrant community, and relegated to a secondary role in archdiocesan attention (see Dolan 1975, 72–73). The aspects of pastoral care not conducted in Latin, such as preaching and the administration of sacraments, especially confession, were given to non-Irish clergy because it was the easiest way of relieving the burden placed on the archdiocese by the new immigrants. Moreover, it was generally expected that funds necessary to attend to social concerns for the non-English speaking would likewise come from their own resources. These often started with a church building society and sometimes blossomed into successful credit and cultural associations (Gleason 1978, 11, 19–21).

Hughes's interest in the national parish seemed to be stirred only when there was a threat to either his economic authority or canonical privileges. When an Italian priest appealed to Irish patrons for funds in order to build a church for the small Italian community in the city, Hughes promptly closed the parish and disciplined the priest (Dolan 1975, 23). He abolished a German Catholic cemetery, asserting diocesan control over all Catholic burials and threatened to close the church if Germans continued in search of a "German" cemetery not run by the Irish (Dolan 1975, 89, 90). Nor was he willing to share funds for either church or school with black Catholics; it was suggested they pay to go to a segregated school run by the Vincentians (Dolan 1975, 24 n. 61). The archbishop's disdain for blacks as a race, which led him to oppose the abolition of slavery, was not very different from racist attitudes common at the time among Irish Catholics. Even if it is unfair to judge Hughes by the standards of today on this score (see Gleason 1978, 4–5), the coolness of African-Americans toward Catholicism in New York has been considered a legacy of that era (Dolan 1975, 25; cf. Greeley 1972b, 226–30).

Ironically, the numerous Irish churches of New York were not officially designated national parishes, although they generally served the same socializing function for the Irish as the German and Italian parishes did for their parishioners (Greeley 1972a, 125). Dolan suggests that what at first may have seemed a negative measure, which would fragment the church by isolating the distinct groups, proved in the long run an effective way of fulfilling everybody's needs precisely because it "provided a safety valve by separating Irish and German Catholics from one another and fulfilling the particular religious needs of each group" (Dolan 1975, 93).

Tomasi considers the function of these parishes that of quasisects, which allowed Catholics to be either Irish Catholics or Italian Catholics, distinct but united (177–84). Symbolized by what was called the "basement church" (Tomasi, 76–84, 102–4), the national parishes of New York had a kind of social distance from the archbishop that bore benefits not unlike those that characterized Puerto Rican Catholicism on the island. Yet even after the passing of Hughes in 1864, the non-English-speaking national parishes tended to lose parishioners as the second generation learned English and imitated the Germans in joining the territorial parishes, a phenomenon described by Gleason as "generational transition" (Gleason 1978, 16–19). In a sense, the religious production of the "Irish" church, offering larger Catholic schools, more impressive buildings, more upwardly mobile membership, better neighborhood and professional organizations outstripped what was available in the national parishes.

This paradigm of the successful New York brand of Catholicism informed the vision of the bishops in Puerto Rico under

United States rule. As already described, the disdain for traditional Puerto Rican devotions and customs, the ignoring of native clergy, the English-language instruction of the island's Catholic schools, the identification with eventual statehood for the island, and a host of other policies brought to Puerto Rico can be traced to the mentality inherited from New York and Eastern Seaboard Catholicism. The entire Puerto Rican church was treated as a sort of national parish, with inferior ecclesiastical and religious standing, until Puerto Rican Catholics could learn English and become full-fledged American citizens.

Meanwhile, in New York the Irish pastors and prelates who controlled the territorial parishes and their resources, continued their hegemony over other ethnic groups, even when the parish membership was integrated. The non-English-speaking immigrants were in a subordinate ecclesiastical world. Whether viewed by the archdiocesan officials as unfortunates requiring paternalistic care or as unwanted reminders of the less prosperous days of the Irish majority, non-English ethnic immigrants were generally considered to be less important to the archdiocese than the successful Irish majority. Cardinal McCloskey, for instance, refused a request for a Polish church from new immigrants, adding that "what they needed was not their own church but a pig shanty" (Tomasi, 46 n. 17). One Irish pastor wrote of the Italians:

> The Italians are not a sensitive people like our own. When they are told that they are about the worst Catholics that ever came to this country, they don't resent it or deny it. If they were a little more sensitive to such remarks they would improve faster. The Italians are callous as regards religion (cited in Tomasi, 45 n. 14).

It may be said that the clerical elite of the New York Archdiocese confused social class and ethnic origins. The poverty of the newer immigrants was usually considered to be the result of persistent ethnic and cultural traits. Americanization, it was thought, would bring prosperity.

Such class distinctions were not reserved to Italians. Among the Irish, Dolan reports that distinctions between "shanty" and "lace-curtain" Irish became common in New York after the War Between the States (Dolan 1975, 102–4). The identification between being Americanized, middle class, and upwardly mobile helped create the so-called Irish-American (Greeley 1972a, 92–

94). However, the changing nature of the rapidly industrializing United States as well as the emergence of New York as a cosmopolitan city modified the four characteristics of political power and affluence, United States nationalism, the Irish paradigm, and the national parish.

Michael Augustine Corrigan, who became auxiliary to the ailing Cardinal McCloskey in 1880 and succeeded him in 1885, was the first New York archbishop to have studied in the North American College in Rome, which was founded in 1859. Corrigan utilized contacts and friendships in Rome throughout his ecclesiastical career. Yet the flow went both ways; that is, Corrigan could be influenced by the Vatican to introduce polices Rome desired for the United States as well as persuade Rome to support his. This communication system between Rome and the Archdiocese of New York, well established since the last quarter of the nineteenth century, has affected archdiocesan leadership until the present (Curran 1978).

Corrigan's about-face on the national parishes and archdiocesean policies toward the Italian immigrants to New York serves to illustrate the importance of Vatican influence. Initially Corrigan had forbidden Italian Catholics to hold public processions or festivals on the grounds that they were non-religious in character, excessively noisy, and a public nuisance (Tomasi, 143). When the Italian missionary Sister Frances Cabrini requested a foundation of her congregation in New York City, he had rebuked her, suggesting that the archdiocese was capable of attending to the spiritual and social needs of the Italian immigrants. He told the future saint that she could best serve her people by getting on the next boat and returning to Italy (Maynard, 149). Furthermore, at the Third Plenary Council in Baltimore in 1884 Corrigan argued against the national parish as a formal instrument for pastoral care to the Italians (Tomasi, 144–45). But six years later Corrigan was on the board of Mother Cabrini's hospital, a sponsor of the Scalabrini Fathers, who administered to the Italian immigrants, and a contributor and sponsor of an Italian St. Raphael Mission Society. The apparent reason for this turnabout was his realization after a trip to Rome that the Vatican wanted better care for the Italians in the United States (Tomasi, 93; 130ff.).

But there were limits, of course, to how much the relationship with Europe could alter the American character of the church in

New York. The archdiocese was already encouraging the missionary society of St. Raphael and its many works on behalf of the Italian immigrants when, in 1890, the several St. Raphael Societies from seven countries came together in a conference at Lucerne in Switzerland. Urged on by Peter Cahensly, a prominent German layman, the conference drafted a statement that provoked serious controversy. The Europeans suggested that the social concerns and good works sponsored by the society should be coordinated by bishops from the respective national groups. The seventh part of the Lucerne Memorial reads:

> It seems very desirable that the Catholics of each nationality, wherever it is deemed possible, have in the episcopacy of the country where they immigrate, several bishops who are of the same origin. It seems that in this way the organization of the Church would be perfect, for in the assemblies of the bishops, every immigrant race would be represented and its interest and needs would be protected (Barry, 314).

In a sense the proposal was a logical one. If having Irish bishops rather than French ones strengthened the bond between the Irish laity and their bishop in 1838 when Hughes replaced DuBois, why not amplify the process until all immigrant groups were represented in the episcopacy? However, the proposal established a link between social concerns and canonical jurisdiction, so that the funds from Europe for the immigrants would be dispensed by their own bishops. Assuredly the United States episcopacy was willing to receive funds for good works and allow for the establishment of charitable agencies, which were voluntary in nature and lay outside the scope of ecclesiastical jurisdiction, but Cahensly intended more.

The tenor of the Lucerne Memorial was to link the church's social concern for immigrants, the question of ethnic (nationality) representation, and the prerogatives of clerical power. Just as social help to the immigrants in the United States was better administered by independently controlled ethnic missionary societies, the Lucerne Memorial suggested that pastoral care would be better served by bishops who were identified with these social concern agencies. Implicit in the proposal was some form of ecclesiastical jurisdiction based on national origin. Tomasi describes the Lucerne suggestion of apostolic vicariates, which was proposed to a reluctant Archbishop Corrigan in 1888. The proposal would have linked all the national parishes together to form, in effect, a "national diocese" for all Italians (see Tomasi, 86 n. 97: 88 n. 98). The proposal, once implemented, would have divided jurisdiction nationwide between the centralized authority of the largely Irish American church and various non-English-speaking Catholics in the United States. The Archbishop of St. Paul, John Ireland, who was considered a liberal Americanizer, called the memorial a "conspiracy." He added, "We are American bishops.... An effort is made to dethrone us and to foreignize our country in the name of religion" (cited in Maynard, 95, 96).

Corrigan took a much lower profile in his correspondence with his Italian contacts, but because yellow journalism newspapers like the *New York Herald* pressed the issue, New York joined in the episcopal protest (Tomasi, 91 n. 114). The Lucerne Memorial was not adopted. Hence, although the national parish in New York acquired a more positive role in pastoral terms, it was prevented from bestowing canonical power parallel to that of the existing episcopacy. It is small wonder that the same American bishops who had railed at Cahensly's proposal refused the petition from Puerto Rican Catholics for a native Puerto Rican bishop on the newly acquired island scarcely nine years later.

Curiously, the "conservative" New York archbishop was courted by Italians interested in fostering the Cahensly proposal (Tomasi, 146). By today's standards the tolerance generated toward the national parishes in New York would qualify for a "liberal" position, and the nineteenth-century Americanizers, like John Ireland, would be the "conservatives." This shift in political meaning for the policies of the archdiocese at the turn of the century is part of the change in the leadership role for New York in American Catholicism.

The road to change was not always smooth, however. Another controversy of the archdiocese during the years of Archbishop Corrigan was the excommunication of Father Edward McGlynn, who had publicly supported Henry George's campaign for mayor of New York in 1886. George had created a stir with his book *Progress and Poverty* within the ranks of the secular reform-minded, who were concerned with the social conditions of the urban working class. Neither George, with his single property tax theory, nor Terence Powderly and the Knights of Labor, were socialist, although both attracted socialists to their causes. But both movements challenged the role of the Democratic Party bosses in representing the working class (Herreshoff, 111–13, 120–22). Corrigan, in an authoritarian style reminiscent of John Hughes, forbade McGlynn to speak at a political meeting in support of George. In compliance with Corrigan's instructions, McGlynn did not speak. However, he did go to the meeting to announce that he could not speak. This sparked a controversy in the secular press about the political allegiances of Catholics and the right of Corrigan to impose his party preferences on McGlynn. The clerical authoritarianism of the bishop was painted as a violation of McGlynn's rights as an American citizen and brought up once again the charge that Catholicism was essentially un-American.

McGlynn may be pictured as a defender of a parish-based apostolic life, somewhat as Father Varela had exemplified the model of parish priest before the arrival of John Hughes. Like other reformers of his time, McGlynn expected government to assume a growing role in public works of charity and education and suggested that Catholic energies in maintaining parish schools and a separate system of Catholic charities could be better directed at social change (Bell; Hennesey 1981a, 189–90). No less a critic than José Martí, the exiled Cuban patriot and revolutionary leader, pictured the controversy as a conflict between authority and faithfulness to the gospel. In an article written for a Mexican newspaper, Martí wrote:

> When Father McGlynn defended [Grover] Cleveland in the political forum of the elections two years ago, the archbishop did not consider it to be bad because Cleveland was the candidate of the party with which the Church in New York is in cahoots. In cahoots and in complicity! But what in Father McGlynn seemed fine to the archbishop when he defended the Archbishop's candidate—the same manner of expression of a political preference from a Catholic priest—now seems bad to the Archbishop because coming to the defense of Father McGlynn could alarm the rich Protestants who have latched onto the Church and who beseech it to oppose justice for the poor who have built the church! . . . So, because the Archbishop, who has expressed his opinion on property in a pastoral letter, ordered Father McGlynn not to attend a public meeting to treat the land issue, and the priest ignored this in so far as such is his right as a cleric and his obligation as an individual to do so,

> the Archbishop suspended him from his parish duties. To one who had made his parish a haven of love! And because he ignored his ecclesiastical superior in a political matter.... But the Catholics of New York rose up angrily against the Archbishop, readying colossal meetings. They contrasted the undescribable piety of the persecuted priest to the unsavory character of the bishops and vicars that the archbishopric maintains in glory. And with all the intensity of the Irish soul, they reclaimed their right to think freely on political issues and denounced the immoral dealings of the Archbishop with the political mercenaries whose dictates he obeys.... Oh Jesus, where would you have been in this struggle? Accompanying... the rich thief or in the humble house where Father McGlynn suffers and waits? (José Martí, "El cisma de los católicos en Nueva York," in Fernández Retamar, 257, 264, 267, my translation).

A foreign visitor like Martí gives testimony to the cosmopolitan nature of New York. It was not only the largest city of the United States, but it had become a meeting ground for intellectuals, patriots, writers, and artists from all over the world. The authoritarianism common in an earlier age no longer fit an evolving metropolis that depended on tolerance among its disparate population for its prosperity. Moreover, what happened in New York was reported upon worldwide as representative of the American church. The matter of excommunication was eventually resolved in McGlynn's favor, and the powers Hughes had accumulated for the archbishopric were limited by the need for the archdiocese to use its authority in ways more suited to a cosmopolitan city.

Cardinal Farley, who succeeded Corrigan upon the latter's death in 1902 and governed the archdiocese until 1918, was more flexible than his predecessor. Farley reconciled his clergy by appointing a host of McGlynn supporters to be domestic prelates. The years of his incumbency, as those of Cardinal Hayes (1919–38) who followed him, saw the Archdiocese of New York assume a different style of leadership in American Catholicism.

The archdiocese began to use its resources, both human and financial, to initiate projects benefiting Catholicism nationwide. After all, in 1908 Pope Pius X had terminated the missionary status of the Catholic church in the United States with his decree *Sapienti Consilio* (Ellis, 112ff). Not long afterward, John Wynne, S. J., was commissioned by Cardinal Farley to publish the first *Catholic Encyclopedia.* The foundation of a North American mission society at Ossining, New York, later called Maryknoll, as well as the reception into the Catholic church of the Anglican Greymoor Friars, also took place in the early part of the century. These steps, as well as the gradual evolution of the Catholic University in Washington into a respected institution for learning, were projects that affected all of United States Catholicism.

The active support of New York for such projects gained prestige for the archdiocese. Because of his generosity the cardinal of New York was frequently given the prerogative to nominate New York clergy to posts in the emerging national Catholic institutions. For instance, when at the outbreak of World War I the National Catholic War Council was formed to assure Catholic participation in the war effort, it was New York Auxiliary Bishop Hayes who became the first official head of the Catholic branch of the military chaplains (O'Brien, 55 n. 9). The archdiocese promoted progressive undertakings and trained talented seminarians abroad, while at the national level it could call upon its appointees to exert their influence within the national ecclesiastical institutions (Maynard, 220–22; Gannon, 144–46; Murnion, 122–32; Finn). The invitation by Bishop Jones of Puerto Rico to Cardinal Farley to preside at the island synod of 1917 flowed from this new dimension of New York's Catholicism. Moreover, in the newfound cosmopolitan character of New York Catholicism, Cardinal Farley and Cardinal Hayes usually avoided the kind of heavy-handed repression that had characterized Hughes in his episcopacy and Corrigan in the McGlynn affair.

Of the traits of modernization Murnion considers characteristic in ecclesiastical organization, the following can be applied to New York at this time:

> Increasing functional specialization among the members; less diffuse, more specific and pragmatic authority; greater emphasis on rationality and current wisdom in lieu of the previous dominance of tradition; organic integration of interdependent members rather than mechanical integration of somewhat identical members; a sense of options about membership itself and about forms and behavior related to membership (Murnion, 392).

The passage of the Immigration Law of 1921, which brought the virtual closing of the Open Door Policy, hastened the transformation already underway. After 1921 the children of Catholic immigrants grew up in a different kind of New York church, one that no longer had to think of itself as "mostly foreign-born." William Halsey has described the interplay of these social and historical factors of the twentieth century, suggesting that after World War I secular thinkers turned pessimistic on the world's future. The Neo-Calvinism and antirational bent of Barth was a religious expression of this pessimism and permeated the mainline Protestant theology of the United States (Halsey, 5). Catholics in the United States, on the other hand, had been insulated from this pessimism because of the condemnation of Modernism in 1907, which served to keep the sources of skepticism from taking root in North American Catholic theology. Hence, questions of historical relativism in the scriptures, scientific discoveries in evolution and medicine, or exploration of the psychological world were excluded from Catholic philosophy and theology (Halsey, 144 n. 30, 66–67).

James Gillis, Paulist editor of an important national Catholic magazine, addressed himself to this topic when he wrote in 1922:

> We Catholics are more hopeful for modern civilization than are they who built modern civilization. We cannot be said to be the creators of the modern system, yet we do not consider it to be altogether hopeless. We believe that the world has a future. . . . We are more modern than the moderns (Halsey, 48, citing the *Catholic World*).

The twin pillars of this Catholic optimism, says Halsey, were the reliance upon Thomism as the axis of all Catholic thinking and the revival of medieval Christendom as a model for a new world order (Halsey, 141 nn. 15, 16). For instance, the political changes of the New Deal under Franklin Delano Roosevelt were sometimes interpreted by Catholic spokespersons as a practical implementation of the principles of papal social teaching (O'Brien, 173–77; Abell). Eventually, liberal Catholics identified their social concern with a renascence of medieval spirituality. For example, there is extensive use of Latin in the names of liberal Catholic institutions such as *Caritas* House, *Fides* Press, *Pax Christi, Orate Fratres.* One also finds proficiency in Gregorian chant encouraged as a spiritual experience and a suggestion for a home liturgy using the "Chi-Rho anagram" to replace "the Easter bunny in candy baskets" (Wills, 38–60). Until the 1960s vocal spokesmen assured Catholics that "since Scholastic principles were eternal they did not shift with the latest currents of cosmological investigation" (Halsey, 159).

Nor did the church have to direct the brunt of its social concern to newly arrived immigrants. The Depression, the New Deal, and the prosperity after World War II produced new forms of social action more directed to the upwardly mobile children of the earlier immigrants. The church sponsored labor schools, which specialized in adult education by holding classes at night for working people. Catholic lay organizations, like the Knights of Columbus, which had always reflected the political interests of the clerical elite, had considerably more financial and political resources. New Catholic organizations in professional fields also sprang up. There were Catholic lawyer guilds, sociology associations, and a Legion of Decency to police the movie industry.

In sum, by the 1950s Catholics in the United States had come to see themselves as "lantern bearers to American society, carrying messages of future progress and enduring optimism" (Halsey, 78 n. 48). The immense energy of a Catholic population grown middle class had led to a proliferation of separate societies for everything from Catholic anthropology to Catholic theatre (Halsey, 57). As the most cosmopolitan of United States sees, New York was national headquarters to many of these institutions. But in contrast to their projections for prominence within the larger society, these organizations were generally reserved to Catholics only. Poet Francis X. Connolly characterized one of these societies as a "cloister," so that the Catholic "semi-priesthood" would not be obscured (Halsey, 105).

At first glance the trend to be "lantern bearers" to the United States seemed to conflict with the isolation of a self-imposed cloister mentality, which these societies appeared to emphasize. But this contradiction may be explained if one accepts the notion that in order to set an example for others to follow, one must first seek perfection, so to speak, in order to remain ahead or above others, but in any case, apart from them. Michael Harrington, raised in this milieu, called United States Catholicism of this period a "countersociety" (Harrington, 14; see also O'Dea, 127–37).

But if liberal Catholicism was alive and well in New York and in other parts of the United States during the episcopacies of Farley, Hayes, and Spellman, so was conservative Catholicism with its insistence upon tradition and unquestioning support for American nationalism. The binding concept between the two bands in cosmopolitan New York was anti-Communism. Dohen applies to this case the Parsonian premise that for successful social function "a common cognitive orientation, an accepted system of ultimate values and goals, and a means to assure effective social integration are necessary" (180).

Liberal Catholics promoted social change, but—except for lonely prophets like Dorothy Day and the Catholic Worker Movement—also condemned the secular radicalism Communism was seen to represent. Conservatives used Communism as the antithesis of America, so that anything that was tinged with Communism was anti-American, and anything American was, of necessity, anti-Communist (see Grasso). Moreover, Catholicism had become the more perfect image of what America should be, making the support of an anti-Communist United States foreign policy a virtually theological premise (Dohen, 182–84; 124). During the Cold War Catholics often identified the West with Christendom and the Soviet block with the infidels or paganism (see O'Brien, 64).

Even the most progressive of liberal Catholic initiative in the Archdiocese of New York often carried conservative baggage. For instance, labor education schools, such as the Jesuit-run Xavier Institute of Social Sciences (later renamed the Xavier Institute of Labor Management Relationships), joined the impetus provided to labor unions by the Wagner Act in 1935 (Cloward and Piven, 131–47). The school offered trained leadership under Catholic sponsorship to the mushrooming organizations of semi-skilled and unskilled laborers. The avowed purpose, however, was to forestall a Communist takeover of labor unions.

Against this background of an emerging cosmopolitan archdiocese, the first pastoral initiative directed toward the Spanish-speaking population was taken in 1902 by Cardinal John M. Farley, who established the Spanish National Parish of Our Lady of Guadalupe on West 14th Street in Manhattan (Stevens-Arroyo, in Sandoval, 273; Stern 1977, 18; Stern 1982, 5). As with other national parishes in the archdiocese, the chapel was intended as a temporary service under the control but beyond the financial responsibility of the archdiocese. The clergy assigned to the chapel were the Assumptionist Fathers (Augustinians of the Assumption) based in Spain.

Moreover, the chapel was opened for the Spanish-speaking as a general language group. Besides Puerto Ricans, the chapel was to serve all the Latin American and Spanish people in the city, as the title Our Lady of Guadalupe suggests. Thus Puerto Ricans were not the specific focus of this archdiocesan initiative. This highlights one of the key differences in the national parish of the Spanish-speaking and that of most other ethnic groups in New York. With the exception of the German language parishes, which mixed Austrian with German nationals, virtually every other linguistic group was also a distinct nationality. And even if one could argue that the early Italian immigration before the establishment of the kingdom in the 1860s did not come from a nation, this circumstance was only temporary. Puerto Ricans, on the other hand, are still lumped together with Cubans, Argentineans, Mexicans, and Spaniards. Thus, the Guadalupe parish was "a Spanish-language chapel" and not a parish for people of only one nationality. As Stern points out:

> The concept of a Spanish "national" parish is somewhat anomalous. For most nationalities, there is a coincidence between national and linguistic identity. In the case of Spanish speaking peoples there are twenty different nationalities. It is more appropriate to consider these four parishes as centers for the Spanish speaking, rather than as "national" (Stern 1982, 7).

This amalgam of people from more than twenty different nations intensified conflicts of culture, history, and class among them and impeded the kind of unifying process around a national identity that had been part of the national parish experience for other groups (Fitzpatrick 1971, 154–55).

Cardinals Farley and Hayes authorized more Spanish-language chapels: Our Lady of Esperanza in 1912 (served by the Assumptionists); La Milagrosa in 1926; and Holy Agony in 1930 (both served by the Vincentians of Madrid). The first two chapels were located in Upper Manhattan's West Side while Holy Agony was located in East Harlem. Like the Guadalupe chapel, Our Lady of Esperanza was originally intended for Spaniards (Stern 1982, 6). But because it was located uptown, Esperanza, like the Vincentian parishes, came to serve the Puerto Rican community, which had become the largest of Manhattan's Spanish-speaking groups and had been segregated to Harlem, where most colored people in Manhattan lived before World War II (Lankevich and Furer, 234–37).

The political changes wrought by the New Deal afforded the Puerto Rican community in New York greater visibility as a distinct Spanish-speaking group in the city (Sánchez Korrol, 187–99). In 1934 Fiorello La Guardia, who had served as congressman for the East Harlem district, was elected mayor on a Fusion Party ticket, thus interrupting Tammany Hall's domination of the city's political apparatus. Vito Marcantonio, La Guardia's successor in the East Harlem district, had a political base with the union movement that was part of the socialist reform wing, the American Labor Party, which eventually collaborated with the New Deal Democratic Party of Franklin Delano Roosevelt. The political organization of their Puerto Rican constituents followed a strong labor and socialist pattern, emphasizing reform of working conditions, legislation favorable to labor unions, and a strong governmental role in social welfare (Meyer, 88–95).

The social and economic needs of these Puerto Rican migrants before World War II were not met by the national chapels. Inasmuch as financial resources were expected to come from the parishioners themselves, the Puerto Ricans were generally too poor to do much more than finance the ordinary works of pastoral care, mass, and the sacraments. Moreover, with a clergy trained in theologically conservative Spain, social concerns were not often part of the chapels' apostolate. Self-help groups, including the Puerto Rican Brotherhoods (Sánchez Korrol, 8), and the worker movements such as *El Centro Obrero Español* followed a Masonic lodge paradigm and were secularist, when not also anticlerical in attitude (Meyer, 148–49).

When the Catholic church did address the social concerns of Puerto Ricans, it was through the interest of the laity. In 1934 Catholic philanthropists Elizabeth Sullivan Ridder and Georgia Sullivan O'Keefe founded Casita María in East Harlem.[3] Casita María, which at that time was outside the structures of the Catholic Charities of the Archdiocese of New York, functioned as a settlement house meant to provide services to the Puerto Rican migrants until they established themselves in the city. It gathered voluntary donations of food and clothing as well as offers of jobs and housing in order to make the church a beneficent intermediary in the process of accommodation to life in the United States.

Upon entering Cardinal Hayes's episcopacy in 1919, the pattern of pastoral care through national parishes and social concern through settlement houses that had characterized the treatment of non-English-speaking immigrants since the end of the nineteenth century was firmly in place for Puerto Ricans. But while the Catholic church had always utilized social concerns as a means to attract the immigrant to the practice of the traditional religion, government programs of social welfare proliferated after the installation of the New Deal in 1932. In other words, government replaced the churches as the principal distributor of social services.

Social concerns, which had always served to bring immigrants into New York Catholicism, had established a weak base during the pioneer migration of Puerto Ricans to the city. Their needs were addressed from secular sources such as the brotherhoods. The Catholic labor schools did not focus upon Puerto Rican workers as a target group, nor were there classes offered in the Spanish language to attract them. This omission ought not be taken lightly on the premise that Puerto Ricans were an insignificant segment of the labor force in New York at the time. *El Congreso de los Pueblos de Habla Española* was a part of the Marxist wing of the Congress of Industrial Organizations (Stevens-Arroyo 1977, 126–28), and such groups formed part of the political power base of the East Harlem Congressman Vito Marcantonio (Meyer, 149–52).

With the arrival of the Roosevelt's New Deal and LaGuardia's mayoralty, Marcantonio became the chief advocate of Puerto Rican needs in government. As Meyer points out, while Marcantonio was not *puertorriqueño,* he was *latino* by virtue of his strong Italian cultural roots (172). Moreover, his district contained the largest concentration of Puerto Ricans. But his socialist convictions inclined him to champion the cause of the poor and racially oppressed. The Puerto Ricans crowded into East Harlem, suffering from racial discrimination unlike that encountered by European immigrants (Fitzpatrick 1971, 101–14; Domínguez, 2–5), remained a loyal constituency of Marcantonio.

The congressman was the first political leader in New York to take the initiative toward representing the Puerto Ricans politically. In 1937 he sponsored the successful candidacy of State Assemblyman Oscar García Rivera, the first Puerto Rican elected to political office in New York (Sánchez Korrol, 190–91). But although Marcantonio was the first prominent politician to support the newly visible Puerto Ricans, it would be unfair to characterize the church as unconcerned. When the Great Migration of the post–World War II era began, this concern would be turned into action. Certainly by the 1950s the archdiocese had many resources that the church of previous generations did not share. But attention to the apostolate among Puerto Ricans would not simply be a matter of money. The archdiocese had to work within the institutional framework that had evolved over 150 years. Application of the national parishes to Puerto Ricans had its failings, particularly in terms of providing the social concern apostolate necessary to attract the migrants to their traditional religion in the new urban setting. This set the stage for the attention given to the Puerto Ricans by Catholic liberals in the early 1950s.

The observations O'Dea (153–61) makes about the role of a Catholic intellectualism apply to the encounter with Puerto Ricans in the archdiocese. How to view the Puerto Ricans in New York became a battlegound between those clergy "whose main interest was the advancement of knowledge, or the clarification of cultural issues and public problems" and those who would "show hostility toward the critical side" (O'Dea, 22, 24). The liberals advocated a closer linking of pastoral care with social concern, and even if they did not agree with the agenda put forth by Marcantonio, they recognized the hold that his radicalism exercised over a desperate community. In urging action in the Spanish-speaking apostolate, intellectuals felt that outreach to Puerto Ricans represented "the razor's edge of creativity for the society in terms of meeting the challenge of the unknown and unstructured future," even if fraught with the fate of Socrates, delivered over "to the charge of subversion or, as it was called in Athens, impiety" (O'Dea, 23). Despite its perils, ministry toward Puerto Ricans offered escape from the formalism, authoritarianism, clericalism, Neo-Jansenism, and defensiveness of which O'Dea speaks.

Murnion's survey of priests ordained in the decades 1920–29 and 1960–69 revealed a leaning toward such social action among the newly ordained. Although his study did not specifically focus upon ministry to the Puerto Ricans, this type of ministry exercised in New York relatively the same role as the Mexican-American apostolate served in Los Angeles and San Antonio (McNamara 1970, 470–72).

A summary overview of the archdiocesean perspective on Puerto Ricans on the eve of a major initiative toward the ministry can be found in Theodore Maynard's *The Catholic Church and the American Idea.* Maynard, a respected voice of Catholic opinion, wrote in 1952 of the Catholic immigrant past. His thoughts reflect a favorable view of Catholic policies in terms of Americanization and ethnic diversity:

> Though it must have been made entirely plain that I consider the Americanization of the immigrant eminently desirable, I certainly do not believe that Americanization should mean standardization. While being encouraged to adjust themselves to American institutions, immigrants should be encouraged to retain their traditions—and I would say the tongue spoken by their ancestors at least as a second language —so as to avoid that dead level which is so marked a feature of American life. It has never been properly understood that variety is capable of giving vivacity, color and charm, and that much of every great value may easily be lost by too rigid a uniformity. The melting pot should not melt people down so completely as to result in something like a porridge —wholesome, no doubt, but uninteresting. Rather it should be something like a goulash, in which the flavors are blended but in which the component parts yet remain distinct. Just how this is to be effected I am not prepared to say, but I would like it to be understood that I am not advocating the production of stereotypes but rather of types. I believe that in the Americanization aimed at by the Catholic Church in America this has been more generously allowed for than in any other of the Americanizing agencies (Maynard, 113).

Maynard also recognized the presence of the Spanish-speaking as "among the earliest immigrants," but explained that United States immigration authorities had not recognized their existence. Maynard is at pains to distinguish the "pure-blooded Spaniards" from Mexicans and Puerto Ricans; the latter, he says, receive "the contempt formerly meted out to the Italians" (Maynard, 180–87). In contrast to the triumphalistic description in his book of the upward mobility of American Catholic groups such as the Irish, Germans, Italians, and Poles, Maynard pictured the Mexicans and Puerto Ricans as victims of poverty and racial discrimination.

Moreover, the author was less sanguine about the future of Puerto Ricans in the United States than about the future of the blacks. He called the Puerto Ricans "devout in somewhat superstitious fashion" due to the shortage of priests and lack of religious education. He saw the Archdiocese of New York as "totally unprepared and therefore largely powerless" (187–88) to halt the multiplication of Protestant, mostly Pentecostal churches. He did not question the effectiveness of the United States Catholic missionaries already in Puerto Rico, nor did he explore why Protestants seemed to be able to keep up with the new wave of immigration and the archdiocese did not. Yet he reflected upon the standard conceptual limitations of the church's immigrant policy: the centralized Catholic Charities system and the national parish. He suggested that Catholic Charities was an archdiocesan agency overwhelmed by the suddenness of the immigration with little immediate opportunity to provide enough Spanish-speaking services.

Maynard called "manifestly preposterous" the 1952 estimate of 700,000 Puerto Rican migrants in New York on the grounds that such a figure would represent 35 percent of the entire population of Puerto Rico, which ironically was even less than the 40 percent that is now estimated to have left the island (see chapter 1). He calculated that the combination of racial discrimination against Puerto Ricans, who were perceived as "colored half-breeds," and the conditions they suffered were unlikely to be remedied without regulation of the migration. Moreover, he expressed the conviction that some Puerto Ricans "clutch at Communism, though usually they go no further than backing Mr. Marcantonio" (187).

Maynard stated that only a plan of controlled migration (much like that proposed a century before by the liberal Catholic prelates), would disperse Puerto Ricans "over a large territory"; a planned "colonization" was the only remedy for their plight, since "neither they nor we ourselves can much longer endure the present state of affairs" (188–89).[4]

As I hope to explain, the Spanish-speaking apostolate vitalized the contact between intellectuals and parish priests, particularly by integrating social concerns with pastoral care in the apostolate. Despite its institutionalization, Catholicism in New York had not allowed its compassionate heart to be shriveled up like the old bean that Don Chago feared in *"La Carreta."* Moreover, it was in responding to the Puerto Ricans that New York Catholicism prepared itself for the changes of the Second Vatican Council in ways few would have anticipated. To arrive at this opportunity, however, the Archdiocese of New York had to pass through the episcopacy of Francis Cardinal Spellman.

4. The Missionary Impulse and the Basement Churches

JUANITA: No gahte máh saliva, "mihter." Mamá, ehte señor eh protehtante y lo que trata eh de venderte propaganda de su iglesia americana incorporá.
MINISTRO PARK: ¡Vender! ¡Señorita, le estoy regalando a su madre la palabra de Dios! ¡Gratis, completamente gratis!
DOÑA GABRIELA: Lo siento mucho, señor. Aquí somoh católicoh.

JUANITA: Don't waste your breath, mister. Mamá, this man is Protestant and he is trying to sell you propaganda about his American Church, Incorporated.
MINISTER PARK: Sell! Miss, I am giving your mother the Word of God! Free, completely free!
DOÑA GABRIELA: I'm sorry, sir. We are Catholics here.

The Oxcart, Act III

The roaring twenties brought significant change to New York City. The closing of the Open Door Policy of immigration at the beginning of the decade drastically limited the number of newcomers to the city from Europe and witnessed a new kind of migration of black Americans from the Southern states and immigration from the West Indies. In 1920 there were 150,000 blacks in New York City, about 3 percent of the total population. But twenty years later the black population had swelled to 450,000 and doubled to 6 percent of New Yorkers (Glazer and Moynihan, 25–27). This new presence was a response to the need for low-cost wage laborers to replace the tides of European immigrants that had previously supplied the cheap labor for the city. In many ways this black migration to New York served a similar economic function before the Second World War as the Puerto Rican Great

Migration after it (Rodríguez, in Centro, 197–221). In the segregated patterns of residential housing which then obtained, these blacks—and many Puerto Ricans of color—were forced to live in Harlem, north of Central Park.

Accompanying the coming of black and Caribbean workers, including Puerto Ricans, there was an emigration of Euro-Americans to the Bronx, Brooklyn, and Queens. Manhattan lost an average of forty thousand inhabitants each year during the 1920s, while the outer boroughs experienced a growth of seven times that number (Jackson, 208 n. 15). The extension of the subway system and the more common ownership of automobiles permitted this shift (Jackson, 208). Moreover, the development of larger portions of central Manhattan as prime commercial space drove rents so high that average workers could no longer afford them. By 1940 half of all the people in the United States who paid the then exorbitant sum of two hundred dollars or more in monthly rent lived in Manhattan (Jackson 208–9 n. 16).

Most Catholics in New York belonged to the middle class, and it was this income group that was leaving Manhattan for the Bronx and Queens, where 80 percent of the rents fell in the middle range (Jackson, 209). Cardinal Hayes was the first prelate of the New York Archdiocese to witness a drop in Catholic population in Manhattan. Hayes used to say jokingly that half of his diocese had moved to Queens. This population shift away from Manhattan to the outer boroughs had important effects on the New York Archdiocese, however, because Brooklyn, Queens, and Long Island were administered by the Brooklyn Diocese. Thus, except for those who went to the Bronx, Staten Island, or Westchester County, Catholics who left Manhattan left the New York Archdiocese.

The Roaring Twenties, which began with prosperity, ended with the stock market crash of 1929 and the beginnings of the Great Depression. Together with the New Deal, which followed, these events from 1920–40 profoundly altered the face of New York. Ironically, the reformers of the New Deal after 1932 hastened the transformation of Manhattan into the residence of the country's most affluent. In his history of New York housing, Anthony Jackson notes that "during 1926–1929, the ratio [of demolitions to new apartments built] was roughly 1:2; during 1934–1937 it was 5:2. That is, old-law tenements were now being torn down not to make way for new [housing] developments but because they were slums" (Jackson, 210). The same author dramatizes the effects of this slum clearance on Harlem, which was the neighborhood for people of color in Manhattan. Harlem replaced the Lower East Side as the neighborhood with the highest population density in the world.

> In 1921 an observer [Rollin L. Hartt] had described Harlem as giving "an impression of spaciousness, of cleanliness, of prosperity, of success." ... By 1932, 12 percent of its inhabitants were out of work, families were doubling up or moving into one room, and it had the highest rate of infant mortality, twice the normal venereal disease rate, and three times the tuberculosis death rate of the city. ... Harlem's problem was not that its buildings were physically obsolete ... but that its tenants could not afford or make proper use of what they had (Jackson 210).

Ironically, the most affluent part of New York, Manhattan, was also home to the poorest New Yorkers, where 45 percent of Manhattanites paid less than thirty-one dollars a month in rent (Jackson, 210).

Such changes affected New York City and the archdiocese. New York Catholics usually voted with the Democratic Party, and the New Deal was generally welcomed. In fact, as described in chapter 3, the reforms initiated by Roosevelt were interpreted by some Catholic leaders as consonant with papal social encyclicals (O'Brien 1972, 173–77). Making adaptations in the Catholic Action approach that had been urged upon Europe, cooperatives and credit unions were encouraged to aid the national recovery launched by Roosevelt. The restructuring of the Democratic Party by the New Deal made the urban political machine less important than union leadership and special interest groups (Cloward and Piven, 126–80.) Hence, after 1932, the institutional church found that Catholic labor leaders, intellectuals, and educators were often more influential allies than political bosses (Glazer and Moynihan, 213–87).

The penchant to develop Manhattan for expensive commercial and residential building was also of concern. In the intensive public works undertaken by the New Deal, the properties of the church as well as influence over Catholic labor leaders became important considerations for political figures like Robert Moses and James A. Farley, who carefully cultivated a close relationship with the head of the archdiocese. The hierarchy of the Catholic church forged agreements with government and construction firms in designing subsequent changes in neighborhoods (Caro, 740, 911).

Catholics came to identify themselves with a wider and wider range of political and social options, and in the process the cohesiveness of the 1900s disintegrated (Halsey, 176–80). The tenor of the times even generated substantial Catholic radicalism in the United States, as is seen with the Catholic Worker Movement. Dorothy Day and Peter Maurin, founders of the Catholic Worker Movement, used papal social thought to advocate social reform as a substitute for capitalism in the United States, and they did so from within the New York Archdiocese. The entrance of the United States into World War II was opposed by these leaders, and they came to interpret the Catholic mission as one of pacifism rather than of blind patriotism (O'Brien 1972, 220–21).

Into this scenario of New York Catholicism in flux was introduced the powerful personality of Francis Spellman, who was named to succeed Cardinal Hayes in 1939. A native of the Boston Archdiocese, Spellman was an outsider to New York's close-knit clergy. Gannon points out that his appointment to the most influential and powerful of the episcopal sees in the United States was based on the strength of his close association with Eugenio Pacelli, who had been elected Pope Pius XII that same year. A role as conduit between Washington and Rome was to be a part of Spellman's career for the rest of his life and would serve to identify the head of the Archdiocese of New York with political issues of international importance (Gannon, 132–36).

Pope Pius XII was quick to align the church with the pro–Western side of the Cold War that characterized the post–World War II era. By his close identification of the church's resources with Christian Democratic parties, the pope opposed vigorously the emergence of Communist parties in Europe, especially in Italy. This policy of Pius XII came to characterize the Catholic Action approach to social concerns. The broad outlines of this approach will be detailed below. Suffice it to say here that where Socialism stressed confrontation of classes, the papal encyclicals urged a Catholic Action effort at inter-class harmony. Educating and organizing workers to this alternative was viewed as an antidote to Communism.

In the United States Spellman sought to link Catholic political support for foreign policy decisions that emphasized this postwar anti-Communist thrust emanating from the Vatican (Gannon, 339–53). This led Spellman into political causes that in retrospect might seem suspect. Critics have used Cardinal Spellman as an example of excessive nationalism (Dohen), but in fairness he was scarcely the most strident of Catholic conservatives. Before coming to New York as cardinal, Spellman had assisted President Franklin Delano Roosevelt in obtaining a well-publicized interview with the then Secretary of State in the Vatican, Eugenio Pacelli. The interview was meant to lend Catholic support to Roosevelt at a time when the architect of the New Deal was under attack from the popular radio priest Edward Coughlin. On the other hand, Spellman's political applications of Catholic doctrine definitely prejudiced him against many struggles for social justice that opposed United States policy.

For example, Cardinal Spellman was a participant in the independence negotiation for the Philippines in 1948, and he intervened with church influence in 1956 to protect United States bases and economic investments from a tide of nationalism. He said, "It would certainly be catastrophic if the Philippines which we have twice helped to liberate and for which we have done so much economically and in other ways would obligate us to withdraw from the bases we have built at such great cost" (Gannon, 398). During a 1956 visit to the Dominican Republic, he warmly supported Rafael Leonidas Trujillo, the dictator of that Caribbean nation, with a laudatory address for his anti-Communist policies. Subsequently, he merited having a street in the capital named Avenida Spellman (Gannon, 403). Spellman's visit to Guatemala in 1959 helped legitimate the pro–United States military junta that had come to power by a United States–encouraged coup d' etat the previous year against the elected government of socialist president Arbenz (Gannon, 399).

Certainly the cardinal's approach to Latin American politics stood in direct contrast with the advocacy of East Harlem Congressman Vito Marcantonio, who represented most of the city's Puerto Rican population in the House of Representatives. In 1938

Marcantonio had been reelected after a brief absence. Besides his outspoken support of the Republican side in the Spanish Civil War, he was defender of the Puerto Rican Nationalist leader Pedro Albizu Campos and had presented legislation in Congress to grant the island its independence (Meyer, 150–71).

The harsh policies of the then military governor of Puerto Rico, Blanton Winship, set in motion a persecution of the Nationalist Party after 1934. The party under Albizu Campos announced the inevitability of armed resistance to United States rule of the island. The announcement launched a cycle of violence that resulted in the sedition conviction of Albizu Campos and the killing of twenty-one Nationalists by the National Guard in a bloody incident known as The Ponce Massacre of 1937 (Corretger, 77–96). In an effort to neutralize a growing popular sentiment for independence on the island, Roosevelt empowered Luis Muñoz Marín to direct New Deal policies in Puerto Rico. Muñoz's reformist approach to Puerto Rico's very real economic problems resulted in the foundation of the Popular Democratic Party (PPD) in 1938. Under its ascendancy, the island initiated economic development and adopted a constitution in 1952 that established a Puerto Rican political identity under the commonwealth status (Wells, 114–31, passim).

United States Catholic missionaries to Puerto Rico generally distanced themselves from the independence movement, (Beirne, 7; see above, chapter 2). This was especially true of one of the Redemptorist superiors on the island, James McManus, who was later to be named bishop of Ponce (Julián de Nieves, 153–56). Bishop McManus not only opposed Puerto Rican independence, but he was later to excommunicate Catholics who voted in favor of the moderate commonwealth arrangement as designed by Luis Muñoz Marín (see chapter 5). McManus was an avid advocate of statehood for Puerto Rico (Ocampo, 4:42–45), and this became the position of Cardinal Spellman also.

Spellman's advocacy of the statehood position was known among the island's political leadership. Some expressed great dissatisfaction with his political stance, and he was criticized on the island for his advocacy of the statehood position. For example, upon Spellman's visit to the island in October 1948 to dedicate the Catholic University of Puerto Rico, the leader of the Nationalist Party, Pedro Albizu Campos, strongly criticized Spellman's intrusion of religion into politics. For Albizu, Catholicism was threatened by the power of a Protestant United States (Stevens-Arroyo 1991). His remarks question the compatibility of pro-Americanism and the Catholic missionary impulse:

> I would like to tell Cardinal Spellman that he should give careful thought to what the scope of his mission in Puerto Rico could be. Let not Cardinal Spellman come here to repeat the role of the Redemptorists in Puerto Rico who stripped the Puerto Rican clergy of their parishes and do everything except to redeem [the people of] Puerto Rico. I trust that Cardinal Spellman will tell the people gathered at the $100.00 per cover banquet that the first thing they have to respect in Puerto Rico is the Hispanic language, the language whose grandeur brought light upon the world. Let him not come here [without taking into account the fact that] the University of Santa María should not allow even its application forms to be in the English language, for such would constitute a sacrilege even though English is the language of the Cardinal. I appeal to Cardinal Spellman's Catholicism because it is his duty as a Roman Apostolic Catholic to give here a lesson of his own apostolate and of the post he represents in the Sacred College; so that the Catholic conscience of Puerto Rico, the Hispanic conscience of Puerto Rico, the freedom and independence of Puerto Rico may be respected (Albizu Campos, recorded speech edited by Dávila and Rondón, my translation).

Despite such criticisms the cardinal remained consistent in his conception of Puerto Rico as subordinate to the United States and anticipated the unqualified assimilation of the island into the federal union. In ecclesiastical matters Spellman viewed the Puerto Rican church as an appendage to that of the United States, a perception which persisted till his death. During John XXIII's papacy, rather than advocating for a separate apostolic delegate for Puerto Rico, Spellman urged Rome to place the island church directly under the jurisdiction of Washington's apostolic delegate. Archbishop Davis of San Juan and the pontiff, however, felt that such a move would not help the development of the local church in Puerto Rico (Beirne, 84), and today Puerto Rico shares its apostolic delegate with the Dominican Republic.

Ironically, one of Spellman's first pastoral decisions as ordinary of the archdiocese was directed toward the care of the Puerto Ricans. In 1939 he turned over the administration of St. Cecilia's parish in East Harlem to the Redemptorist Congregation. Scarcely a year before his appointment, Spellman had taken a sea voyage to South America and had spent a brief time in Puerto Rico. His journal of the visit shows both his appreciation of the work of the Redemptorists and his appraisal of Catholicism on the island.

> Less than ten percent of the people go to Mass and only one percent of those who go are men. Think also of the difficulty of supporting the Church in Puerto Rico. There are priests there who receive only thirty cents a month from people of their parish. And since these are not considered foreign missions, the priests receive no help from the Propagation of the Faith Society. However, the American Province of the Redemptorists is doing superhuman and supernatural work both in Brazil and Puerto Rico. And I am consoled by the generosity of Americans who in thirty-five years have contributed two and a half million dollars to build churches and schools in Puerto Rico (cited in Gannon, 126).

Spellman was confronted with a city that commonly pictured the Puerto Ricans as led astray by Congressman Vito Marcantonio's support of Communist causes (see above, chapter 4). Spellman viewed church activity in Harlem in light of a necessary effort to stop the spread of Communism among the poor,[1] and such a notion was doubtlessly part of his motivation to take a new initiative among the Puerto Ricans. Thus Spellman's missionary thrust toward the Puerto Ricans in his own archdiocese ran parallel to the presence of North American Catholicism in Puerto Rico. It was an Americanizing effort, based on the implicit premise that Puerto Ricans had much to gain by assimilating the Catholicism of English-speaking Americans.

As in Puerto Rico, those in New York with nationalist aspirations came to assail the political agenda of the archdiocesan initiative, even if they welcomed the new concern for a needy community. Baptized, as it were, with this Americanizing dimension in 1939, the apostolate toward the Puerto Ricans in New York during the episcopacy of Spellman did not enjoy immediate acceptance among the recognized political leaders of the Puerto Rican people in Harlem. A decade and a half later in 1954, when Marcantonio died of a heart attack in the city streets, he was denied a Catholic burial by Cardinal Spellman on the grounds that "he had not practiced his religion for many years" (*New York Times*, August 11, 1954). This extraordinary penalty was imposed even though the congressman had received confession and the last rites of the church (Meyer, 182–84). Some Catholics perceived Spellman's action as a political decision rather than an ecclesiastical one. The cardinal was openly criticized, and more than one priest decided to celebrate Mass in their own parishes for the repose of Marcantonio's soul (Meyer, 183–84).

However much one may regret his politics toward nationalist aspirations, Spellman's great contribution to the Puerto Ricans was to recognize the need for the archdiocese to adopt a missionary character to the apostolate. In effect, he had declared St. Cecilia's "missionary territory" for the Puerto Ricans and had requested the island's principal missionary order, the Congregation of the Most Holy Redeemer, to begin in the heart of New York City what they were already doing in Puerto Rico.

The parish had originally served a German congregation but now found itself with a large number of Puerto Rican migrants. Spellman's decision to cede the parish to a religious order may be interpreted in various ways. It certainly broke with the tradition of keeping non-English-speaking groups confined to national chapels they financed themselves. The Puerto Ricans were endowed with a church property already built and paid for—a prize that would have taken some time to accumulate if the previous patterns had been observed. Yet, in another sense, disposal of the building to a religious order was a solution for the archdiocese (Fitzpatrick 1971, 125; see Tomasi, 98–102). The German and Irish population was no longer supporting the parish, and the East Harlem area had a plethora of Italian national chapels. This was a quick solution to accommodate the Puerto Ricans without upsetting other parishes in the East Harlem neighborhood. St. Cecilia's parish, however, would not be another Spanish national parish; it would also continue to serve the earlier German and Irish parishioners (Stern 1982, 32). Thus the "problem" of national parishes without a congregation because of changing neighborhoods was avoided. Should the Puerto Ricans move on as other immigrant groups had done, St. Cecilia's would remain unchanged canonically.

But what on the one hand can be seen as Spellman's great contribution can also be seen as having inherently a serious defect, at least initially. As Stern points out:

> It's interesting to note that in the period before the Second World War, the time when the four national parishes were founded and St. Cecilia parish was entrusted to the Redemptorists, pastoral responsibility for Hispanic Catholics was being delegated almost in its entirety to religious congregations. The diocesan clergy, with few exceptions, did not seem to be conscious of any special, personal responsibility to serve Spanish speaking Catholics, nor were they being challenged to do so by the archdiocesan authorities. If there was a fault to be found, perhaps it was that of complacency. The thriving and booming predominantly Irish American parishes seemed to be the main business of the New York Church; Hispanics and other ethnic groups seemed only to be a kind of special interest and apostolate for those so inclined. In so far as they were integrated into the general population they were served by all the institutions of the archdiocese, otherwise they were left, for the most part, to the care of the Spanish speaking religious (Stern 1982, 13).

Perhaps more significant was Spellman's decision to entrust the parish to the Redemptorists. They certainly had been missionaries in Puerto Rico, but they were not Puerto Rican clergy. In fact, the Redemptorists had not accepted a single Puerto Rican native for the priesthood in 1939 and were not to ordain the first Puerto Rican Redemptorists until 1955 (Julián de Nieves, 80; see above, chapter 3). Apparently, both Cardinal Spellman and the Redemptorist superiors believed that the missionary impulse rested principally upon a knowledge of the Spanish language on the part of the clergy. It will be seen in the next chapter that the cardinal came to accept the importance of cultural sensitivity to Puerto Rican values as well.

If anti-Communism were part of Cardinal Spellman's motivation in providing services to the Puerto Ricans in 1939 and his support of the Catholic University of Puerto Rico in 1948, it could only have intensified by the events of 1950. In October of that year an island-wide insurrection by the Nationalist Party required mobilization of the National Guard and several days of intense fighting in the island's mountainous interior. The Nationalists also attempted to assassinate President Truman at the Blair House (Ribes-Tovar 1971, 105–18.)

Moreover, with an influx of more than a quarter of a million Puerto Rican migrants in successive years from 1946 to 1952, immediate action on a grand scale was necessary, especially since the migration gave no signs of abating (Centro, 126–30; see also 17–20). This sudden and continuing growth of the Puerto Rican population meant that it spilled out of Harlem into the Lower East Side, on both sides of Second Avenue between 14th to 58th Streets, peripheral areas of Harlem as well as East Harlem itself, now known as *El Barrio,* or Spanish Harlem. Small Puerto Rican communities were found in Greenwich Village and Chelsea, and the area on the Upper West Side between 125th and 150th Streets including San Juan Hill on Amsterdam Avenue had the second largest concentration of Manhattan's Puerto Ricans outside Harlem (Mills et al., 220–21). Although nearly 60 percent of New York's Puerto Ricans lived in Manhattan at the time, there were also significant communities in the Morisannia and Mott Haven sections of the Bronx, which also falls under the jurisdiction of the New York Archdiocese.

This dispersal of Puerto Ricans into so many neighborhoods rendered the repetition of the St. Cecilia's experiment relatively useless. The archdiocese could not continue to "give away" parishes, even had it been able to find religious congregations willing to assume them. Meanwhile, the entry of Puerto Ricans into these neighborhoods implied the exodus of middle-class Euro-American Catholics. Catholics who had provided the archdiocese with a strong and trustworthy financial support base were abandoning the neighborhood parishes.

The church in New York had faced the problem of financially strapped parishes in the early nineteenth century by making the archdiocese into a highly centralized urban institution. The solution now appeared to lie in turning the institutional strengths of the archdiocese toward the Puerto Rican apostolate. This implied more than attention to pastoral care. Clearly, if the parishes were ever to be supported by Puerto Ricans, these newcomers would have to receive social assistance so they, like previous immigrants, could progress economically.

In his search for a solution, Spellman could not help but be influenced by the Bishops' Committee for the Spanish-Speaking in the United States (Walsh 1952). This committee had been proposed in the annual bishops' conference held in Washington, D.C., in 1944, and its first meeting took place in Oklahoma City the following year. As the location of the meeting suggests, the focus of the committee was upon the Mexican-American population of the southwestern United States. This committee had wrestled with the inadequacy of national chapels and the importation of Mexican clergy (Walsh 3,1). In 1946, under the aegis of Cardinal Stritch of Chicago, steps were taken by the committee in its care for Mexican-Americans that were also reflected in Spellman's policies toward the Puerto Ricans. The committee assumed an interdiocesan character, and in addition to offering the sacraments through pastoral care, it also attempted programs of social concern. These were coordinated by the committee, which also established lines of communication between the migrants' sending dioceses and the receiving dioceses. The committee undertook a major role in the delivery of social services provided to Mexican-Americans in the Southwest (McNamara 1968). As a means of better understanding the plight of the people it served and of justifying foundation money in order to carry on its work, the committee undertook a sociological survey. This study emphasized that the church's social services were independent of works of evangelization, although as Walsh points out (39), the proposal to the Rockefeller Foundation failed to generate funds because the work was not perceived as nonsectarian.

On the other hand, the committee's work merited a strong letter of support from the apostolic delegate in 1948, who commended the anti-Communist impact of its good works (Walsh, 40 n. 15). Since Mexican-American farm workers were residing both in the Southwest and in farmland further north and west, a major interdiocesan convention in Washington, D.C., sponsored by the committee that same year, encouraged collaboration by Midwestern dioceses in the Spanish-speaking apostolate (Walsh, 60 n. 2). In 1949, the committee formally proposed that dioceses receiving the migration of Mexican-Americans appoint a Spanish-speaking vicar general. Although at first sight this may appear similar to the Cahensly proposal in the nineteeth century, in this case there is no suggestion of the formation of a separate diocese with its own Mexican-American ordinary. In 1949 the bishops were more secure in their power and the suggestion received considerable attention. In his address to the bishops Archbishop Robert F. Lucey of San Antonio, one of the first supporters of the committee, focused on the need for clergy training. He volunteered his Texas diocese as a training ground for Midwestern clergy who wished to learn the language and customs of the migrant people in their home state. So effective was its work that the committee acquired a national reputation for representing the interests of Mexican-Americans. In 1950 Archbishop Lucey was named by President Truman to a national commission for the study of migratory labor, crowning the labors of the committee with presidential recognition.

Thus, when Spellman considered his options toward the Puerto Ricans in 1950, he had the Bishops' Committee for the Spanish-Speaking in the United States as a model. The focus of the committee made it impractical to attach New York's problems to the same agency, however. For one thing, migratory farm labor was the principal concern of those working with the Mexican-Americans, while the Puerto Ricans in New York were largely urban factory workers. Second, the interdiocesan connections were between the Southwest and the Midwest; they did not affect the immense majority of Puerto Ricans who traveled on airplanes between San Juan and New York. However, the model of a broad social-concerns focus, the use of sociological analysis as a mode of planning, and the clergy education through exchange with the home base of the migrants were significant characteristics of an organized apostolate.

This was the genesis of Spellman's new missionary initiative. He had decided to allow the St. Cecilia's experiment to begin in every parish where Puerto Ricans were found, but to use archdiocesan priests, not Redemptorists, as the clergy. In order to analyze the scope of the commitment that was necessary, a sociological study was commissioned by New York Coadjutor Archbishop John J. Maguire in 1952. Father George Kelly began the survey the next year and completed it in 1955.

The data collected in the first year alone presented "a bold and blunt challenge to the archdiocese," says Stern, and was "remarkably prophetic about the growth and development of New York's Puerto Rican population." Kelly was correct in anticipating that Puerto Ricans would one day represent the largest Catholic group in the archdiocese, and that only a massive clergy training program would supply for the pastoral needs of Hispanics (Stern 1982, 16–18). This and the advice of other educators and religious and lay leaders had a positive impact upon the decision of the cardinal (interviews with Fitzpatrick, January and December

1982; Stern 1982, 19). In respect to the cardinal's decision, Stern gives much weight to George Kelly's findings and Archbishop Maguire's recommendations. The sociological soundness of the study was underscored by Joseph P. Fitzpatrick, S. J., a graduate of Harvard and professor of sociology at Fordham University. Recognizing Spellman's political acumen, Fitzpatrick arranged a meeting for the cardinal with Encarnación Padilla de Armas, whose activism had given her various posts in city government. Unlike many of the Puerto Rican political leaders at the time, Mrs. Padilla was unabashedly Catholic.

Even though the study was not to be completed until 1955, Spellman decided to establish a chancery-based office in 1953 under the directorship of Monsignor Joseph F. Connolly to coordinate an apostolate that was both pastoral and social. According to Stern, an important factor in this decision was that of "image."

> The new office was clearly meant to be a high level and prestigious one. The appointment in itself was an important message to the Puerto Rican community and reflected a new sense of responsibility on the part of the archdiocese for Puerto Ricans. Msgr. Connolly was an intelligent and dynamic priest of the archdiocese, Roman trained, a former faculty member of the seminary, and a domestic prelate . . . and his designation was well received by the spokesmen for New York's Puerto Ricans (Stern 1982, 20).

Monsignor Joseph F. Connolly was appointed to this post by Cardinal Spellman on March 24, 1953, and served in this capacity until 1956. Connolly, according to documents cited by Robert L. Stern, one of his successors, brought to his new position a wide vision and much enthusiasm (interview, October 1982; and Stern 1982, 26ff.). A "Plan of Coordination of Spanish Catholic Action for the Archdiocese of New York," which bears his signature, was designed six months following his appointment. In Stern's words, it was a carefully formulated "grand design . . . especially dear to Msgr. Connolly's heart." Connolly himself described his efforts as:

> [A] plan . . . formulated only after careful thought about the survey of Father George Kelly, after deliberate reflection upon the functions of the various Archdiocesan departments, and after six months of active personal experience with many of the priests, people and problems of the Spanish-American Catholic population of New York (Stern 1982, 24 n. 31; Connolly, 1953a and 1953b).

To ensure representation of the archdiocese at any and all "ecclesiastical and secular Spanish American societies," and "at all and sundry 'conferences,' 'workshops,' 'seminars,' 'committees,' etc.," one part of the plan called for the creation of a Committee of Laymen for Spanish Catholic Action. Another section defined the role of the office of Coordinator of Spanish Catholic Action (Stern 1982, 26). Accordingly, the office's role was "to serve as the clearance center for all liaison between the Spanish American people and our own Coordinating Council and Committee of the Laity, as well as the many ecclesiastical, civic and social agencies in New York pursuing similar activities" (Stern 1982, 26 n. 35).

A special value of the plan was that it avoided the Cahensly dilemma by articulating a principle of unity for pastoral action on behalf of Hispanics and calling for "an integration of these, our newest and numerous Catholic citizens, into the existing pattern of archdiocesan life" so as to "avoid the unhappy and undesirable evolution, in effect, of a separate diocese within the archdiocese" (Stern 1982, 25–28).

The office had three functions:

1. Clearance of all matters affecting the Spanish-American population to the proper department of the archdiocese;
2. Contact with all agencies and individuals, ecclesiastical and civil, concerned with matters affecting the Spanish-American population of the archdiocese, active or passive;
3. Communication with all agencies and individuals, ecclesiastical and civil concerned with matters affecting the Spanish-American population of this archdiocese.

Connolly submitted his plan to the cardinal archbishop and to the heads of the departments of the archdiocese for comments and suggestions. These were subsequently incorporated into the first draft, followed by a discussion of the final plan at a meeting of priests for the Spanish ministry (Stern 1982, 24, 25). Although Connolly states with enthusiasm that the plan was approved in "its basic elements," according to Stern it was never implemented in all its details (interview with Stern, October 1982; Stern 1982, 28). Such "details" included "the Coordinating Council and the Laymen's Committee," which "were never set up as Msgr. Connolly had hoped." As Stern also points out, this council would have consisted of the priests representing the various departments. In connection to the plan, Connolly had devised a kind of table of organizations of the archdiocese with eleven major department heads. "Briefly, the principle underlying the plan of a 'Coordinating Council' is the principle of unity. There should not be two distinct departments performing the same function" (Connolly 1953b, Plan 4, 5).

The name Office of Spanish-American Catholic Action established the ideological credentials of the ministry. While Catholic Action in the United States had been modified so that the church did not sponsor separate Catholic political parties, as had been done in Europe, Catholic Action represented the political involvement of the laity under the guidance of the bishops (Abell). The hierarchy in the United States sought to integrate labor unions, parish-based social action groups, and papal teaching on economic and social relations. In the pluralistic United States the church did not take an integralist approach that addressed the whole society as a target for Catholic principles and institutions. Instead, loyal Catholic citizens in the United States were expected to vote for programs and candidates representing the church's interests as defined by the bishops. This was the basis of a "Catholic vote" in the Post–World War II era (Fenton, 132–40).

Although Puerto Ricans were newcomers to New York and its Catholic church, they were identified as Catholics. Moreover, because they had been United States citizens since 1917, they had a right to acceptance as a constituent part of Catholics in New York City. The Office of Spanish-American Catholic Action was expected to educate Puerto Ricans into these functions, including their political role as voters for church interests.

From an institutional perspective Spellman was responding to the same pressures experienced by his predecessors. If Catholicism were to continue as an urban institution representing all of the city's Catholics, it had to expand its services to the Puerto Ricans. Governmental and political institutions were accepting responsibility toward the Puerto Ricans, as were Protestant and Pentecostal churches. Hence, if the Catholic church did not actively pursue its role as integrator and Americanizer of the Puerto Ricans, it would sacrifice its role as the leading denominational institution of New York City.

Despite his efforts, Monsignor Connolly was unable to wield sufficient clout to have all the chancery offices open themselves to the needs of the Puerto Ricans. The amount of work was immense. Besides the meetings with chancery officials, he was also supposed to oversee the parish apostolates and supervise clergy training for the Spanish-speaking ministry. His outreach to the city's Puerto Rican civic leadership was impeded by his lack of facility in speaking the Spanish language (interviews with Fitzpatrick, January and December 1982).

For these and other personal reasons, Connolly served as Coordinator of the Office of Spanish-American Catholic Action for scarcely three years, leaving the post in 1956. Father James Wilson was named acting coordinator in November of that year and permanently assigned to assume responsibility in May of 1957.

Connolly had provided a good start to the chancery-based office, even if not all of his vision was implemented. The ministry to the Puerto Ricans was firmly established as an innovative apostolate that committed the archdiocese to a missionary form of activity. Moreover, when the archdiocese could not supply quickly enough one of its own priests to an integrated parish, it encouraged pastors to recruit a native Spanish or Latin American priest to serve as a regular, if not incardinated, member of the parish clergy. Some of these Hispanic priests were on temporary assignment in New York because they were graduate students at one of the many universities; others, like the Canons Regular of the Lateran, came as members of a missionary society in response to a missionary need.

While such pastoral measures were not unlike those taken in the parishes of the nineteenth century, they were now enriched with sociological perspectives and archdiocesan chancery support. In some ways the Office of Spanish-American Catholic Action was the equivalent for Puerto Ricans of the Bishops' Committee for the Spanish-Speaking in the United States, which had been founded to serve the Mexican-Americans. Yet while the latter was funded nationwide, New York took upon itself much of the financial responsibility for ministry to Puerto Ricans in the northeastern United States, basically because most of the Puerto Rican population resided there.

Second, the office represented an initiative toward incorporating Puerto Ricans into the fabric of church and city life in accord with the path taken by previous European ethnic groups. Third, the effort to aid Puerto Ricans, who were now generally viewed as a racial group, gave the apostolate to the Puerto Ricans a particular attractiveness to Catholic liberals, who advocated a stronger commitment to social concerns. As explained in chapter 3, the cosmopolitan nature of New York in the middle of the twentieth century implied a role for intellectuals who wanted Catholicism to identify with progressive social policies. The participation of these liberals in the Office of Spanish-American Catholic Action resulted in two particular initiatives: sponsorship of a massive public celebration in the traditional Puerto Rican style of *fiestas patronales,* which began in June of 1953 as *La Fiesta de San Juan;* and the Conference on the Spiritual Care of Puerto Rican Migrants, held in Puerto Rico in April of 1955. These will be described in detail in the next chapter.

But the most important of the changes brought by the office to the New York Archdiocese was the installation of an integrated territorial parish to serve both English-speakers and Spanish-speakers with bilingual archdiocesan clergy. This meant that as Puerto Ricans moved into poor areas from which older residents had departed, the existing parish resources—church buildings and parochial schools—could be used for the newcomers (Fitzpatrick 1971, 125).

> Wherever Puerto Ricans lived, the local parish would adapt itself to them! Wherever necessary, parishes would begin to function in a bilingual, bicultural way. The model of St. Cecilia was now made normative for the archdiocese, except now it applied to the parishes staffed by the diocesan clergy as well. The implications of this pastoral decision were enormous: local clergy and religious would have to acquire new communication skills, and adjunct Spanish-speaking clergy and religious would have to be recruited; all diocesan programs, offices, and agencies would have to begin to address themselves to a bilingual, bicultural reality: these new immigrants would not be ecclesiastically isolated but involved immediately in the life of the local parish (Stern 1982, 32).

The advantages of this plan lay in its avoidance of duplication of existing resources as well as the aforementioned effort to begin immediately the process of integrating the Puerto Ricans into the practice of New York Catholicism.

With parish life serving as the fulcrum for the ministry to Puerto Ricans, it is not surprising that Connolly's successor, Father (later Monsignor) James Wilson was noted for his pastoral attention to parish life. Remarkably fluent in the Spanish language, Wilson also had experience as a missionary to the Philippine Islands. Less focused upon chancery influence, his directorship of the office focused upon developing parish organizations and movements consonant with pre–Second Vatican Council Catholicism.

Monsignor Wilson coordinated a city-wide program that brought the traditional preaching of the parish mission to virtually every parish that served Puerto Ricans. Father Saturnino Junquera, S. J., with six other Spanish-speaking priests preached *La Gran Misión.* Distinguished in Puerto Rico for his sermons on piety, devotion to Our Lady of Providence, and traditional fire-and-brimstone calls for repentance, Junquera attracted large crowds of Puerto Ricans to New York churches where they could be ministered to by the ever-increasing number of Spanish-speaking priests enlisted by the Office of Spanish-American Catholic Action. Wilson also founded the Knights of San Juan, modeled after the successful movement in Chicago. But this attempt at a Catholic substitute for the self-help that had been delivered by the Puerto Rican brotherhoods during the Pioneer Migration failed to materialize (Stern 1982, 47–49).

The most significant of Wilson's initiatives was the introduction into the archdiocese of the Cursillo Movement. Founded in Mallorca, Spain, in 1949,[2] the Cursillo arrived in New York in 1958 when Father Gabriel Fernández and a team of lay persons gave the first three-day training session of spiritual renewal to Puerto Rican Catholics of the archdiocese. Convinced of the movement's potential, Wilson arranged for the movement to be founded in New York. The Cursillo began on a regular basis in the archdiocese in September of 1960, when a group of Mexican-American laymen from Nuevo Laredo, Texas, came to give a Cursillo. This was followed by a second and third celebration in December led by laymen from the Cursillo Movement in Spain (Stern 1982, 45).

The Cursillo Movement emphasizes singing in its celebrations, adding religious lyrics to secular melodies. In the New York experience, Puerto Ricans adapted for their own special compositions, patriotic and nostalgic songs that were sometimes identified with political parties on the island. More important, lay men and women were given roles as preachers and organizers of the movement. The Cursillo provided a bridge between a cultural

Catholic and a practicing Catholic, so that the initiated not only identified with the general tenets of Catholicism but adopted an active and informed embrace of that religion with all of its moral implications. The Cursillo is, in religious terms, a conversion experience. Once the experience was structured into a movement in the archdiocese, however, it appears to have functioned as a sect within Catholicism (Stevens-Arroyo, in Rodríguez et al. 1980, 129–39; cf. Fitzpatrick 1977, 21ff.).

The success of the movement was "spectacular," to the point that within a few years "in the Puerto Rican community to be a *cursillista* and a Catholic was almost one and the same" (Stevens-Arroyo, in Rodríguez et al. 1980, 133). Cursillo Center records show that by 1978 about thirty thousand Puerto Ricans had made the Cursillo. Since the lay person was instructed that activism was always to be limited by the approval of the hierarchy, the *cursillistas* sought direction from the clergy. Moreover, the autocriticism, the local focus of the parish groups, and the financial low cost of the Cursillo Movement promised a high return in apostolic and spiritual zeal for very little institutional commitment. As Stern points out:

> During the past two decades and more, the Cursillo Movement has been the chief instrument of Hispanic lay leadership formation within the archdiocese. Several thousand lay men and women have "made" a Cursillo, and thousands of them have received further and specialized formation for the apostolate in the associated programs of the Cursillo Movement at Saint Joseph's Center. The "cursillistas" have provided the nucleus of Hispanic lay leadership in almost every Hispanic parish of the archdiocese. Perhaps one reason for the rapid spread, great popularity, and considerable impact of the Cursillo among New York's Hispanics is that this diocesan-wide, city-wide movement provided a framework and community to the individual Hispanic immigrant otherwise submerged in New York's dominant non-Hispanic culture and in danger of losing his identity as Hispanic and Catholic. Its religious celebrations and great rallies and assemblages both made each Hispanic cursillista very aware that he was not alone in New York and gave him great opportunities for self-expression, recognition, and leadership (Stern 1982, 46–47).

However, the Cursillo Movement in New York had its problems. As is usually the case with changes or new activities being introduced into an established traditional setting, the Cursillo was the object of suspicion among some, especially pastors of an older generation.[3] But the newness of the Cursillo was not the only cause of distrust; it was also something which had not first been tried upon the English-speaking Catholics. Moreover, some saw Communism in the movement, especially when César Chávez and the United Farm Workers identified themselves as *cursillistas* while organizing strikes and a national boycott (Rendón, 323–25).

As the movement developed in the archdiocese, however, the thrust toward social concern and political activism that characterized the Cursillo among the Mexican-Americans was absent (Stevens-Arroyo 1980, 143). Clergy in the parishes were sometimes indifferent to the Cursillo, seeing constant supervision as superfluous. Those most comfortable with the Cursillo Movement were traditionalist clergy from Spain. Moreover, the excellent leadership provided by the Augustinian Recollect Fathers of Spain from St. Joseph's Center made it appear at times that they, and not the coordinator of the Office of Spanish-American Catholic Action, were the leaders of the Spanish-speaking Catholic community.

Although there was an incipient Puerto Ricanness and cultural identification with Oxcart Catholicism among many *cursillistas,* the movement in New York generally perpetuated the traditional Spanish power of a conservative clergy (Stevens-Arroyo 1980, 175–79).

Overall, the Cursillo Movement can be considered to have strengthened Catholicism among the Puerto Ricans of the New York Archdiocese. The Cursillo galvanized cultural Catholics and made them practicing apostles of religion. A sense of sect, or church-within-a-church, was a practical result among Puerto Ricans. Together with other lay parish organizations, the Cursillo served Puerto Ricans as an extra-geographical ethnic community. Indirectly, it fostered the consciousness that Puerto Ricans practiced Catholicism in ways that made them different from the non-Hispanic immigrants before them. The Cursillo reinforced cultural traits in religion and thus diluted the Americanization focus of the archdiocesan ministry toward the Puerto Ricans (Stevens-Arroyo 1980, 269–82, 288–91, 315).

In order to understand the practical effect of these policies upon the Puerto Rican laity, it might be useful to analyze the history of a "typical" Puerto Rican parish of the Upper West Side in

Manhattan. Sometime in 1950, Puerto Ricans living in the neighborhood approached the pastor with their need for a Spanish-speaking priest to celebrate Mass on Sundays in the local church rather than forcing Catholics to travel nearly forty blocks to a Spanish-language chapel. Even though parish rectories at that time were administered in a style that made the pastor distant and even lordly, most of the Puerto Ricans had been active in their island parishes before coming to New York.[4] They had some general anticipation that they had a right and responsibility to bring their needs to the attention of the pastor. The response was, "First come to our Mass [in English] and show yourselves worthy. If you are as many as you say you are, we want to see that. Then we will talk again."

After more visits and petitions the pastor invited a priest from one of the Spanish religious orders in New York to celebrate mass in the Spanish language on Sundays. The liturgy was held after all the regularly scheduled masses in English and utilized the basement chapel rather than the main, upstairs church. But the mass was not enough. Because it attracted satisfying numbers of Puerto Ricans for services, the Puerto Rican leaders were eager to have their own organizations and parish activities. Moreover, newly arrived Puerto Rican children were in the need of a Spanish-speaking catechist in order to prepare for their First Holy Communion.

The need for a catechist opened the way for further communication with the pastor in 1953. The commitment of one member of the community every Sunday to prepare children for the reception of the sacraments necessitated that the basement church be left open after the celebration of mass. As more and more people asked for their children to receive religious instructions, a group of permanent catechists was established and asked to meet aside from the Sunday classes. It was agreed that they should meet one night a month in the lower church. Since at that time, most of the catechists were young unmarried women, the congregation of *Hijas de María* was a logical offshoot. Soon to follow were *La Sociedad del Santo Nombre* (Holy Name Society) for the men, *Las Damas del Sagrado Corazón* (Ladies of the Sacred Heart) for married women, and the Legion of Mary, where both men and women, married and unmarried could meet. A parish not unlike one in Puerto Rico had been established.

With the increasing attendance at the mass celebrated in Spanish, the pastor came to recognize the permanence of Puerto Ricans in his parish. A native Spanish priest was named as a resident in the rectory to minister to the needs of this growing Puerto Rican community. Furthermore, he was assigned regular parish duties, as were the other clergy. This meant that besides the care of the Spanish-speaking parishioners he had responsibility for daily mass for the total parish congregation, visiting the sick at home and the hospitals, receiving parishioners at the church rectory, and even counting the Sunday collections.

Usually such a non-incardinated Spanish-speaking priest would serve for a period of approximately three years and then be reassigned to a different parish. Priests from the Society of Jesus, Augustinian Friars, the Augustinian Recollects, the Dominican Order, and from other dioceses in Latin America and Spain were either entrusted on a regular basis for pastoral care of this community or came to serve for the summer months. While in most instances the work of these clerics was exceptional, the fact that they moved in and out so quickly created a sense of instability in the community. Eventually priests from the archdiocese, trained in the language and sensitized to Puerto Rican culture by intensive preparation courses in Puerto Rico (see chapter 5) augmented the bilingual clergy. In some parishes the only priest unable to speak Spanish was the pastor.

Nonetheless, the community grew and was fortified by the good example and strength of those ministering to them, surpassing oftentimes the English-speaking community in the number of people attending Sunday services as well as membership in sodalities and societies and parish activities. Some of the movements, such as the Cursillo, were new to the New York church and had no English-speaking equivalent; others, such as the Holy Name Society and hospital volunteers, already had existed in the parish, but founded a separate organization just for the Spanish-speaking. Eventually non-apostolic associations like a theater group and a choir were formed. Parish picnics, attendance at the *San Juan Fiesta* as official parish representatives, cross-town journeys to *Cursillo Ultreyas* and other inter-parish activities completed the picture of typical parish life. As these activities, movements, and organizations flourished among the Puerto Ricans, their success attracted more of the Spanish-speaking to belong to the parish.

On the one hand, such a "basement church" was the center of a living community. Since many of the parishioners were related by blood, marriage, or friendship, it also functioned as an extended family. It was the place to worship and celebrate religious events, and also where parishioners could see and speak in their own language to cousins, aunts, uncles, and friends after a week of hard work in a world foreign to their traditions and way of life.

On the other hand, the faithful in the basement church often felt treated as second-class citizens and second-class Catholics, because the basement represented social distance from the upper church. *Las misas de sótano,* as masses in the lower church came to be referred to, served as a constant reminder that despite their Catholicity and United States citizenship, discrimination against them existed in the church (Anson, 33; Stern 1982, 35). While mass in the upper church was the definition of upward mobility in the context of church community, it also required abandoning the Spanish language in worship and Puerto Rican Catholic customs. The Puerto Ricans were conscious that as long as they practiced Puerto Rican Catholicism, they were stuck in the basement. Indeed, the inferiority attributed to the Puerto Ricans in the lower church was often extended to the priests who ministered to them.

Older members of the English-speaking congregation would sometimes complain that the "people from the lower church are too loud; they do not seem to know that Holy Mass is not a *fiesta;* that *Ite Misa est* means go home to your business and stop obstructing the passage of the parishioners who want to worship in the upper church." Happily, this was not always the case. Some would comment on the "friendliness of the Spanish-speaking." There were even cases of a member of the upper church joining the lower church and one of their parish societies because "the people are so much more alive and the congregations seem to do so much."

For the most part, however, the lower church conferred upon the Puerto Ricans a sense not so much of integration as one of internal colony. Even when the lower church and the activities of the Latino community far surpassed those of the upper church, in terms of clergy and accessibility of parish resources, its members came second. At the practical level the "integrated" parish became synonymous with the basement church.

The distance from the upper church also awarded Puerto Ricans the time and place to develop their own mode of worship in this country. In this new isolation, so close yet so far from traditional New York Catholicism, the Puerto Ricans borrowed from their own age-old traditions of the homeland and tempered them with their experiences as migrants. From these adaptations they fashioned a new mode of Oxcart Catholicism to fit their needs in the great metropolis. In fact, the lower church assumed the role of the hills of the homeland, keeping the community secure and at the familiar social distance from hierarchical structures. In a sense, the basement church for the Puerto Ricans was like the basement church of the Italian immigrants, an expression in New York of their own brand of Catholicism (Tomasi, 80, 76–81, 167–68).

The Puerto Rican faithful were often responsible for the physical upkeep of the basement church. For instance, if an organ or a paint job was needed, it was the responsibility of those meeting in the lower church to provide for it. Raffles, donations, and dances were activities initiated by the Puerto Rican parishioners to secure necessary funds. Thus, although segregated in their own chapel with their own organizations, the Puerto Ricans were "separate but equal" with the English-speaking of the parish.

Eventually pastors were coaxed into giving permission to use the school auditorium and other facilities. Then the community would congregate every Sunday for a quick breakfast after mass, perpetuating the *fiesta* and communal spirit some non-Latinos frowned upon. Usually the parish society that held its monthly meeting that Sunday was also responsible for the breakfast. Eventually, with much work and sacrifice in some parishes, bilingual masses were celebrated on special occasions where lectors, choirs, and concelebrants represented both communities. In the meantime, the number of Puerto Rican children in the parochial school slowly increased, socializing these children and their English-speaking classmates into a mutual acceptance.

Cardinal Spellman viewed such a parish as an adaptation of the traditional role of the archdiocese in "Americanizing" the immigrant. The archdiocese intended that the Puerto Ricans would become assimilated into the church and the city, eventually without the need for the Spanish language. Until his death, he requested information on the annual number of communions, baptisms, confessions, and mass attendance, repeating the pastoral measures of his own spirituality. But in his structuring of the apostolate to the Puerto Ricans, Cardinal Spellman introduced an intellectual function that bestowed on the Chancery Office a leadership role toward the archdiocese. As I hope to show in the next chapter, the missionary concept of Spellman was gradually expanded by church intellectuals to represent a new definition of church mission toward all the faithful as it immersed the younger clergy into the language and culture of the newcomers and forced a degree of mutual integration between Euro-Americans and Hispanics.

5. The Intellectualization of an Experiment

Nunca tuvo un comisario e barrio que lo protogiera.
Hay gente que nase coja o manca o jorobá.

He never had a district commissioner to protect him. Some people are born lame or crippled or hunchbacked.

—Doña Gabriela, in *The Oxcart,* Act I

This book has addressed social distance in chapter 2 and the increasing specialization of church leadership as Catholicism evolved an institutionalized archdiocesean structure in chapter 3. Both topics—the social distance of the Puerto Rican faithful from the institutional church and the evolution of a cluster of village parishes into a cosmopolitan institution—are related by the installation of United States institutional Catholicism on the island of Puerto Rico after 1898 and the migration of large numbers of Puerto Ricans to the Archdiocese of New York. In this way the Oxcart Catholicism of Puerto Ricans and the Fifth Avenue urban institution of the New York church were matched.

This chapter analyzes the role of clerical leaders who were invited into the archdiocesean policy process because of their standing as intellectuals. As described in chapter 4, the influence of these leaders was significantly greater in the shaping of an archdiocesean response toward Puerto Ricans that might have been anticipated. Rather than simply expand the existing national parishes to meet the needs for pastoral care, in 1952 New York's Cardinal Spellman turned to clerics with special academic training in order to formulate a long-range plan. The basis for the selection of clerics like Ivan Illich, George Kelly, and Jesuit Joseph P. Fitzpatrick was their status as intellectuals, specially prepared by university education to analyze Catholicism. Thus, the Spanish-speaking apostolate in the Archdiocese of New York was shaped from the beginning by intellectuals.

It is important, I think, to analyze the leadership role of these intellectuals, since in great measure the trajectory of the Spanish-speaking apostolate as a forum for innovation in ministry can be traced to these beginnings. The status of clergy who were also academics was problematic for United States Catholicism in the 1950s and 1960s, as O'Dea (1962) has explained. The church is not a democracy; it maintains a power structure based on a feudal and medieval monarchy even while it faces the challenge of adapting to the political values of the United States. Neither does the church operate with cost analysis or volume of sales as the determining factor in decision-making, as in a business corporation. The leaders of the church do not stand for election from the populace, as in the political arena. But although the church is not a business or political institution, neither is it completely alien to such operational modes. In a sense, the multiplication of nonvoluntary associations that constitute the professionalism and the staff of an archdiocese like New York creates a complex web of competing motivations and self-preserving interests that the sociology of religion has only begun to study in detail (Hargrove, 266–67).

But if Catholicism were to be analyzed in its institutional functions, its essentially religious orientation would have to be included in order to portray accurately its decision-making process. As Otto Maduro points out, the clerical, social class, and financial interests of church activity are constantly subject to demands and alternating support from the diverse Catholic public, which expects fidelity to the gospel.

> Any religion, then, must maintain continuity with its history. It must maintain its tradition, respect the limits of its foundational doctrine, reproduce its organization, guard its power, satisfy the exigencies of its functionaries, adapt to the demands of its heterogeneous public, and use its resources in a rational manner. The reality of a determinate religion in a specific context is the geometrical result of the polygon of these forces, and perhaps others as well, drawing this religion in different directions and with various degrees of traction. In certain historico-social circumstances, this *result* may be the self-perpetuation, simple or extended, of the re-

> ligious system, or its adaptation of reform. In other circumstances, on the contrary, the result may be the regression, asphyxiation, decadence, dismemberment, or division of the religion concerned. In either case, it is only by keeping account of the complexity of the facts of reality that we shall be able to grasp how far a determinate religion's possibilities can take it in the direction of self-reformation, and why they take it only this far—independently of the desires and intentions of the religious agents (Maduro, 112).

The various layers of competing interests that had coexisted for generations under the various guises of social distance and national parishes were now brought into contact by a changing demographic pattern that rapidly substituted Puerto Ricans for Euro-American Catholics in New York. But even if the archdiocese had become increasingly pluralistic in the expressions of clerical leadership since the end of the nineteenth century, the decision of the cardinal archbishop still remained the single most important factor in determining church policy. Access and influence upon the cardinal were crucial to any apostolic efforts. The contributions of Ivan Illich, George Kelly, and Joseph P. Fitzpatrick have been described as parts of the historical events that led to the institution of a Spanish-speaking apostolate office, but their importance as intellectuals merits special analysis as a sociological process.

The role of church intellectuals can be considered from several different sociological perspectives. McNamara utilized the Weberian notions of charismatic and rationalizing leadership in his ground-breaking studies of Mexican-American Catholics (1968 and 1970). Murnion (1978), Vallier (1967) and Stevens-Arroyo (1980) have adapted this Weberian approach to other considerations that link the function of leadership to other factors (see above, chapter 1).

But unfortunately, none of these studies includes the concept of "organic intellectuals" first developed by Antonio Gramsci, the Italian Communist,[1] and successfully employed in recent studies of clerical leadership. Adriance (1986) analyzed the Brazilian church after the conciliar reforms of the Second Vatican Council, suggesting that local clergy provide progressive leadership to grass-roots communities in ways applicable to Gramsci's notion of organic intellectuals. Cadena (1987) applied the same notion to some of the members of PADRES, a Latino priests' association that exercised considerable influence in the United States.

Gramsci's definition enhances studies of church leadership because the dialectical dimension implicit in the notion of an "organic intellectual" explains well both the constraints upon as well as the opportunities for change in a complex institution such as the Catholic church. Hobsawm (1974, 43) notes that Gramsci was "saved from Stalin because Mussolini had him put behind bars." Whatever the reasons, Gramsci's writings generally avoid the heavy dogmatism characteristic of some Marxist writing. Moreover, he was extraordinarily critical of the failures of his own party, often casting a sympathetic eye upon the Catholic church of his youth. He sought to find in the success of religion an answer to effective communication with the masses of working class and peasants in the Italy of his day. I introduce his concept in order to tie this book to the emerging literature on Latino and Latin American Catholics.

Gramsci viewed clerics as important intellectuals in a feudal, rural society. The religious ideology espoused by such clerics largely determined school, education, charity, good works, and morality at that time. In particular, I found his description of Italian attitudes toward the clergy resonant with a Puerto Rican experience, where social distance defined the relationship.

> The peasant's attitude towards the intellectual [cleric] is double and appears contradictory. He respects the social position of the intellectuals . . . but sometimes affects contempt for it, which means that his admiration is mingled with instinctive elements of envy and impassioned anger. One can understand nothing of the collective life of the peasantry and of the germs and ferments of development which exist within it, if one does not take into consideration and examine concretely and in depth this effective subordination to the intellectuals. (Gramsci, 14–15)

The process described by Maduro as institutional adaptation is analyzed by Gramsci. According to his class analysis of church history from the Middle Ages to the Reformation, many heretical movements were "manifestations of popular forces aiming to reform the church and bring it closer to the people" and were "based on social conflicts determined by the birth of Communes and represented a split between masses and intellectuals within the church. This split was 'stitched over' by the birth of popular religious movements subsequently reabsorbed by the church through the formation of the mendicant orders and a new religious unity" (Gramsci, 397, 331 n. 6).

Thus, while intellectuals are limited by church discipline, they also articulate an alternative policy for the hierarchy that allows for adaptation to new social conditions. Clerical intellectuals sometimes force the church to face up to a problem in the institutional support for the status quo and the need to speak to the simple people (Gramsci, 331). This alternative policy is framed by the intellectuals as theology, harmonizing traditional belief with new concerns. Such clerics serve the institution's interests by preserving continuity and power, but they also legitimize the concerns of the faithful by elevating popular religious movements to the status of theology.

> The strength of religions, and of the Catholic church in particular, has lain, and still lies, in the fact that they feel very strongly the need for the doctrinal unity of the whole mass of the faithful and strive to ensure that the higher intellectual stratum does not get separated from the lower. The Roman church has always been the most vigorous in the struggle to prevent the "official" formation of two religions, one for the "intellectuals" and the other for the "simple souls." This struggle has not been without serious disadvantages for the Church itself, but these disadvantages are connected with the historical process which is transforming the whole of civil society and which contains overall a corrosive critique of all religion, and they only serve to emphasize the organizational capacity of the clergy in the cultural sphere and the abstractly rational and just relationship which the Church has been able to establish in its own sphere between the intellectuals and the simple (Gramsci, 328–29).

Gramsci sees theology in the church as an ideology that binds together thought and action. Usually the intellectuals and the hierarchy are in harmony, because they reflect the same class interests. But both are responsible to the gospel and must maintain the loyalty of the mass of the faithful. If the gap between the interests of the hierarchy and the religious needs of the faithful grows too large, the intellectuals are capable of developing a theological legitimacy for a new course of action that will reconcile conflicts, allowing the church to act collectively. Intellectuals exercise the key intermediating function in the process. Theologizing clergy "put themselves forward as autonomous and independent of the dominant social group" (Gramsci, 7), and in so doing they provide to the church a way of transcending the interests of the dominant class.

Gramsci introduces specialized vocabulary for his concepts, which I feel is not necessary to introduce here. His unorthodox approach to social change, however, is of particular value in understanding contemporary movements in Catholicism. Gramsci insists revolutionary action includes changing culture, that is, "superstructure." In a society that had restricted the understanding of philosophy to specialists and professionals, he was an avid advocate for a revolutionary education that took seriously the capabilities of common people to think for themselves about ultimate human values. Gramsci awarded cardinal importance to "popular religion, and . . . the entire system of beliefs, superstitions, opinions, ways of seeing things and of acting, which are collectively bundled together under the name of 'folklore' " (Gramsci, 323). He repeated Schopenhauer to the effect that "religion is the philosophy of the multitude, whereas philosophy is the religion of the elect" (Gramsci, 407). And while he recognized that popular religion is not the same as philosophy, a revolutionary "new culture" offering an alternative to existing conditions could emerge out of the accumulated sense and beliefs of ordinary people. "For a mass of people to be led to think coherently and in the same coherent fashion about the real present world, is a 'philosophical' event far more important and 'original' than the discovery by some philosophical 'genius' of a truth which remains the property of small groups of intellectuals" (Gramsci, 325).

Albeit the appropriation of specialized roles for intellectual and educator, every person in society was not only capable of being an intellectual (Gramsci, 9), but society was in need of creating a new social role in which common persons could share in a group articulation of the most essential goals of human activity (Sassoon, 134–141). By supplying in religious form the answers to fundamental questions about life, destiny, and social purpose, Catholicism has in fact accomplished this goal throughout the centuries (Gramsci, 328–29; 351–53). Peasants have been connected to intellectuals by a common loyalty to the faith that united them. Catholicism has thus developed new forms of organization, ritual, and artistic expression that echo changing social conditions without sacrificing internal continuity. Ultimately it is this common loyalty to the faith that establishes a dialectic process in which both sides need each other to function effectively—the intellectuals supplying theory, and the masses, practice. (Gramsci, 334–35) The dedicated cleric, therefore, focuses his intellectual functions upon the legitimation of church action to benefit his parishioners, while the faithful consider the parish priest to be the spokesperson for a corpus of shared values that at times they are not able to explain fully. Gramsci's emphasis, however, does not seem to be so much on the ability of the cleric to explain (that is, reason) as that of the faithful to trust in his ability (that is, faith) (Gramsci, 339).

In such a community of faith the class distinctions between intellectual and masses are eroded. Borrowing on the concept of popular leadership taken from the unlikely source of Machiavelli, Gramsci developed the notion of a "modern Prince" (Gramsci, 125–205). Such leadership was not a single individual (129), but a group that, far from allowing its members to be co-opted or coerced into a perpetual situation of subjugation, through an acquired consciousness of itself would produce its own intellectuals and vanguard, set liberating goals, and propel its members toward shared success in changing aspects of social life (177–78, and 204–5).

In this case the dynamic of change is supplied to the group by success in its work, wherein the new ideas provided by the intellectuals prove to be effective when employed by the ordinary persons in everyday life (Gramsci, 34–35; Entwistle, 137ff.). The functions of intellectual and ordinary persons were bound together "organically" so that they essentially need each other (Sasson, 152–57). "The mode of being of the new intellectual," says Gramsci, "can no longer consist in eloquence, which is an exterior and momentary mover of feelings and passions, but in active participation in practical life, as constructor, organizer, permanent persuader" (Gramsci, 10).

This is the context for Gramsci's "organic intellectual." Such a spokesperson is organically linked to the masses to the degree that legitimacy depends upon an identification of interests. An upper-class person may embrace the agenda of the masses and gain acceptance as their leader, so that the organic connection should not be confused with class origins (Entwisle, 116–18). Of course, such an upper-class leader may later turn against the interests of the masses and sever the organic connection (Entwistle, 120–22). Likewise, working-class people who acquire the capability to be intellectuals may abandon their origins (Entwistle, 125–27). This kind of organic unity is not a simple perpetuation of a traditional society's subordination of the peasant to the religious ideology of the curate (Entwistle, 113–16), nor is it a situational use of the masses to justify the predefined goals of the upper class—what he calls "conjunctural leadership" (Gramsci, 177–78; see 408–9; Sassoon, 182–88). Under conjunctural leadership there is a struggle among upper-class intellectuals for control of a course of action. Each group of intellectuals uses its interpretation of the real conditions of the ordinary people as the "terrain" upon which "the forces of opposition organize" (Gramsci, 178).

To avoid betrayals and subordination to conjunctural leadership, the organic leaders must never become bureaucratic. Gramsci advocates "democratic centralism" as the ideal condition for preserving an effectively revolutionary leadership (see Sassoon, 162–72). Such centralism requires "a continual adaptation of the organization to the real movement," "thrust from below" matched by "order from above," and the "accumulation of experience" that results in "an organic unity between theory and practice, between intellectual strata and popular masses, between rulers and ruled," rather than "a mechanical juxtaposition of single 'units' without any connection between them" (Gramsci, 188–90).

Gramsci saw a place for religious renewal in his revolutionary scheme. "An important part of *The Modern Prince,*" he said, "will have to be devoted to the question of intellectual and moral reform, that is, to the question of religion or world-view" (Gramsci, 132). Moreover, he offered a simple agenda for developing such organic leadership:

> 1. Never to tire of repeating its own arguments. . . . Repetition is the best didactic means for working on the popular mentality.
> 2. To work incessantly to raise the intellectual level of ever-growing strata of the populace, in other words, to give a personality to the amorphous mass element. This means working to produce *élites* of intellectuals of a new type which arise directly out of the masses, but remain in contact with them to become, as it were, the whalebone in the corset (Gramsci, 340).

The most important problem in creating organic intellectuals comes at the beginning of the process and lies with "the creative contribution [that] superior groups can and must have in connection with the organic capacity of the intellectually subordinate strata to discuss and develop new critical concepts" (Gramsci, 341).

In concluding my exploration of Gramsci's notion of an organic intellectual, it is necessary to advert to Cadena's analysis of Chicano leadership after the Second Vatican Council. He redefines "organic," which for Gramsci was a class description, with ethnic origins. In other words, Chicano priests are organically tied to the Chicano faithful because they share a common culture as birthright. There is cogency to this adaptation of Gramsci by Cadena, although it must be recognized that such ethnic solidarity ought not be presumed to be permanent. Milton Gordon was correct to perceive an "ethclass" phenomenon, in which stronger bonds and interests are found among persons of the same class than between members of two classes of the same ethnic group (Gordon, 51–54). But in fact, part of the importance of considering the role of intellectuals lies in the varying forms of solidarity of ethnic origins and social class.

There is no better way to begin a description of the linkage between intellectual clerics and the mass of Puerto Rican Catholics in New York than with Ivan Illich. Illich had been born in Vienna, son of a titled Dalmatian nobleman and a mother who came from a Sephardic Jewish family. In his childhood during the rise of Nazism, Illich had been enrolled in an Austrian school, from which he was later expelled on account of his mother's background.

In exile with his family in France, during his teens Illich met and made friends with the well-known French philosopher Jacques Maritain, whom he acknowledges as having exercised an important influence upon his life. After the Second World War he studied crystallography at the University of Florence, but his restless soul was not content with an engineering career. He decided upon the priesthood, and by the age of twenty-four he had earned a doctorate in history from Salzburg University and degrees in philosophy and theology from the Gregorian in Rome. This background made Illich a very special sort of candidate for the priesthood, and because his mother and sister had moved to New York (interview with Fitzpatrick, December 10, 1981), he requested ordination for the New York Archdiocese.

Spurning a career in the church's diplomatic corps, Illich sought an assignment to "an obscure position in New York City's most conservative Irish territory," where he arrived in 1952, shortly after being ordained a priest in Rome (Gray, 40–43). Assigned to Incarnation Parish in the Washington Heights area of Manhattan, Illich realized the need for parish outreach to the Puerto Ricans, who were entering the changing neighborhood in significant numbers. He learned Spanish in a manner of months. Illich started employment agencies for Puerto Rican migrants and persuaded Madison Avenue to publicize them; he induced Irish bus drivers to give up part of a weekend to drive Puerto Rican children to the Sunday camps that had been set up for them; and he encouraged young social workers to live among the Puerto Ricans in *cuartitos,* or boarding rooms, in the homes of Puerto Rican families, where they could observe and partake of Puerto Rican life in New York City (interview with Fitzpatrick, December 10, 1981; see Gray, 42–43). This commitment to the social welfare of Puerto Ricans may have had its roots in Illich's intellectual formation with Jacques Maritain, but it was also the bedrock for his identification with the class interests of Puerto Ricans, beginning his journey toward a Gramscian role as intellectual within the Puerto Rican community.

Cardinal Spellman, however, was not content to allow the talents of Illich to be buried in parish affairs. The cardinal called upon the Roman-trained cleric to mobilize his Vatican contacts for tasks of delicate diplomacy in church affairs (interview with Fitzpatrick, February 1982). In return, he allowed the Yugoslav a free hand in expanding his apostolate on behalf of the Puerto Ricans into wider spheres of influence. In one of history's strange coincidences, Monsignor Joseph Connolly, who was later chosen to head the archdiocesan office for the Spanish-speaking apostolate, was stationed in Incarnation Parish with Illich. Fitzpatrick strongly believes that Illich influenced not only Spellman in relationship to the programs and policies of the archdiocese toward the Puerto Ricans, but Connolly as well (interview, December 10, 1981).

Among the first concessions Spellman made to Illich was the integration of the San Juan Fiesta as an event sponsored by the archdiocese. As a European, Illich had a fresh perception of New York's oldest traditions. He came to appreciate the celebration of St. Patrick's Day, with its customary festivities and parade, as positive elements in the Irish-American's identification with the church. Likewise, the continuation in New York of Italian feasts, such as that of San Gennaro, enhanced Italian solidarity with Catholicism in New York. Constituted as the American Puerto Rican Saint John Day Observance Association, the Puerto Rican civic leadership of New York had already held such an event on Saturday, June 29, 1950, on the other side of the river from Illich's parish, at Hunts Point Stadium (Randall and Hunt's Point Ave, Bronx). Recognizing La Milagrosa as the "Hispanic church," they invited their priests for a ten-minute opening blessing. During that initial fiesta, the artistic and cultural predominated. And yet, when organizers of that event, such as the poet Juan Avilés, were invited, they eagerly welcomed the archdiocesan support. In fact, Juan Avilés stayed with the fiesta for many more years to come, eventually receiving the San Juan Fiesta Medal, an annual recognition to outstanding members of the Puerto Rican community.

Illich assumed that the archdiocese should sponsor this local event, devoting its resources to maintain the fiesta as a city-wide Puerto Rican annual celebration. Recognizing Puerto Rican culture's strong identity with Catholicism, Illich realized that the celebration had to maintain the cultural idiom of the Puerto Ricans. A willing ally in this project was the Jesuit sociologist Joseph P. Fitzpatrick, who has already been introduced as the intellectual who solidified Cardinal Spellman's commitment to an integrated parish as the option to the national parish (chapter 4). The two priests were not only to collaborate in terms of the apostolate to the Puerto Ricans but to become friends.

Rather than destroy the folkloric expression of the faith on the way to assimilating Puerto Ricans to urban Catholicism, both Illich and Fitzpatrick wanted to build upon this religio-cultural foundation. The social distance that had come to characterize the relations between the migrants and the institutions of the New York church had to be reduced. If the New York Archdiocese showed itself to be sympathetic to the traditions of the island, it was reasoned, Puerto Ricans would respond by seeking in the city the practice of the faith they once had in Puerto Rico.

Neither of these clerics would have described himself as a Gramscian intellectual, but their efforts to serve the Puerto Rican people through culture initiated the kind of identification with the needs of the common person that Gramsci advocated. Both clerics learned to speak Spanish, virtually as natives. Fitzpatrick, a sociology professor at Fordham, turned the social science interests in ethnic experience within the American mainstream into a manifesto for cultural pluralism within the archdiocese. There was a need to demonstrate the acceptance of New York Catholicism to the Puerto Ricans. Thus, the sponsorship of a traditional patronal feast-day celebration in New York for Puerto Ricans was expected to be a symbolic representation of how the archdiocese had committed itself to recognizing the value of Puerto Rican Catholicism.

The traditional celebration of the feast days in different Puerto Rican towns is derived from European medieval Christendom.[2] The celebration of the *fiestas patronales* allows each town to make the liturgical commemoration of a saint or feast day into an occasion for reaffirmation of the communality of belief. These celebrations in Puerto Rico, like their counterparts in medieval Europe, are part of what has been called by Christopher Herlihy, a "civic Christianity" (Herlihy, 1967). Organized under the guidance of the hierarchy, the sermons and ceremony of these feasts also emphasize one or other aspect of fealty to the church, often in consonance with agricultural or other seasonal cycles.

But in addition to the specifically religious functions of such observances, the *fiestas patronales* usually invited other social manifestations of communal solidarity. In the Middle Ages the town feast day was often used to conclude marriages, finalize property exchanges, settle inheritances, and end feuds (Gurevich, 231–32). Communal solidarity was enhanced by legitimizing the celebration in honor of a saint who had some connection to the town or its people, usually on account of a relic or some miracle worked on behalf of a suppliant (Brooke, 334–35). Pilgrimages often became the fulfillment of vows taken to the saint, either imploring or rendering thanksgiving for a favor (Brooke, 336). These devotions to personalized saints served as an antidote to a highly clericalized religion that emphasized reception of the sacraments as the primary expression of faith (Matthew, 210–18; Brooke, 347–49). One historian's description (Herlihy, 257–58) suggests that rituals of the medieval feast day united with common values in what Durkheim called "a single moral community" (cited in Parsons, 434). Such a community, Parsons observes, is larger than the organized church and includes the whole society (Parsons, 434).

The *fiestas patronales* of late nineteenth-century Puerto Rico echo the basic functions of the medieval feasts. The patronal feasts were usually sponsored by Spanish merchants, who profited from the increased trade in the villages stimulated by the celebrations. Moreover, by appearing as a kind of aristocracy, legitimized by church and government symbols, these commercial elites cemented their political and social hegemony. Hence, while the *fiestas patronales* were occasion for much community celebrations, they underscored the class structure and emphasized the dependency of the peasant farmers (*jíbaros*) and blacks upon the ruling Spanish and white *criollo* aristocracy. The carousing, drinking, and gambling fostered by the largesse of the wealthy reinforced notions of the lower classes' incapacity for the responsibilities of social power.

The invasion in 1898 and subsequent annexation of Puerto Rico somewhat altered the political and religious meanings of the *fiestas patronales*. Embarrassed by the popular excesses that generally accompanied these celebrations, even Bishop Blenck sought to discourage them (chapter 2). However, as United States Catholic missionaries began to increase their influence in Puerto Rico after the synod of 1917 (which coincided with the United States giving Puerto Ricans citizenship), the patronal feasts were resurrected along with traditional processions and other Catholic devotions as a means of reaffirming the Catholic nature of Puerto Rico's culture.

While not losing completely its affirmation of the power structure, participation in the celebrations—at whatever level—became a symbolic protest against the Protestantizing and liberal influences upon Puerto Rican society. The popularity of the feasts on account of their secular festivities, such as eating, dancing, and drinking, became ammunition in a battle for the Puerto Rican masses. The Catholic missionaries viewed the fiestas as residual evidence that, at its core, Puerto Rico was Catholic. The public feast day was the first step in a process of evangelizing and catechizing that would eventually restore a regular practice of the faith to most Puerto Ricans.

For years to come the San Juan Fiesta would be one of the two main pillars upon which the newly created Office of Spanish-American Catholic Action would function. The archdiocesan-sponsored event was inaugurated by a mass in St. Patrick's Cathedral in 1953, and repeated until 1955. In 1956, seeking to enhance participation, it was again returned to an outdoor celebration at Fordham University open-air facilities at Rose Hill Campus in the Bronx, where the Jesuit Fitzpatrick was professor. The spacious public stadium on Randall's Island was first used in 1957 in order to accommodate the overflowing crowd, which according to some estimates numbered as many as fifty thousand (Ribes Tovar 1968, 1, 125–27).

To the first outdoor celebration of the archdiocesan-sponsored San Juan Fiesta at Fordham, the archdiocese invited the flamboyant mayor of San Juan, Doña Felisa Rincón de Gautier, who once had snow flown into San Juan to make a tropical Christmas merrier on the island. Her presence gave an unmistakably Puerto Rican character to the celebration and extended the legitimacy of San Juan as municipality and as cultural capital of Puerto Rico to the community in New York.

At subsequent celebrations other political figures from the island were invited and appropriately participated in the public celebrations. In addition to the liturgy, some speeches, civic awards (the San Juan Medal), and other honorific displays were scripted into the celebration. Thus the San Juan Fiesta once again included an extraliturgical dimension, while maintaining a strong religious component. Local political leaders also figured in the feast, so that in many respects it became the Puerto Rican equivalent in New York of the Irish celebrations of St. Patrick's Day, just as Illich had anticipated.

A key part of the *Fiesta de San Juan* was the procession of all of the lay parish organizations around the stadium track. The sodalities, confraternities, societies, clubs, and later the *cursillistas* organized year-round for this kind of visible participation in the feast. The city-wide celebration, moreover, gave an identity to Puerto Ricans that transcended the narrow boundaries of parish life. The palpable evidence of the numbers and the organization of so many Puerto Ricans in the city strengthened the social cohesiveness of the people who had migrated from the island.

The thousands of Puerto Ricans who paraded at the fiesta were among the first grass-roots leaders of the community in New York. Despite the very real limitations in their leadership role from the perspective of church institutional power, these men, women, and children were leaders whose religious production in the everyday events of life was recognized on the grand scale. Even if the feast celebrated their subordinate role to the hierarchy, it none the less attributed to them a visible role, which was a remarkable improvement over the neglect of Puerto Rican customs that had characterized previous archdiocesan policy. Moreover, given the chronic lack of native Puerto Rican clergy, lay participation alone was the link between Puerto Rican traditions and the Catholicism practiced in New York. This was the stated purpose of Illich and Fitzpatrick, who had suggested the sponsorship of the celebration as intellectual advisors to the cardinal. The popularity of the *Fiesta de San Juan* demonstrated that the practice of religion in New York could be modified to reflect Puerto Rican culture.

The feast assumed a structure that varied only slightly from year to year but preserved a clear-cut division among the following events: the procession, leading up to the sermon and celebration of the mass, with closing remarks by the cardinal; the civic ceremony, in which leaders were honored with the awarding of the San Juan Medal by the cardinal; an organized recreation period, sometimes using the *piñata,* usually focused upon children; a cultural celebration, including performances by theater, music, and dance troupes. Importantly, the clergy, and sometimes even the cardinal, attended the recreational and cultural celebrations. Hence the communitarian nature of the feast served to consolidate the identification of the non–Puerto Rican clergy as members of a human community composed of Puerto Rican Catholics.

The San Juan Fiesta satisfied the goals of Spellman, Fitzpatrick, and Illich. Numbers of Puerto Ricans and visible proof of their return to Catholic practice in New York were among the cardinal's concerns. The presence of political leaders also continued the high profile of Catholicism as a part of the urban structures, even as the population shifts away from Euro-American groups began to refashion New York politics. Fitzpatrick could see in the feast a confirmation of his thesis that "a strong community has been the condition from which assimilation has effectively proceeded among earlier immigrants" (Fitzpatrick 1971, 42; 1987, 152–57). By creating an ethnic turf for Puerto Ricans, the San Juan Fiesta was the first step in absorbing these people into the daily life of the church. The vitality of parish organizations and the growing numbers of faithful, both Catholic and Puerto Rican, who were integral parts of many parishes gave evidence of a sociological process not unlike that of previous Catholic immigrant groups.

Illich, however, was the most restless of the three. He seemed to have been preoccupied with the changes the Puerto Ricans could make upon the life of the church in New York, rather than with the impact the church made on the life of Puerto Ricans. In this sense the Puerto Ricans were the "terrain" for Illich's first pastoral effort at creating a new culture for Catholicism. He assiduously explored the reasons why the church in New York had generally responded in what he deemed a negative fashion to the Puerto Rican presence. He concluded by criticizing the church in the United States for its complacency, arrogance, and tight bureaucratic apparatus. Fitzpatrick was also forthright in his confrontation of bigots.

> Those less favorably disposed [toward the Puerto Ricans] repeat the familiar accusation that they are the cause of our delinquency, that they ruin every neighborhood they move into, that they will not learn English and mingle with "Americans"; in brief, that with the coming of the Puerto Ricans, the great experience that was New York is coming to an end (Fitzpatrick, in Ferrée et al., 4:63).

But while Fitzpatrick could address his concerns against discrimination to an intellectual audience, Illich was a parish priest on the West Side with a limited public. His own intellectual formation made him restless, since as a parish priest he could not correct the chauvinistic tendency he perceived in the North American Catholic church's personnel and policies, which imposed its own values upon Puerto Ricans and other minority groups. He manifested his irritation at the "ecclesiastical conquistadores," whose ignorance and lack of interest in native customs, traditions, and idioms were so appalling to him (Gray, 44). According to Illich, the methods employed by the New York clergy to evangelize and carry on the ministry of the church had to be radically transformed.

This *metanoia*, or change of heart, could only come when missionaries realized that they themselves needed to be poor in order to preach to the poor. This poverty was not only in terms of material comfort, but most important, in a style of ministry that learned to transcend the values and the customs predominant in the missionaries' own backgrounds. This he called "total cultural indifference." In equating the process of stripping oneself of one's cultural values to that of obtaining grace, Illich called the fruits of this intentional effort "a beatitude of cultural poverty." More than the preaching of beautiful spiritual words, a missionary's testimony through everyday living is the true message. Failure to live this poverty is total failure as a missionary (Gray, 44). Clearly, these goals approximate the identification with the working class advocated by Gramsci for the organic intellectual.

In order to practice what he preached, Illich embarked upon a project of immersion into the Puerto Rican culture. During his vacations he traveled to Puerto Rico, where he stayed away as far as possible from the big cities and centers of tourism. Illich would make his way into *La Isla*, or rural parts of Puerto Rico, knapsack on his back, by foot or horseback or by hitchhiking. He would spend days at a time sleeping in the open air, on the steps of *barrio* chapels, where at sunrise he would offer mass. These trips strengthened his commitment to a cultural adaptation of church ministry to the Puerto Rican's rich Catholic legacy. They brought him face to face with something he had already experienced among the Puerto Ricans in that other island of Manhattan, that is, their distinct mode of being Catholic.

Daniel Levine, in speaking of religious motivations of secular actions, says that one must "take account of the fact that actions which appear identical when seen from the outside often spring from quite diverse motivations" (Levine, 13). I believe the same can be said of this case, where Illich, Fitzpatrick, and Spellman agreed on a similar plan of action for the apostolate to the Puerto Ricans, and yet each had a different motivation and goal.

Following this logic, the *Fiesta de San Juan* affirmed for Spellman the traditional role of the hierarchy as patriarch of the Catholic community. An intellectual himself by formation, Spellman was by function the supreme hierarch of the New York church, pressed to maintain its institutional power. But his own intelligence brought him to recognize the need for innovation and adaptation to preserve the hegemony of Catholicism in New York. Fitzpatrick's notions of an eventual integration of Puerto Ricans into the fabric of city life as with the immigrants before them was congenial to Spellman, who could thus rationally defer the final goals of assimilation. The popularity of the San Juan Fiesta, which was so faithful to the medieval-derived patronal feast day strengthened for Fitzpatrick the sociological functions of cultural continuity. For Illich, the fiesta fostered the development of a new culture in which Puerto Ricans gained respectability and acceptance as equal partners with previous immigrants to New York.

The 1955 Conference on the Spiritual Care of Puerto Rican Migrants became a springboard for Illich's ambitions to make the entire archdiocese respond to the ministry to Puerto Ricans. The conference was held April 11 to April 16, 1955, in San Juan, Puerto Rico, largely at the Caribe Hilton Hotel. One day consisted of travel around the island and a final session at the Catholic University of Puerto Rico in Ponce. Officially convened by Bishops Davis and McManus of Puerto Rico, local arrangements were made by Redemptorist Father Thomas Gildea in San Juan. All sessions were chaired by Marist Father William Ferrée, then rector of the Catholic University of Puerto Rico.

The participants from the United States included representatives of virtually every place where Puerto Ricans had elicited church response. The conference welcomed clergy from diverse parts of the country to which Puerto Ricans had migrated in numbers significant enough to have been recorded by the Division of Migration of the Puerto Rican Commonwealth. These included the sees of Boston, Bridgeport (Connecticut), Brooklyn, Buffalo, Camden, Chicago, Cleveland, Detroit, Hartford, Harrisburg (Pennsylvania), Newark, Philadelphia, Pittsburgh, Saginaw (Michigan), Saint Augustine (Florida), Trenton (New Jersey), and Youngstown (Ohio). Of these eighteen dioceses, nine responded to the Puerto Rican migration largely in terms of seasonal farm labor. The representatives from Buffalo, Camden, Cleveland, Hartford, Harrisburg, Saginaw, St. Augustine, Trenton, and Youngstown fell into this category. The pattern for the apostolate in virtually all of these dioceses was for a Spanish-speaking priest, usually not native to the United States, to visit the camps seasonally. Often Catholic Charities sponsored a social services center to attend to material needs. In a sense, this continued the traditional division between pastoral care and social concerns, the first "spiritual" and the latter "temporal."

The striking exception to the rule was the parish in Lorain, Ohio in the Diocese of Cleveland. A mission church erected under the Apostolic Constitution *Exul Familiae* (1:13), this parish gave to its pastor the canonical functions of ordinary and had personal jurisdiction over all the Spanish-speaking in the diocese. The Lorrain parish was ministered to by four Trinitarian priests, of whom two were native Puerto Ricans (Ferrée et al., 3/5). Thus, although it had a total number of only four thousand Spanish-speaking persons to serve, the parish enjoyed the advantage of native Puerto Rican clergy.

Of the larger city archdioceses (Boston, Chicago, Detroit, Newark, New York, and Philadelphia) and dioceses (Bridgeport, Brooklyn, and Pittsburgh), only Chicago and New York had archdiocesan-wide programs. The Brooklyn Diocese sent no report and was represented only by one North American Redemptorist and a Spanish Vincentian, neither of whom were empowered to speak for the diocese. Detroit and Pittsburgh sent representatives, but they made no presentations at the conference. The Archdiocese of Chicago, which had stimulated the establishment of a national office for Mexican-Americans (see chapter 4), also reported on an apostolate specifically matched to the needs of Puerto Ricans. This was the Knights of San Juan (*Caballeros de San Juan*), which enlisted large numbers of lay leaders in its outreach, social help, and pastoral care efforts (Ferrée et al., 3/4). An extensive assessment of the Knights has been made by Felix Padilla in *Puerto Rican Chicago* (126-66); further analysis of the organization and its founder, Fr. Leo MacMahon, lies outside the scope of this book. Significantly, in terms of developing Puerto Rican leaders, the concept of the Knights of San Juan in Chicago was more focused than the plan explained by Monsignor Connolly for New York. Doubtless, the Knights suffered from a deference to clerical authority that proved inadequate to the challenges of the 1970s, as Padilla has shown. But in the context of the pre-Conciliar era, Chicago's efforts were the most clearly organized around the development of lay Puerto Rican leaders of any of the participant sees at the conference.

New York's report on efforts to address the needs of Puerto Ricans was so extensive as to need three presenters. Monsignor Connolly presented the overall picture (Ferrée et al., 2/21–2/28), while Father Edward Head explained in detail the direct services of Catholic Charities (Ferrée et al., 3/9–10) and Father Harry J. Byrne explained what the tribunal of the archdiocese was doing to meet the special needs of the Puerto Rican migrants (Ferrée et al., 3/11–14). If one were to use today's post-Conciliar values and commend Chicago for its emphasis upon lay leadership development, still the commitment of clergy to New York's apostolate among Puerto Ricans would have to be judged as impressive by pre-Conciliar standards. The scope of Connolly's plan for the chancery-based Office of Spanish-American Catholic Action has already been described (chapter 4), and the omission of the Committee of Laymen for Spanish-American Action has been analyzed. The contrast between clergy commitment in New York and lay leadership development in Chicago is further underscored by the non-implementation of Connolly's original suggestion for a lay council. Not surprisingly, it is noted in the summary of the conference (Ferrée et al., 1/5) that Chicago initiated a coordinating plan afterward.

The New York concept of coordination was also present in the way the conference selected participants from the island, which included seventy-seven priests; the two bishops; Luis Muñoz Marín, the governor of Puerto Rico and his spouse, Inés Mendoza, who offered a reception at *La Fortaleza*, the governor's official residence; and an impressive parade of government officials and academics. A comprehensive analysis of religion, culture, social conditions, and Puerto Rican history were woven together in a volume that remains readable and informative more than a generation later.

The guidance of the Fordham University Jesuit, Joseph P. Fitzpatrick, can be seen in the central role afforded to social science data in the framing of pastoral questions. Fitzpatrick prompted the participants that "in the long run you will be amazed at the knowledge which will be accumulated from a meeting such as this" (Ferrée et al., 1/26). The meeting was conducted much in the manner of an academic conference, with formal papers and sessions organized around clearly defined themes. Nonetheless, the data were presented with an intensely pastoral focus. Several of the appendices carried over this pastoral focus, with titles such as "Suggestions for the Preparation of Non–Puerto Rican Parishioners for the Influx of Puerto Rican Migrants" and "Study Club Outline for Report on Conference." A careful bibliography of important social science studies on Puerto Ricans was included (Ferrée et al., 4/74–80), the first of many such contributions by the Fordham Jesuit to the study of Puerto Ricans.

Perhaps most important, Fitzpatrick prepared a scholarly interpretation of the Puerto Rican migration that was published in *Integrity* magazine in 1955, but also was included in the conference final report (Ferrée et al., 4/63–71). This keystone presentation outlined the concept subsequently developed and defended by Fitzpatrick throughout his career, that the Puerto Rican migration could be compared sociologically to the influx of European immigrants to New York. While careful to note differences related to history, Fitzpatrick detailed the discrimination and social problems of previous immigrant groups. He showed that in the normal course of events problems related to delinquency, dependency on relief, adequacy of housing, and fidelity to religious practice were gradually overcome as newcomers became New Yorkers.

Fitzpatrick held out the expectation that Puerto Ricans would accommodate to life in New York more or less as Euro-American Catholic groups had done before them. It was crucial, he maintained, to integrate them with the rest of the Catholic faithful. Discrimination against the Puerto Ricans, he warned, would be likely to push them out of the church and "the responsibility will rest heavily on our consciences in the years ahead" (Ferrée et al., 4/64). He concluded on a note of self-interest for the institutional church. After citing the dramatic numbers of demography for New York and the Puerto Ricans, Fitzpatrick noted: "For one who has eyes to see and the mind to understand, this picture of the future is much more than a shadow. If New York is to remain a vigorously Catholic city two generations from now, it will do so only if the great majority of Puerto Ricans remain faithful to the Church" (Ferrée et al., 4/70).

Some Puerto Ricans have criticized Fitzpatrick for this premise that the Puerto Rican migration can be understood by comparison with previous European migrations to the United States (Centro, 17 n. 2, 16–26). Certainly, it is easier to change such an altered perspective in 1979 than it was to have done so in 1955. And in fairness to Fitzpatrick's notion of assimilation, he also expected the church to do for the Puerto Ricans what it had done for the Irish. As he told me in an interview in 1982, "What Puerto Ricans need is a Puerto Rican John Hughes." Nonetheless, academic controversy cannot becloud the enormous pastoral contribution of Fitzpatrick's work to the advancement of Puerto Ricans. His priestly zeal and unwavering moral uprightness are deservedly admired by three generations of Puerto Ricans, both those who are leaders and those who are simple members of the community.

These notions of Fitzpatrick's diagnosis are evident in the introduction to the final conference report, which was prepared by the cardinal. Spellman had not abandoned the Americanizing function of the archdiocesan institutions with his innovations for the ministry among the Puerto Ricans. "The Catholic migrant helped make America great," he told the conference participants, and "the Catholic Church helped make the migrant a great American" (Ferrée et al., 0/6). But he had seen that the size of the Puerto Rican migration and the lack of native priests to accompany the migrants had forced the archdiocese into a new role. Puerto Rican neighborhoods had become missionary territory, and the proud New York Archdiocese would have to send missionaries to these Catholics,

> for the Archdiocese of New York "The Sidewalks of New York" have become a mission field "white with harvest." By Divine Providence every priest in New York has become a missionary to these people of Puerto Rico, so desperately in need of the priestly ministrations the heroic, zealous priests on their own little island could never have given because they are so few in number (Ferrée et al., 0/8).

The effects of this 1955 conference were felt for nearly two decades. First, it wedded the "spiritual" needs of pastoral care to the "temporal" dimension of social concern. The apostolate relied upon diagnosis of social needs by scholarly research, and the office supplied the coordination of how to apply the remedy. The coordination was generated at the level of a chancery office that oversaw strictly parish activities. Once having marshaled the sociological, demographic, and theological arguments for such an office, it would not prove easy for the archdiocese to dispense with it.

Second, the conference established a connection between New York and the island of Puerto Rico for interdiocesan cooperation in ministry to migrants. Just as Southwest Texas had been linked to Chicago for the sake of the Mexican-Americans, Puerto Rico and New York were linked in the Northeast.

Third, the New York Archdiocese took upon itself an apostolate virtually equal in scope to that the National Council of

Catholic Bishops had entrusted to the Bishops' Committee for the Spanish-Speaking in the United States. The visibility of New York as champion of the Puerto Ricans helped solidify the impression that Puerto Ricans were urban dwellers and not migrant farm workers, just as the emphasis upon migrant farm workers in Texas and the Midwest had created the impression that Mexican-Americans were migrant laborers and not urban dwellers. Anyone who cared to study the facts knew, of course, that there were Puerto Rican farm workers, just as they knew that there were Mexican-American urban dwellers. But the images created by the type of apostolate organized by the church created lasting stereotypes.

Fourth, the conference confronted United States Catholicism with the differences among the Spanish-speaking groups. The sociological and culture-sensitive pastoral approaches that were fashioned by this conference for Puerto Ricans, and which were already in formation for Mexican-Americans, stressed to an English-speaking church the need to distinguish among Hispanic groups. The large-scale Cuban migration after the success of the 1959 revolution added a third major group to Catholic awareness that the Spanish-speaking could not be lumped together.[3]

Curiously, the name of Ivan Illich does not appear as one of speakers or organizers of this 1955 conference in Puerto Rico. Listed only as a participant, under the name of "John D. Illich, Incarnation Parish," his role began to take shape in the preparation of the conference report. He was largely responsible for the summary of the conference's deliberations. He showed remarkable insight, for instance, in discussing canonical options for national parishes (1/6–14). These discussions have periodically resurfaced in the struggles of the Hispano church nationwide in the United States (Carrillo, in Stevens-Arroyo 1980, 154–57; Deck, 59–63; Vidal, 329–33, 334).

Illich's acumen in summation and articulation of the conference report greatly impressed the rector of the Catholic University of Puerto Rico, William Ferrée. As a result of this contact and negotiations with Cardinal Spellman, in the fall of 1956 Illich was appointed as vice-rector of the newly founded Catholic University of Puerto Rico, which was indebted to Cardinal Spellman for valuable assistance and financial support. Illich began preparations to open a center for the training of United States priests in the Spanish language and the Puerto Rican culture. The first step in this direction had been taken in 1953 and had been continued in following years "when each year two newly ordained priests of the Archdiocese were sent for one year of residence and ministry in Puerto Rico." In fact, at the 1955 conference, Monsignor Connolly had noted with some pride that "New York now has more Spanish-speaking clergy, very many of them native New Yorkers, than the Diocese of Ponce in Puerto Rico" (Ferrée et al., 2/26). Furthermore, in 1956 "one half of the number of the newly ordained priests of the Archdiocese were sent to Georgetown University in Washington, D. C. for an intensive, two-month, saturation training in spoken Spanish" (Stern 1977, 18). The cardinal was counseled on the advisability of sending "one half of the class of newly ordained priests and a large group of seminarians and religious to a similar two-month program" to be directed by Illich at the Catholic University in Ponce, Puerto Rico: "In addition to their linguistic studies, these students had other courses in Puerto Rican, Latin American, and American culture and in the particular problems of intercultural communication. Most of them remained on the island for a further month of residency and ministerial apprenticeship" (Stern 1977, 18).

This clergy training program gave Illich considerable influence over the newly ordained priests of the archdiocese. He strove to mobilize church resources into a wider apostolate than the one-day annual celebration of the San Juan Fiesta. He was convinced that the missionary task the archdiocese had taken upon itself in the ministry to Puerto Ricans in the city required more far-reaching changes than a better use of church buildings and available clergy. Accordingly, in the program he initiated at Ponce the outlines of a Gramscian "new culture" were evident. While Fitzpatrick remained an academic teaching sociology, Illich became an intellectual matching new theories of ministry to the practice of the apostolate among Puerto Ricans.

During their training on the island, Illich encouraged and even pushed the young priests and religious to do what he had done in previous years. It was his intention to have them taste Puerto Rican mountain life, to talk to the people, to observe first-hand their daily routine, to partake of their diet, and tune themselves to the people's cares and aspirations.

In 1959, with the full support of Cardinal Spellman, these efforts were enlarged to continue and sustain the language studies initiated in Puerto Rico through the academic year program conducted from Cardinal Hayes High School in the Bronx, and later even in the archdiocesan seminary and other regional centers. Illich's efforts carried the cardinal's approval. The effectiveness of the clergy he trained in ministry to the Puerto Ricans was remarkable, and although Illich may have seen it as a long-range effort at changing the church itself, the cardinal was satisfied that the emphasis upon cultural identification produced full churches, abundant baptisms, confessions, communions, and funerals within the rites of Mother church.

Election year 1960 in Puerto Rico, however, brought open conflict between the Catholic church on the island and the popularly elected government of Puerto Rico. The Catholic church, under the leadership of an island hierarchy almost exclusively North American, had come to odds with the liberal administration of the Popular Democratic Party (PPD). Longstanding issues over the teaching of catechism in the public schools came to a head when the island government sponsored birth-control clinics (Silva Gotay 1988).

The case resulted in the excommunication of any Catholic in Puerto Rico who voted for the party in the 1960 election (Ocampo, 4:225). Although the canonical grounds for such an excommunication were suspect (see Silva Gotay 1988), it became an almost passionate obsession with the island's North American hierarchy to have unquestioning support from all the clergy in Puerto Rico. Such a statement was never offered by Illich. Finally Bishop McManus informed Illich by letter that he was to remove himself from the Diocese of Ponce, where the Catholic University was located.

Illich returned to New York where, on the recommendation of Fitzpatrick, he was appointed to the position of Assistant to the Director of Research and Development at Fordham University. This allowed him to travel and continue to work on his projects. Puerto Rico, however, was no longer to be the focus of his work and interest. Illich eventually left for Cuernavaca, Mexico, to start a center modeled somewhat along the lines of the one he had started in Puerto Rico, and which in later years was to gain an international reputation for its controversial ideas (See Gray, 40–42, 50, 83–92).

But the Puerto Rican apostolate was the genesis to much of Illich's thinking. Many of his views are summed up in the article "The Vanishing Clergyman." First drafted in the summer of

1959, Illich expanded it in 1962. Somewhat later he used this article as the basis for a talk delivered to a group of clergymen who were considering leaving the priesthood, many of whom were in the Spanish-speaking apostolate of the Brooklyn Diocese.[4] Subsequently, several ideas central to this article were adduced by the Holy Office as grounds for condemnation of Illich and his work (Zizola and Barbero).

Illich attacked the luxury and the security of the clerical state. He declared that the church has "too many clerics" but perhaps not enough priests. The distinction that Illich made between a priestly vocation and the clerical state is essential to an understanding of his position. For Illich, the true priest came from the people; his vocation was sustained by the service he rendered to the people. It would also follow that the prophet, whether lay or ordained, would have to come from the people and be God's spokesperson on their behalf. It almost seems that, for Illich, the call to be a priest was also a call to be a prophet, but neither did he exclude the laity from the prophetic call, thus blurring the distinction of roles (see Zizola and Barbero, 146–48).

When the priesthood was institutionalized in the form of the clerical state, the candidate became an ecclesiastical bureaucrat whose main function, whether at the parish level or at any other post, was to perpetuate the existence of the institution. Because the priest received his calling for the sake of the people, Illich urged a degree of "lay responsibility over the hierarchy." This could possibly have been perceived to mean that the bishops were in part accountable to the grass-roots community. Thus some saw Illich as denying a distinction between church-teaching and church-learning, between pastors and flock, as well as lending support and advocacy to the emergence of a democratic church "without class distinctions" and stripped of "ecclesiastical bureaucracy" (Zizola and Barbero, 149).

Illich believed that by renunciation of privileges and the institutional needs of professionalism the church could replace the territorial parish with a new and spontaneous form of service or *diakonia* (Zizola and Barbero, 149). He also questioned the structure of present-day seminaries and seminary training, whose clerical-state orientation he saw as separating the priestly candidate from the real world, maintaining him in the celibate state, giving him a rather conservative theological formation, and transforming him into a full-time functionary of an organized institution, none of which is essential to the real priesthood (Illich, 67–68).

In "The Vanishing Clergyman" Illich argued that "during our generation, at least, there is no need to consider the ordination of married men to the priesthood." But Illich was speaking only of his generation, and the reason he gives for his stance is that "we have more than enough unmarried ones" (Illich, 78). Illich said this although he was aware of the shortage of native priests among the Puerto Rican people and the other Latin American nations. Apparently Illich feared that the ordination of married men (or allowing ordained priests to be married) would do little to stop these candidates from becoming merely "clerics." Illich saw no need for the continuation of ordained clerics; rather it was a "clerical mass exodus," with no permission to marry, which was needed. "During this time, ordination of married men would be a sad mistake," he argued, since "the resulting confusion would only delay needed radical reforms" (Illich, 78). Illich saw married priests as too facile a solution to a complex situation. The radical reforms he refers to would probably go better under the rubric of transformations. In fact, from the tone of this and other writings, it seems as if Illich was more concerned with sweeping structural change rather than gradual reforms.

In subsequent articles, "The Seamy Side of Charity" and "Yankee, Go Home: The U.S. Do-Gooder in Latin America," Illich also attacked the collusion between missionaries from the United States and political interventionism in other lands on the pretext of anti-Communism. A number of his articles, such as "The Vanishing Clergyman" (1962) and "Yankee, Go Home" (1968), were derived from talks to specialized groups. "The Seamy Side of Charity" was first published in *America* (January 1967), meriting comments by fellow clergymen (see Fitzpatrick 1967). These and others like them eventually found their way into published collections. Regardless of his intentions, these pronouncements, dating from his involvement in the Puerto Rican apostolate of New York, led to the interventions and ultimate suspension by the Holy Office in Rome.

This chapter began with a detailed, but (I trust) useful analysis of the kinds of leadership as defined by Gramsci. My intention was to enable the reader to assess with me not only the contributions of intellectuals to the formation of an archdiocesan office for the Spanish-speaking apostolate in New York, but also the how and the why of the real changes that were the results. And although categorization of living persons is always a difficult task, I feel I would be remiss in not concluding with some evaluation of the type of leadership that these clerics brought to the Puerto Rican Catholics of New York.

All Catholic priests, to the extent that they hear confessions, preach in the pulpit, and administer the sacraments, share in aspects of cross-class solidarity with the faithful. But as has been said, in itself this does not constitute organic leadership. From an institutional perspective, it must be asked if the source of influence is with the people, or rather uses the *need to be with the people* as "the terrain upon which the forces of opposition organize" (see above, page 144). This is the distinction between "organic" and "conjunctural" leadership. In the case of Father Fitzpatrick, I think it is clear that his was a conjunctural leadership. The Jesuit never developed a pastoral identity for the archdiocese independent of his academic post as professor of sociology at Fordham University. By remaining in this professional status, he was never an "organic intellectual" and part of the Puerto Rican community. This does not demean his contribution; in fact, it helps explain why he has continued in the role of leadership for so long. Insulated from chancery structures by his academic position, he has maintained autonomy in his quest to explain to the archdiocese the crucial historical role of Puerto Ricans.

It is a much harder task to decide if Ivan Illich was an organic or conjunctural intellectual leader. He effectively redefined the intellectual role for the priest in the Spanish-speaking ministry at the pragmatic level of parish involvement. The effect of Illich's pastoral training institute was to urge upon the young archdiocesan clergy a closer cultural and class identification with the Puerto Rican people. Yet, although Illich had once enjoyed this identification himself, by accepting the influence of the position at Ponce's Catholic University, he also was deprived of the role as "organic intellectual." I believe the notion of conjunctural intellectual fits him best. He was able to promote the wider vision of an altered church, apostolic clergy, and lay leadership while the conditions for pastoral training were thriving. But once that opportunity vanished due to political circumstances, he had no base from which to continue his struggle on behalf of Puerto Ricans. He transferred his identification with the people to those at the Institute in Cuernavaca, Mexico. This change in venue does not mean that Illich rejected Puerto Ricans or their pastoral needs, but it serves to demonstrate that he was not an organic intellectual himself, no matter how fervently he urged such a role upon others.

Philip Murnion has documented the differing character of the theological education provided to the clerics who were prepared by Illich for the Spanish-speaking apostolate (Murnion, 157–277). Murnion shows that the Illich-influenced clergy were more inclined to a dynamic understanding of ministry than their predecessors among the archdiocesan clergy. Their education included a greater sensitivity to psychology and cultural differences, while orienting them more toward social concerns and political activism than to sacramental rituals. All of these dispositions are necessary steps in the development of organic intellectuals in Gramsci's definition. Illich's most permanent contribution, then, was in the way his ideas about the Spanish-speaking apostolate altered the overall vision of younger clergy in the archdiocese toward the church as a New York institution.

In summary, it may be said that the missionary character of the apostolate to the Puerto Ricans in New York provided the crucible for much of Illich's radical thinking about Catholicism. It may seem strange that a conservative like Cardinal Spellman protected Illich through much of his career. Still, Illich was never put in charge of the Office of Spanish American Catholic Action in the archdiocese, nor was he promoted to the episcopacy, as might have been expected. Spellman kept Illich in Puerto Rico, where his role was important, but not institutionalized. Yet, although the cardinal could keep Illich out of the archdiocesan structures, he could not keep Illich's thinking from having a far wider impact on the clergy in the apostolate. As will be seen in the next chapter, the altered vision of a priestly role in a renewed church was to become identified in a special way with the Office of Spanish-American Catholic Action during the years after the Second Vatican Council.

6. *Culture as a Sacrament: An Apostolate of Magical Realism*

> *PACO: Lo único que necesita entender es mi soledad.*
> *JUANITA: No sea idiota. Si tu soleá se junta con la mía tendriamoh una soleá mah grande. ¿Qué ganamoh con eso?*
> *PACO: Dos soledades juntas dejan de ser soledad.*
> *JUANITA: Habla ubté ahora como en lah novelah de radio.*
>
> PACO: All you have to do is understand my loneliness.
> JUANITA: Don't be an idiot. If your loneliness is joined to mine we'll only have a greater loneliness. What would we gain by that?
> PACO: Two lonelinesses together cease to be loneliness.
> JUANITA: Now you're talking like the soap-operas on the radio.
>
> *The Oxcart,* Act III

Contemporary Latin American writers like Nobel Prize winner Gabriel Garcia Márquez have created a new dimension in literature. Called "magical realism," it is a mode of weaving together symbols and reality with romantic aspirations and subjective perceptions. As a result, the world created by the novelist becomes surcharged with meanings, some of which are imaginary and some are actual. Magical realism makes symbolism the integrating force for human behavior. Deciding whether imagination or actuality is more important becomes impossible, because in the novelist world, both are real.

The ministry to Puerto Ricans in the Archdiocese of New York was to adopt a premise toward the importance of symbolism not very different from the underlying assumption of magical realism. This change was nonetheless built upon prosaic foundations. In previous chapters I have outlined the social distance characteristic of Puerto Rican Catholicism and traced the trajectory of the Archdiocese of New York in the establishment of a North American Catholicism that incorporated the immigrants into the church and American society. Particular attention was paid to the roles of intellectuals in the response of this archdiocese to a new migrant group in the twentieth century, namely the Puerto Ricans. Entering the 1960s the ministry to the Puerto Ricans in New York had five basic components: an office in the archdiocese to coordinate the efforts of the parishes; the parishes themselves, no longer seen as national or territorial parishes but as integrated communities, with separate societies for the Spanish-speaking; the Institute of Intercultural Communication to acculturate and integrate New York clergy into the Puerto Rican and Hispano community; semi-autonomous movements like the Cursillo and *La Fiesta Patronal de San Juan Bautista*, which offered the Puerto Ricans a means to identify themselves and celebrate their uniqueness as both as Catholics and as a *pueblo* ("people").

These were the remedies adopted to alleviate "one of Cardinal Spellman's biggest headaches" (Gray, 42–43). While the establishment of a chancery-based office was innovative, at the parish level pastoral care was often of a conservative nature. The model of church often remained traditional in style and hierarchical in structure. With some exceptions, much of the older clergy, especially pastors, persisted in their attachment to the well-established norms of New York Catholicism. They anticipated a clerical direction over the laity that resulted in political power, fostered a pro–United States nationalism, and usually repeated the Irish paradigm in their expectations for ethnic groups. Even Spellman's break with the national parish in the effort to integrate Puerto Ricans into territorial parishes found resistance. In 1955 Kelly reported to the cardinal: "There is almost a reluctance on the part of the pastors of diocesan parishes to plunge into Puerto Rican wholeheartedly or to have their parishes known as Puerto Rican, even when a large minority of the Catholics, and in some places a majority are Puerto Rican" (Kelly 1955).

Thus, while there was much that represented positive change in the outreach to Puerto Ricans, the overall policy was unevenly applied. The emphasis of Monsignor Wilson on parish life, pious organizations and apostolic movements, did not challenge this unevenness. Where pastors permitted the younger clergy a certain level of autonomy and shared resources with the largely Puerto Rican faithful, Oxcart Catholicism made a successful adaptation to life in New York. But where clergy members were divided or ineffective or even hostile, the Spanish-speaking apostolate suffered accordingly. The great vigor of Puerto Rican Catholicism was felt primarily in the semi-autonomous Cursillo Movement and the lay-dominated *Fiesta de San Juan.* Such vitality was encouraged by the clergy trained by Ivan Illich at the Institute of Intercultural Communications at Ponce.

When Monsignor Wilson left the administration of the office to a younger man in 1963, it was the eve of important changes in the nation, the city, and the church. The first Catholic president in the history of the United States, John F. Kennedy, had been tragically gunned down in Dallas. With Kennedy's death a long period of self-doubt was to appear in the country's psyche, leading to more assassinations, race riots, and the anti-war movement, which forced a retreat from Vietnam and the beginnings of a sharp turn to the political right.

In New York city politics the power of Tammany Hall had been dealt a death blow by the defeat of boss Carmine DeSapio (Lankevich and Furer, 266–68). Even though Mayor Robert Wagner had been a part of the political machine, he cast his lot with the reform movement, which eclipsed Irish Catholic political power in the city (Glazer and Moynihan, lviii-lxiv; 272–74). An augur of things to come was the new party leadership in the deposed DeSapio's own district; he was replaced by a young politician named Ed Koch, later to become mayor of the city.

The reform movement in 1960s' politics opened the doors of power to a new generation of Puerto Rican leaders. Some Puerto Ricans working in government positions had founded the Puerto Rican Forum in 1957 to serve as a focal point for social programs designed for Puerto Rican needs. In 1960 this led to the funding of the Aspira organization. Led by the dynamic Antonia Pantoja, Aspira was a cultural-awareness program for Puerto Rican young people, motivating them to continue schooling into college and to return to the community for service once they achieved professional success (Stevens-Arroyo and Díaz-Ramírez, 215–16). Similar efforts by young Puerto Rican leaders to create programs for the community also provided the training ground for a new generation of political leaders (Rivera, 95).

In Rome, the grandfatherly John XXIII had decided to "throw open the windows of the church." In the ensuing Second Vatican Council, far-reaching reforms in liturgy and theology, as well as a redefinition of Catholicism's role in the world, were to sweep away the church archbishops from Hughes to Spellman had defended. Cardinal Spellman's advancing age led to whispers about his eventual successor and a certain amount of jockeying for position in the ecclesiastical politics of the archdiocese.

On the face of it, the appointment of Monsignor Robert Fox in 1963 as Director of the Office of Spanish-American Catholic Action was probably intended to do little more than provide a new, fresh energy to an existing model. Fox belonged to the same generation as the new Puerto Rican secular leadership, while Monsignor Wilson was tied to older and less ambitious community leaders. Yet, because of the changes in church and society, much more was to happen than a simple changing of the guard.

In the person of Robert Fox, the Office of Spanish-American Catholic Action had its first charismatic personality. Articulate, young, strikingly handsome, Fox was a diocesan priest educated as a social worker. He had received special training at Catholic University and spoke Spanish flawlessly. He had been prepared by Illich in 1958 with other priests of the archdiocese and had been assigned for three years in the Family Service Division of New York Catholic Charities. In 1961 he was appointed to a Fulbright lectureship in social work in Uruguay, one of the most progressive Latin American nations of that time (Stern 1982, 56–57).

As a social worker conversant with the Catholic Action approach of Latin America, Fox encountered contradictions between the policies shaped or handed down through the Office of Spanish-American Catholic Action and the actual practice in the local parishes. He said, "Some pastors went to their graves denying they had any Puerto Ricans or Hispanics in their parishes." Fox must have witnessed not only the condescension and paternalistic tolerance toward Puerto Ricans so aptly described by Edward Rivera in his autobiographical novel *Family Installments,* but in some cases the open hostility and total rejection of this community by some recalcitrant clerics and clerical personnel. Whatever his personal experience in this respect, Fox came to the conclusion that the social distance between the Puerto Ricans and the reluctant clergy could never be eliminated without attempting a new approach for the apostolate (interview with Robert Fox, February 1, 1983).

The scope of Catholic Action in the United States has been briefly sketched above (chapter 4). The reader is reminded here that it had been modified from the European counterpart so that instead of founding separate Catholic political parties, the hierarchy in the United States sought to integrate labor unions, social action groups, and minority and ethnic enclaves into the larger core society. Catholic citizens were expected to form a distinct voting bloc.

In Latin America, however, Catholic Action was closer to the European model both in its scope and approach. It established a Catholic ethos for society through the work and influence of church-sponsored Christian Democratic parties. Catholic Action in the Latin American context treated the masses as a unified group, which would work toward the acquisition of a particular principle—social justice—through Christian values as the core basis for society (Vallier 1970, 64–73). The focus was not upon limited political influence to protect Catholic interests and institutions, as in the United States. Latin American Catholic Action sought to influence and transform all of society.

Bolstered by the progressive clergy and religious working in the Spanish-speaking apostolate, Fox decided to shift the emphasis in his office in the direction of transforming social attitudes. This was a course very much indebted to the vision of Ivan Illich. There was a basic difference, however. While Illich's emphasis was upon the structures of the church and complete shift in the training of its clergy, Fox's approach emphasized societal shifts. Fox banked heavily on personal conversion and presumed that it, together with the innovations of the Second Vatican Council, would bring the necessary structural change.

At the beginning of his archdiocesan apostolate Puerto Ricans remained the target population. But, because his emphasis was upon societal shifts, he soon began to include the entire society in the scope of this redefined apostolate. The effort, time, personnel, and funds invested by the office in this new direction for ministry constituted a major shift in its mission. The first evidence of this shift was the change in the name of the office from the Office of Spanish-American Catholic Action to the Office of Spanish Community Action. The focus of the office was shifted from the religious practice of Puerto Rican Catholics to the needs of the Spanish-speaking considered as a special group among the urban poor, from the inner mechanism of the official church to society at large (church as community), and from an objective structural approach to a more personal and subjective one.

In 1964 Fox was approached by the superior of the Sisters of Charity, Sister Margaret Dowling, who wanted her sisters to work with Puerto Ricans on a volunteer basis during the summer months. Fox coordinated a plan of home visitations and youth work among residents at the Lillian Wald Houses, a city project, on the Lower East Side (Stern 1982, 57). Already, at this time, the Puerto Ricans would be one group among many. According to Dowling, the initial format was simple indeed:

> Msgr. [Fox] told us to go to a city owned housing project, Lilian Wald, filled with people of all races and religions, and just be with people. "Don't give lessons," he said. "Don't do nursing, don't try to teach anything. Tell your sisters to just be with the people. Go to the playground there and draw with the children when they feel like drawing and swing with them when they come around and spend the whole summer like that (Cole, 131).

The program provided contact between the church, represented by the sisters, and the community of Puerto Ricans. The success in reducing social distance between the people and those who officially served Catholicism was particularly important. The new definition of church mission and a liturgy close to the culture of the people were essential parts of the conciliar message.

Fox made the Puerto Rican culture into a kind of sacrament; it was to be venerated as a sign of something sacred. Those who recognized the human values of Puerto Rican customs and traditions were placed in the presence of God's work among the poor of this earth. According to Fox's vision, the Puerto Ricans did not need evangelization from the official church, because their own rich religious culture had kept them close to Catholicism in spite of antiquated hierarchical traditions. With an expression of sensitivity and openness from the church, these values would blossom into the full practice of the faith.

Progressive clergy and religious saw the experience of the Sisters of Charity in the summer of 1964 as a paradigm for a new post-Conciliar church. Besides the Sisters of Charity, other religious congregations asked Fox for similar opportunities. Accordingly, Fox worked during the winter to expand the program for 1965. Thirty-five parishes were scheduled to serve as hosts for the program, which was given the name "Summer in the City." Mary Cole's book by the same title gives a detailed account, which I cite here for reasons of analysis.

From the outset, this outreach was meant to be comprehensive. Rather than limiting the attention to Puerto Ricans and Hispanics, as was the case with the Institute of Intercultural Communication and the San Juan Fiesta, Summer in the City took on a multi-ethnic and interdenominational orientation from its inception. Furthermore, it did not specify any type of activity, but left itself open to any response to the needs of the people. The program also represented an innovative attempt to use neutral rather than church-controlled or church-owned sites (interview with Robert Fox, February 1, 1983).

The use of the street as a public forum was one of three basic principles employed by Fox in Summer in the City; creativity and human relationship were the other two. These three principles represented Fox's underlying rationale or philosophy and a comprehensive commitment for collaboration in his future ministerial work among the Puerto Ricans, Hispanics, and other minority groups. All of these groups together would be seen to constitute the urban poor. The organizational manual described the program as

> a combined effort of many persons attempting to establish an environment conductive to increased relationship and communication between persons and among groups within a neighborhood.... Too frequently barriers, deeper than language, separate persons one from the other. External pressures rising from social censures, living standards and even norms of dress combine with internal forces founded in traits of personality, differences of background to form seemingly insurmountable obstacles to genuine communication of ideas.... Spontaneous creative expression is an

important element in the growth and development of human relationships. . . . The need of such a response is seen in all areas but especially in depressed sections where withdrawal and escapism in their varied forms are evident. Growth in appreciation of oneself and appreciation of another's individuality are the foundations of genuine relationship. . . . All aspects of the program—education, recreational, and cultural—must be infused with creativity. . . . The composite group of distinct persons making up the staff is a deliberate effort to foster relationship among persons of varied backgrounds. . . . Another factor necessarily connected with the concepts of relationship and creativity is the visibility of the program. By its very nature, if the program is to make a worthwhile contribution to the neighborhood, activities must be conducted in the open forum. Every effort must be made to involve people in places where they naturally congregate (Stern 1982; see also Cole, "Information for Center Directors, Board Members," etc. [Summer in the City Manual], Record Retention Center of the Archdiocese of New York, box 99:9).

Fox defined the public forum as the area—street or project square—where a person leads a public life, as opposed to a private life with family and close friends. In his philosophy this area is defined as one that is both threatening and vital. Its circumstances are often beyond a person's control. Yet, at the same time, the person's self-estimate, confidence, and self-respect or lack of it, derive from the figure he or she feels is projected in the public forum. Throughout his apostolate Fox believed that, however hostile, this area holds a promise for humanity. It offers the opportunities that can be used to promote personal as well as community development (interview with Robert Fox, February 1, 1983). Out of necessity, a good deal of time has to be spent where people naturally congregate, especially in poor neighborhoods where many of a person's waking hours are lived in the street.

Fox felt that, with imagination and daring, people would be brought into communication with one another in the public forum, where they could be unified to work simultaneously for personal and community development. Moreover, he believed that people do not identify with their environment when it is too hostile and threatening. Most of people's daily lives are superficial at best, because they are afraid to "be themselves," or to "share their richness" in public. Instead, they save these for the family circle.

The end result is a deprived and more hostile environment and more threatened and alienated individuals.

Fox also believed that if people realize that their environment and other people have something to offer, the opportunities for the public forum to create community will be successfully realized. In this way, as a person is brought to identify positively with the public forum, anomic behavior will be diffused and both the environment and the person will be changed for the better (Cole, 101; see Alers-Montalvo).

A second principle undergirding Fox's philosophy was that of creativity in art. According to Fox, everyone has a need to express joy, pain, problems, and victories. When a person is prevented from doing this, says Fox, feelings, passions, and emotions turn into threats and weakness rather than into healthy manifestations that contribute to growth. The commercialization of art, on the one hand, and the quasi-cult of the fine arts, on the other, prevent the poor from expressing themselves artistically—the way most people did in pre-urban societies and still do in some parts of the world today. Therefore, freeing persons to express themselves is also freeing them to grow. The importance of art in the liberating process and the need for art are not to be taken as an individual or private matter (Cole, 134ff.).

Fox's views on the link between the street as public forum and art as the means of universal self-expression were summarized in this way:

> Creativity is defined in the dictionary as the act of bringing into existence; and when creativity happens in the streets, and in the public domain, it brings into recognized, realized existence, talents and therefore strengths of the individual and of the community. Beginnings are made toward solving certain concrete daily problems: preparing for a project circus can ease racial tensions in public housing, for example. And foundations are laid for profound, permanent, basic change (Cole, 135).

Moreover, art lays the foundation for a third principle.

> People brought together through participating in a creative act begin letting down barriers. They gain in mutual respect of one another that revelation of their individual and group talents engenders. A start is made toward erasing isolation and alienation and in

> creating community, a community which because it is founded on the discovered richnesses and strengths of an area and people, can accept the challenge of change and development—more than accept, can plan for them (Cole, 135).

In summary, Fox believed that self-expression is at the core of all human activity. Without this ability there is no chance for the individual to assimilate further humanizing experience. In the community, art is a vital tool for self-expression, and thus it is an instrument of growth, development, and human liberation.

The third component and all-encompassing principle guiding the program was that of human relationship. It was the cornerstone of the 1964 pilot project in which Fox told the sisters just to be with people. He testified to it by the 1967 peace procession (described later in this chapter). Human relationship grounded the other principles—the public forum—which brought together people of diverse backgrounds and creativity, enabling them to share and participate in the benefits of each other's richness. Fox thought that deepening human relationships among different races and nationalities, even for one occasion or single activity, was not an ephemeral event. Such a small beginning "has time and again laid the groundwork for lasting friendships making life on a poverty-stricken, depressing block simply more enjoyable for its residents" (Cole, 137). Such human relationship he believed, was the key to making otherwise depressing surroundings into the sacramental presence of God's love.

In President Johnson's War on Poverty, Fox acquired a tool for the expansion of the ministry among Puerto Ricans. The Federal Office of Economic Opportunity opened in New York that same winter, 1965, and was eager to dispense money to community organizations in accord with the president's ambitious program of self-development for urban minority groups. It decided upon Summer in the City, which formally applied for and was granted funds. Suddenly, a church volunteer program had a quarter of a million dollars with which to rent and purchase recreational and artistic materials (Stern 1982, 58).

In the fall of 1966 the decision was made to extend Summer in the City throughout the whole year. A more formal organization was set up to deal with this expansion, namely the Institute for Human Development. It was designed to act as an umbrella organization, encouraging and cooperating with the now autonomous and almost completely self-operating Summer in the City program. It was also to act as a kind of brain trust, open to developing and operating new programs in all kinds of areas, wherever and whenever a new need appeared. Following in the footsteps of other anti-poverty, social, and community organizational units, the institute was legally incorporated under New York State laws. It was also felt that this would facilitate the funding process from the government. The new corporation was tied to a structure of boards and committees (Cole, 101). That year seventeen storefronts were rented, and the program began operating from these under a winter program called Project Engage.

Fox's initial success in moving from the role as coordinator of an apostolate into one as leader of a crusade in the larger society has various explanations. In personal terms he was every inch a charismatic leader and the image of all that was progressive in the days of the Second Vatican Council. Those who chose to work with him often fitted the description of disciples. And this charisma extended into the secular community as well. *Nueva York Hispano,* a Spanish-language monthly magazine first published in 1964 by the Spanish Assumptionist priest, Marcelino Pando, made Fox's activities part of the secular news. The pages of the magazine reflected the vitality of the Catholic church as the leading institutional advocate for the Spanish-speaking, and Fox was frequently featured in articles on community activities.

Perhaps more important, Fox reaped the harvest of many years of apostolate in which the church had assumed leadership among New York's major institutions in addressing the Puerto Ricans as new members of the urban community. The prominence of the San Juan Fiesta as the grandest grass-roots mobilization of the Puerto Ricans in the city gave the church an organizational advantage over the Puerto Rican agencies that existed in 1964 (Stevens-Arroyo and Díaz-Ramírez, 215, 216; Estades 1978, 39–43). The secular Puerto Rican organizations, such as Aspira and the Puerto Rican Forum, were highly professionalized and specialized; they did not have a community base. The hometown clubs were organized around loyalties to the island and to the annual Puerto Rican Day Parade, but they lacked the city-wide visibility necessary to compel a political presence before federal agencies. Herman Badillo, elected Bronx Borough president in 1965, was the only Puerto Rican to hold office at that time. While there was a growing number of Puerto Rican appointees in the new Lindsay Administration, none had yet acquired the clout to rival that was conferred by the archdiocese on its appointed leader of the Office of Spanish Community Action (Ribes Tovar, 2:155–66).

Fox, it should be noted, never saw himself as the leader of the Puerto Rican community. His efforts were directed at making the local parish and its resources a base from which Puerto Ricans would form community organizations. The archdiocese lent its prestige to take advantage of federal funds. But while Summer in the City had flourished as a basically volunteer program, once it became a part of the bureaucratic administration of poverty funds, its identification with the church did not free it from the problems inherent in political organizations.

The local boards composed of Puerto Ricans took control, and conflict began to surface when a number of the non-Hispanic artists were fired from the staff (Cole, 101; Stern 1982, 65). The same was true of the relationship of religious and clergy with lay leadership, since apparently the authoritarian role of clergy among Puerto Ricans persisted in image and, at times, in fact. Moreover, to comply with governmental regulations, the directorship had to be shifted from the priests and religious sisters to the lay people. Fox soon found the program too diffuse and the paper work too demanding to handle from the office at the chancery, even if he had desired to do so. Planning sessions and coordination of the day-to-day work of the centers transformed the office and its staff into bureaucratic administrators of programs dealing with the city's anti-poverty office—a task that took an enormous amount of time and energy. Furthermore, the paper work and collaboration with city officials did not meet the expectations Fox had set for the program (Cole, 101).

Monsignor Fox began delegating some of the coordination that had been focused in the office and which indeed formed its very raison d' être. Moreover, because Ivan Illich had departed for Cuernavaca, Fox inherited a larger share of responsibility in shaping the clergy for the Spanish-speaking apostolate than his predecessors. Since he was focused upon the streets of New York as the primary forum for encounter with Puerto Rican culture, the institute in Ponce seemed less important to him. He assigned the first archdiocesan priest of Puerto Rican and Cuban descent, Father Peter Ensenat, to coordinate the summer segment of the Ponce program. Filling the shoes of Illich was not an enviable task in any context, and for a young, newly ordained priest it was impossible. Yet the naming of a native Puerto Rican to a position of leadership was a symbol of the direction Fox intended for the office. It was expected to prepare the way for Puerto Ricans to become leaders of their own apostolate within the church. In actuality, however, Ensenat's appointment only called attention to the appalling lack of native Puerto Rican leadership within the archdiocese (Anson 1974, 31).

Fox invited Spaniard Angel Pérez, one of the musical artists who had participated in Summer in the City, to take charge of providing music in accord with the liturgical reforms of the Council. Mr. Pérez also developed opportunities on a fledgling Spanish-language television station for religious programming, as well as preparing radio shows on a regular basis.

But the most significant of Fox's withdrawals was his 1967 resignation from the board of the Cursillo Movement in New York (Stern 1982, 70). Fox had never excluded Cursillo members or the generally Spanish-origin clergy who served them. He had originally worked with the Cursillo secretariat as the official representative of the cardinal. He even began the Cursillos in English. But the principal purpose of his ministry was in the community, and the Cursillo Movement did not respond to his invitations for planning Summer in the City. The focus of the Cursillo Movement upon ecclesiastically sanctioned activities and its narrow sacramental theology made it difficult to integrate into Fox's programs. In many ways it reacted against Fox, as if Puerto Rican social concern was outside the apostolate, just as the Chicago-based Knights of San Juan also failed to integrate themselves into an emerging Puerto Rican leadership (Padilla 1987, 126–37).

The dynamics of the decade enabled the charismatic and talented Fox to give the office a leadership function in the archdiocese that went beyond its stated role of coordinating pastoral care and social concerns for Puerto Ricans. But in this new post-Conciliar configuration of the church and the world, the role of the clergy required redefinition. Where was the vigor of priestly and religious commitment to be centered—on the church or on the world? Increasingly, the apostolate became for clergy and religious a theater for their own transformation. The public forum of the street and the spontaneity of interaction with the people became a place for self-discovery. The essential service to preserve the faith among Puerto Ricans was subordinated to vocational soul-searching for adults recently freed from the cloister (Fitzpatrick 1966).

Thus, the Office of Spanish Community Action became a source of identification for clergy in transition in the aftermath of the Council. The aims articulated by Fox helped accentuate the gap between such clergy and an older, conservative clergy. This attention to transformation of clerical attitudes, unfortunately, overshadowed the empowerment of the Puerto Rican laity. This, in turn, weakened community support for Fox's apostolate, as can be seen in the changed role for the San Juan Fiesta.

The new immigration law in 1965 has already been described (chapter 1). With it came an unprecedented influx to New York of Spanish-speaking people from the Dominican Republic in the Caribbean and from Central America.[1] While Puerto Ricans remained the largest Spanish-speaking group in the city, it became important for the church to reach out to these other Hispanics through the Spanish-speaking apostolate. The Catholic church in New York thus began to address itself to Latinos in general, subsuming Puerto Ricans under the classificatory term of Hispanos.

The office had never been intended exclusively for any particular Spanish-speaking group. The emphasis upon Puerto Ricans was the result of their overwhelming proportion of New York City's Hispanic population throughout the Great Migration. In the new context of increased immigration from other countries, inclusion of all the Spanish-speaking in the ministry was to be expected. This was especially true for Fox, whose vision of community action emphasized the unity of neighborhoods and cooperation among all peoples.

The *Fiesta de San Juan,* which up to that time had been a Puerto Rican celebration in content and style, was transformed through Fox's efforts into the *Fiesta de la Comunidad Hispana.* He tried to integrate all members of the Hispanic community through this celebration, so that the Fiesta would become an event for the entire Spanish-speaking community, with greater emphasis placed upon "Hispanicity" than upon "Puerto Ricanness."

The adoption of the term *Hispanic* by Fox was intended to forestall the need for the archdiocese to plan a separate *fiesta patronal* for each of the different Latin American nationality groups in the city. Instead of a plethora of traditional feasts, such as Our Lady of Charity of the Cove for Cubans and Our Lady of High Grace for Dominicans, the single feast of San Juan would suffice for all—as long as it was "de-Puerto Ricanized." Hence, the cultural particularity of the fiesta as a manifestation of Puerto Rican identity was stripped away.

In all programs directed by Fox, he attempted to forge an authentic unity for all the Spanish-speaking groups, transcending their cultural and national particularities. Thus in this quest for solidarity among the urban poor, Fox even inserted symbols from the black community into the fiesta. Felix Padilla has studied a similar phenomenon in Chicago (Padilla 1985), where the use of *Latino* rather than *Hispanic* is the common term for such an identity. It is his conclusion that "Latino ethnic identification is not the combination of various group's behavioral patterns, nor does it persist independent of their intergroup social behavior. Rather, Latinismo represents a collective-generated behavior which transcends the individual group's national and cultural identities" (Padilla 1985, 162).

Padilla criticizes ethnic labeling of all Spanish-speaking as basically the same because such a process neglects the formation of what he calls "Latino consciousness" on the part of the people. He considers such lumping together of groups as "political ethnicity [which is] a manipulative device for the pursuit of collective political, economic and social interests in society" (Padilla 1985, 163). Such a manipulation usually meets with little success. Only when a sense of ethnic consciousness is constructed upon an existing set of positive relations and interaction among Hispanic groups can it be converted into Latino solidarity. Chicago's neighborhood politics placed Mexican-Americans and Puerto Ricans in relative parity before government, and they cooperated in programs such as the Spanish Coalition for Jobs. Leaders of each group saw advantage rather than disadvantage in forming a common front, so that Latino unity was formed out of common success (Padilla 1985, 84–87, 155, 163–64).

From Fox's actions one can deduce that he not only anticipated changes but at times presumed such changes to have occurred when in fact they had not. This is his greatest flaw. I believe he not only hoped but actually believed that the radical structural changes Illich had proposed were taking place, even coming to full fruition in the archdiocese. He seems to have held the same belief in terms of Latino unity. Certainly he had worked for greater understanding among the urban poor, but the process of discovery of mutual interests and strengths, of which the Dworkins and Padilla speak, had not yet produced the objective conditions for Latino group unity and identification in New York.

From a sociological perspective Fox's immediate action in forming one fiesta for all Hispanics was premature, just as he was premature in focusing most of his attention outside the structures of the church while presuming that these would acquire the needed transformation to include Latinos as equal to other groups within the church. In other words, he presumed there was a unified Latino reality and a unified community of the faithful. But while he might have been interested and worked arduously in creating intergroup unity, the process of discovery of mutual interests had not yet produced the objective conditions for Latino unity in New York. The difficulties of achieving such cohesion have been recorded by Estades (in Rodríguez, et al.) in her study of the Puerto Rican Day Parade. The change in the title of the fiesta was interpreted to mean that Fox was diluting attention to Puerto Ricans by including Dominicans and Central Americans within the celebration. Furthermore, he was forcing the Puerto Ricans to fuse with other Hispano groups before any group had fully identified itself as a community.

In all fairness to Fox, however, we must acknowledge that his call to unity was a prophetic advance toward a common front that is now increasingly a part of political strategies for Latinos in New York (Calitri et al., 7–11). Fox always intended to make the apostolate prophetic and to be on the leading edge of social trends. As insistent as he was on allowing the disenfranchised to speak for themselves and to advance at their own pace, he had a different set of rules for those of his own calling. The church was to present an alternative behavior, if only symbolically, so that the reality would follow. In the fabrication of Latino unity, the group cohesion symbolized in the San Juan Fiesta would serve as an example or proof that this integration was possible.

Moreover, Fox's sense of unity went beyond Hispanic identity to include all of suffering humanity. His political vision of society supported the causes espoused by César Chávez, Martin Luther King, Jr., and the Kennedys. With the rise of black and Puerto

Rican militancy, the anti-war movement, and radicalism, the San Juan Fiesta assumed a decidedly anti-establishment tone. The mirth and frivolity of the crowds of people who annually came to picnic at the fiesta was seen as inimical to the higher purposes Fox had set. Nor did the coordinator of the office believe that the archdiocese should provide a platform for the bevy of office-seeking politicians who opposed the causes supported by the Office of Spanish Community Action. Accordingly, in 1965 and for the next two years, a special mass was held at five o'clock in the morning (Stern 1982, 67–69).

These changes robbed the *Fiesta de San Juan* of the medieval form that had served as an expression of social solidarity among different elements in the society (see above, chapter 5). Instead of symbolizing the harmony of conflicting classes in an ordered, hierarchical church and world, the fiesta now reminded participants of the struggles going on against the status quo.

Fox's changes accelerated a drastic drop-off in attendance and provoked criticism from both secular and Cursillista leaders of the Puerto Rican community. The alterations in the fiesta antagonized Puerto Ricans but did not produce loyalty from the other Latino groups Fox had included. Rather than celebrate on San Juan's Day, they eventually sought their own feasts (see chapter 7). Moreover, conservative Puerto Rican Catholics and certain civic leaders found the political message of change contrary to their view of church and state. Further, since Fox avoided identification with the Puerto Rican independence movement and the Puerto Rican Nationalist heroes, he also failed to rally progressive Puerto Ricans to the fiesta. His support for controversial causes was divorced from the passion of Puerto Rican politics and proved unsatisfactory to a specifically Puerto Rican agenda for change. Alienated from virtually every segment of the native Puerto Rican and Latino public, the new form of the celebration symbolized more what Fox hoped or assumed the people would want rather than their own agenda.

Fox's "mistake" lay in pressing for a unity of Spanish-speaking groups, African-Americans, and the urban poor in general when the objective conditions for such unity did not yet exist. Yet he was not alone in such an error. Faced with a plan to organize all anti-poverty programs along ethnic rather than territorial lines,

Mayor Lindsay in 1965 had rejected the plan for a Puerto Rican Community Development Project. Instead of opting for essentially a black agency and a Puerto Rican agency in nearby neighborhoods, Lindsay placed the two groups together in the same local agency for administering common funds (Fitzpatrick 1971, 62–69, 180–81). In 1967 a similar decision to decentralize the school boards and allow local elections of community leaders led to increased racial and ethnic conflict rather than cooperation (Fitzpatrick 1971, 113–14, 151–54).

The San Juan Fiesta was to meet with a similar fate. Competition with a purely political and secular Puerto Rican Parade gradually eroded the wide popularity of the fiesta. The parade, generally held the first Sunday in June, had greater appeal to the many Puerto Ricans who were not affiliated with the Catholic church than the San Juan Fiesta, held two weekends later. Even with its rank commercialism, it was public revelry. Moreover, the music, symbols, and leadership of the parade were exclusively Puerto Rican at a time of rising ethnic pride and increasing mobilization for political goals. Thus Fox's so-called changes toward a Hispanic Fiesta accelerated the substitution of the political parade as the chief city-wide event for Puerto Ricans.

It should be emphasized, however, that the fiesta's loss of popularity was not simply a matter of nostalgia for ritual. Even when the original format was reinstituted in 1971, after Fox had left the office, initial popularity was not restored. From a reported high of seventy-two thousand participants, attendance dropped to less than ten thousand, causing the archdiocese to relocate the celebration after 1978 to the bandshell in Central Park. Events were limited to little more than the mass, awards ceremony, and some music. From its status as *the* event, which made a part of the city into a Puerto Rican public place, the San Juan Fiesta has become a celebration in search of public recognition.

One may argue that ecclesial and social changes spelled the eclipse of the San Juan Fiesta rather than the change in its structure. But the social function of symbols is to represent some part of reality. As long as Puerto Ricans perceived the world as a clerical and political hierarchy, there was a general appeal in this legacy of the medieval feast. After the Second Vatican Council, however, and because of the cultural and political changes in

United States society after 1964, Hispanics no longer viewed traditional symbols in the same way. Durkheim's bond of "common values" was absent from the San Juan Fiesta (Díaz-Stevens 1990).

This criticism of Fox's use of symbols in the case of the San Juan Fiesta should be interpreted against his successes with symbols in the 1967 Harlem riots. During those summer months, after a series of confrontations in East Harlem, the relationship between Puerto Ricans and the police came to a climax. A Puerto Rican man, Ronaldo Rodríguez, who had just arrived to visit relatives in East Harlem, was killed by the police on July 23, 1967, when he failed to follow their orders. Not knowing English, Rodríguez had unfortunately panicked and run. The police reacted by shooting him. As news of this incident spread, the Puerto Rican response in East Harlem was rebellion. The people demanded that Mayor Lindsay go to their *barrio* to explain what actions he would take. But both the mayor and Puerto Rican Bronx Borough President Herman Badillo were hooted down by the crowds of Puerto Ricans (Cole, 16ff.).

Fox was called upon to intervene, and he made a special appeal through the Spanish radio and television stations. But he urged the people not to stay home, as Badillo, their only elected leader, and Lindsay, the mayor, had asked, but to go to the street.

> If everyone just stays inside, the street will be left to the rioters and those who believe in violence. But if all those who believe in peace, love, and human values go out into the street in a spirit of celebration, then a riot can not take place (Cole, 31).

Rodríguez had been killed on a Sunday. By Tuesday morning there were, according to accounts, a thousand policemen stationed in the area. On different occasions policemen had used youngsters as cover as they were retreating from an area and had attacked adults in the doorways of their buildings. This infuriated even those who at first did not want violence and open confrontation (Cole, 21–26). In all, by Tuesday there had been seven arrests, two deaths, and about thirty injuries. Approximately one out of every three store windows in East Harlem had been broken; the streets were filled with cans and all sorts of rubbish. Many of the public utilities had been destroyed. Most important, feelings were running higher than ever before (Cole, 27). The priests and the sisters were the first to respond to Fox's appeal. They, in turn, urged the people to follow them. Ultimately, the people responded positively to this call.

Fox was very much aware of the symbols he was using: a peace procession where women and their children, venerable old grandparents with small grandchildren, working men and women, would all gather together as family and a *pueblo* to walk in each other's company, reciting the most notable Puerto Rican community prayer, the rosary (See Fitzpatrick 1972, 116 n. 3). Puerto Ricans traditionally engage in public recitation of the rosary, such as in the *Rosario de Cruz,* where the rosary is sung by the people. Processions are also quite common, both during the Christmas octave and the *fiestas patronales* (See Babín, 184–217). They sing traditional Marian hymns while marching in the streets around the public plaza.

Fox consciously chose this Puerto Rican form of traditional religious expression to counter the seething conflicts. On the one hand, he appealed to the Puerto Rican sense of familial ties and peoplehood; on the other, he sought the support and help of his colleagues, the priests and religious who had worked with him. The prayers and the singing were intended to dissipate anger and anxiety, replacing them with a sense of peace and security. The rioters would be inspired by respect for their own people. That it was a very serious and delicate situation, however, is attested by Fox's own words:

> We may be hit with bottles; we may be burned; we may face death. I think we really have to recognize that someone may be killed in this peace procession. But we are going out there to the street to stand up for all the values so inherent in the culture of the Puerto Rican people—peace, love, faith in life. We're going out there to show our love of God, our love of peace and our love of man. We're going to sing hymns, pray, carry lighted candles, smile at everyone. The love we show tonight can stop this destruction and killing. . . .
>
> Walking in the procession tonight I saw a woman with a child in her arms and when I saw this young woman risking the dangers of death to testify for love then I knew that Christ was in the *barrio.* That in a way *she* was Christ and each person here walking in this procession of peace was Christ, that Christ lives in the *barrio,* in the Puerto Rican people's commitment, so deeply ingrained in their religion and their culture, to life, to love, to peace, to human values, and that Christ is here in the *barrio* tonight as we stand up in the face of death to testify to those values (Cole 33–34).

The peace procession brought about the desired results. Unlike many of his other efforts in the street with the people, he did not try to emphasize solidarity among the diverse ethnic groups. The peace procession incorporated symbols of culture and spirituality that were uniquely Puerto Rican in nature, not Hispanic as in the restructured San Juan Fiesta. Fox also overstepped the nonsectarian commitment of Summer in the City to become both religious and traditionalist.

The public forum, creativity, and human relationship—the three basic ingredients in Fox's philosophical approach to the apostolate among the urban poor and Summer in the City—had always been intended as part of all activities related to his ministry. For those who followed him closely and who shared in this work, the peace procession was truly a success beyond expectations. At the outset of the procession even Fox had misgivings regarding the ultimate outcome, something he shared openly among those who followed him. Once over, however, the peace procession left Fox convinced that use of the public forum with the creativity of religious expression and the warmth of human relations could change a hostile environment of conflict.

But besides testing the soundness of Fox's ministerial approach, the peace procession served a second and perhaps unforeseen purpose. It served to prove that religion exercised a powerful influence with the East Harlem Puerto Rican community. Only the procession proved able to contain the hurt, the hate, and the frustration leading to the riots. In one of his last public appearances before his death, Cardinal Spellman came to celebrate mass in *El Barrio* at St. Paul's Church on 115th Street, the place of origin for the peace procession. His visit was in conjunction with a national day of prayer proclaimed by President Johnson for Sunday, July 30, for racial peace in the country. In his last personal message to the Puerto Ricans of the archdiocese, Spellman said:

> I have always looked upon the Spanish-speaking community of New York with affection and respect. Tonight, I look upon you with profound admiration because, in the face of a very dangerous situation, you had the courage to stand up in the name of peace. Our Lord Jesus Christ has said: "Happy are the peacemakers." At this moment, you are happy because you have struggled in the cause of peace (Cole, 192).

Ironically, the peace procession upheld the status quo. Fox was congratulated by New York's mayor, John Lindsay, whose appeal to remain off the street had been challenged by Fox's directive to go outside. Fox's co-workers commented on his surprise that Lindsay would personally call to congratulate him, since the mayor's politics were far from Fox's mind when he organized the peace procession (interview with Robert Fox, February 1, 1983; conversation with Father Raymond Byrne). Yet despite the contradiction between Fox's creative use of the street and the mayor's previous admonition to avoid the street on that occasion, Lindsay was to claim the peace produced by Fox's leadership as one of the achievements of his administration. And in his 1969 campaign for reelection he boasted that there had been no major riot during the four years of his administration.

This unintended political result to the peace procession also highlights the inability of Monsignor Fox to move beyond symbols of social change into an organization capable of achieving these changes politically. Despite his formation in a forward-looking Latin American Catholic Action tradition, Fox did not seem to follow the same road toward greater politicization.

Fox advanced the concept of Catholic Action beyond the scope of a North American Catholicism that had made the lay person, religious, and priest little more than auxiliaries of the hierarchy. With his Latin American experience of a total Catholic society, Fox had dignified *all* persons, whether believers or not, with a role within the apostolate. The church was to be publicly involved with the social changes underway through the War on Poverty and the Civil Rights Movement. Specifically, church leadership was to provide a religious motivation for change and solidarity among all classes (Colonnese, 110–11, 126.) Fox believed that the psychological and personal focus he proposed could be turned into a most important tool for achieving equality among the better-off, the white middle class, and the urban poor. While his views eventually turned more against structures than attitudes, when he was working with Summer in the City he was operating within the institutions of church and government and had to obey concrete guidelines in order to continue his programs.

Nonetheless, throughout his apostolate Fox understood that dealing with injustice at the personal level is the first step toward liberation. For Fox, every poor person possesses an added dimension as symbol that acquires revelatory power if one is disposed in faith to be compassionate. Speaking of a drug addict, he said:

> I'd like to feel myself on top of the situation and on top of him because I'm the social worker and I'm going to solve his problem. But before any problem can be solved, there has to be this experience of compassion—there has to be a liberation of me through experiencing this man as he is, to come in touch with myself the addict. No, I don't use heroin and I don't smoke marijuana but I have a whole bag of psychological tricks that I carry around with me everywhere to coat my nerve endings so that I'm not in touch with what is challenging, embarrassing, painful or shameful to me. And so, as I look at this addict, I have an experience, I have the opportunity to being liberated to experience another part of myself. I have the opportunity of being wrenched away from that little static, idealized, fantasized me that I'm comfortable with and maybe come in touch with the rest of me (Colonnese, 121).

Puerto Ricans and other minorities were catalysts for such change among the better-off. Fox suggested that an experience of the Puerto Rican's sufferings and joys, virtues and vices would reveal to the smug and confident their own failings. Fox made the mission of the Office of Spanish Community Action a social concern focused on attitudinal change. He reduced the traditional social distance between clergy and laity by direct contact between the givers and the receivers of charity. But in his notion of church, Fox did not advocate making Puerto Ricans into middle-class Catholics. He wanted, like Illich, to put the clergy, religious, and middle-class suburbanites on the same level as the urban poor. In this process the roles of giver and receiver of charity would be reversed. Success would be measured in terms of feelings and attitudes.

In a talk at the Conference on Inter-American Cooperation in 1969 Fox identified alienation as the principal source of oppression. "Some people think of alienation in terms of the poor," he added, "but alienation is not exclusive property of the poor" (Colonnese, 113). Thus, despite his shared background with other Latin American activist clergy in the Catholic Action movement, Fox had moved in an opposite direction. While in Latin America the Medellín Conference made oppression concrete by denouncing unequal social structures, Fox personalized injustice. Simply put, Latin American theologians like Gutiérrez preferred a materialist understanding of the church's role in liberation (Gutiérrez, 134), and Fox remained in the framework of an idealistic interpretation of human nature and of the gospel.

> The point ... is that the question of the liberation of others is the question of the liberation of me. Can I, in my relationship with others, allow them to challenge me—to come in touch with me? Can I really come to understand that I'm incomplete—that there's a vast degree of riches within me that I haven't even begun to be in touch with? And that there's a vast degree of poverty and garbage within me that I don't even begin to be conscious of? Can I so believe in love ... that I allow myself to be loved? Can I allow myself to be alive to me, to take the risk of looking at life and looking into reality, to take the risk of coming up with my response to it? And can I do this in a context with other people in which I allow them to write in my flesh the revelation of who they are, and I write in their flesh a revelation of who I am? ... Can all of us so radically believe in love, that we will allow ourselves to get into the developing solution which human experience is, and come more and more to be conscious of who we are? This is what it seems liberation is about (Colonnese, 125, 126).

One could argue that, just as the objective conditions were not present for the kind of Hispanic unity symbolized by the San Juan Fiesta, neither was New York in 1968 the setting for the preferential option for the poor taken by the Latin American Episcopate at Medellín in 1968. Hence, if one criticizes Fox for pushing ahead of the people with the Hispanization of the fiesta, he is to be praised for adhering to his premise of attitudinal change as a preparation for revolutionizing the structures.

Indeed, upon leaving the office Fox developed a program named Mansight, which can be categorized as consciousness raising. It consisted of slide presentations depicting scenes from the city. The idea was to have the people see the picture, try to identify the place portrayed, detect what was wrong in the situation, put themselves into the picture, and think the problem through. Many times the participants thought the photographs had been taken in Latin America or other third world countries. When Paulo Freire came to the United States in the late 1960s under Fox's sponsorship, he visited Mansight and was much impressed with the program. According to Fox, the similarity between Mansight and Paulo Freire's own approach to *conscientizão*[2] was "a coincidence, but a very happy one" (interview with Robert Fox, February 14, 1983).

The need for consciousness raising was evident in the reaction of community leaders on the board of the Institute for Human Development, which officially directed Summer in the City. According to Stern,

> The 1967 street processions to counteract the riots received a tremendous amount of publicity and acclaim, but they also triggered some disturbances within the Institute for Human Development. Not all the staff members were agreed about that intervention or about the role of the newly developed parish centers of the involvement of suburbanites. The internal dissension culminated in the Board of Directors asking for the resignation of the staff. For someone like Msgr. Fox, for whom trusting and open relationships were the essence of any program, the situation was untenable. He left the association with the organization he had founded and during the next six months proceeded to reorganize with the same spirit a new entity, called Full Circle Associates (Stern 1982, 65).

Such tensions reveal the inability of his programs to develop a native Puerto Rican leadership. Under his administration the Puerto Rican was a catalyst in the work of liberation. This was an enhanced role when compared with the client relationship of previous years, but it still filtered Puerto Rican leaders and the people's aspirations through Fox's own vision of solidarity and the needs of a non-Latino clergy to experience a sense of commitment.

Fox himself never attempted to replace native Puerto Ricans as spokespersons. But at the parish level some of the clerics and religious involved in Summer in the City, now renamed Full Circle Associates, sparred with Puerto Ricans from the community over the administration of poverty funds. The native leaders protested that they were the legitimate spokespersons for the Puerto Rican people because they, not the clergy, were Puerto Ricans. This criticism on the basis of ethnic identity alone was often a shallow one, because the local politicians who had recourse to this argument were frequently motivated by base personal ambition.[3]

More telling was the reaction of young Puerto Ricans, such as Alfredo López of the Young Lords. López articulated a more ideological criticism of Summer in the City.

> During every riot they appear, case book in hand, attempting to appease the people, calling meetings which they know will serve no purpose but "communication" and you can't pay the rent with communication, and you don't want communication if it is going to come in the form of a billy club. Instead of talking to those who really cause the riots, the government and its functionaries... [they] talk to the people, those who are answering the long, frustrating years of violence with a little violence of their own (López, 273).

Since the idea of self-help is preceded by another one that says "things are not as bad as they seem and the situation can be remedied," self-help is translated into basketball tournaments, dances, and fiestas, says López. Thus, the people who run these programs,

> are people whose aspirations never question the basis of the system but only the fact that Puerto Ricans aren't allowed a piece of the pie. That the pie has rotten apples is not a question.... "Help" [is] a goal to be reached in a particular context. That context is the status quo, keeping things the way they are, maintaining the system. They will give you all, as long as help does not conflict with the system, but when all help is not enough, when it is obvious that higher more political answers are necessary, the help disappears (López, 275).

López's class analysis criticized Summer in the City for lacking the political consciousness of Puerto Rican militancy:

> Run by nuns, priests, and white adults, Summer in the City did not supply what people felt was needed: political action. Instead, it facilitated "relating to others" and all those other nice liberal phrases. So, in the process of relating, stoops were painted orange, windows were fixed and time was wasted (López, 309).

Monsignor Fox was quick to point out that at times he, too, was aware of the "waste of time" involved in these activities. However, he contended that people must be accepted as they are and that when one works in community organization, "one must let people get certain things out of their system." Oftentimes this means having enough patience and foresight to let people work at their own pace and, if need be, make mistakes in order to better prepare themselves for future tasks and events (interview with Robert Fox, February 1, 1983).

What is relevant here is that after Summer in the City had been disbanded, the experience helped the Puerto Rican participants to confront local issues. Community success in struggles for control of Public School District I, for nursery centers, and to take over and renovate buildings in the Lower East Side can be attributed to the experience afforded the Puerto Rican local leadership through Summer in the City. Success in these and other community actions was possible, said Fox, because the people benefited from the experiences of Summer in the City. Moreover, in most instances, their sense of community process and loyalty to the people was superior to the self-seeking actions of some Puerto Rican politicians (interview with Robert Fox, February 1, 1983).

The problem Fox faced in developing leadership was inherent in Catholic Action and a church in transition. Patricia Cayo Sexton observed in her study of Spanish Harlem (1965, 71–91) that the Catholic church of the time did not allow native Puerto Rican leadership to rise to the highest level of authority within the church because of the hierarchical nature of the clergy, while the Protestant churches were generally more successful in creating a truly Puerto Rican leadership. Stevens-Arroyo detected what he called "levels of leadership" within the parishes of the time (1980, 100–1). According to his analysis, the highest level of leadership was pastoral theologian, and this category was "almost always reserved for non-Hispano clergy who worked as parish priests." Lesser roles serving social and institutional needs such as catechetical classes, money-raising, and census-taking were the "foot soldier" roles allowed to native Puerto Rican leaders. Occasionally some of these persons worked their way up to a higher level, where collaborators were offered posts on school boards and poverty agencies. In Fox's vision of things, however, the role of pastoral theologian was supposed to interpret and give direction to these other leadership functions. The group within the Spanish-speaking apostolate with whom Fox constantly exercised leadership was the clergy that shared the role of pastoral theologian with him.

The issue of symbolism and the legitimatization of leadership becomes critical here. Symbols are a very important part of human reality. But the power over symbols comes from interpreting them. That power was reserved to the pastoral theologians under Fox—largely outsiders to Puerto Ricans as an ethnic/racial group.

Because Fox's ministry was so focused upon symbols as a constituent part of reality, his followers were often satisfied with the symbolic resolution of conflict rather than addressing the material dimensions of the problems.

The people, their needs, and their response were never completely or adequately understood. And because the clergy had control over the symbols, the Puerto Ricans were left with little or no ecclesiastical mode of articulating their conception of the alternatives. The Cursillistas resisted Fox's programs with their hierarchical concept of church, which ironically coincided with the Puerto Rican leadership of the movement. Fox understood such resistance as support for the status quo. As a result, the idea of "progressive" and "Puerto Rican" was an equation for leadership that remained outside the church in the secular arena.

In Gramscian terms, Fox, like Illich, advocated a role of organic intellectual for the clergy and religious committed to the Spanish-speaking apostolate. Fox's focus upon human liberation moved the ministry beyond pastoral care and beyond even social concerns as previously understood. Summer in the City may be interpreted as the genesis of working groups for achieving an alternative society. The Puerto Ricans on the street of Fox's public forum, along with the clergy and religious, were engaged in building new values by experiencing them. Yet, by failing to develop liberation from the perspective of the Puerto Ricans, Fox did not accomplish as much for the people as he did for the clergy. Like the sincere Paco in *La carreta*, Fox approached the people, attempting to solve their loneliness by adding that of the clergy. But the people knew the difference between feeling and reality better than the clergy. In a sense, they reacted by observing, just as Juanita observed, that such talk is "like the soap operas."

Moreover, by emphasizing idealistic notions of culture and subjective dispositions toward liberation, structural change was neglected. So Fox was revolutionary in aspiration and idealization, but not in actuality. Ironically, his charismatic personality may also have limited him. A powerful personality and inspiring presence tend to overshadow the people's articulation of its own agenda. Fox was, I think, not an organic intellectual, but a conjunctural one. His leadership was based on the conjuncture of a political decade of change and the reforms of the Second Vatican Council. He advocated new forms for both society and church from the pulpit of the Office of Spanish Community Action, utilizing the social distress of Puerto Ricans and other urban poor to dramatize a message intended for all.

Ultimately Fox's use of the chancery-based office for such wide goals proved impossible. Fox had to choose between his desire to change attitudes and his mandate to tend to the spiritual care of the Puerto Ricans and other Spanish-speaking groups. There were other factors for this erosion of influence, of course. The increasing national attention on United States involvement in the war in Vietnam gradually eroded the public prominence of those who, like Fox, were considered leaders for civil rights on the domestic scene. Herman Badillo had emerged as an articulate Puerto Rican leader with his first city-wide campaign for mayor; he was shortly to go on to Washington as the first Puerto Rican congressman. Moreover, with the election of Richard Nixon as president in 1968, the Federal government began to cut the funds of the War on Poverty. The Nixon Administration's focus was on individualized help and away from community action. Finally, Cardinal Spellman had passed away and the new ordinary, Archbishop—later Cardinal—Cooke, installed in May of 1968, was gradually replacing officials appointed by Cardinal Spellman with those of his own choice.

In the spring of 1969 Fox renounced his position with the archdiocese to dedicate himself to work for Full Circle Associates, which he had founded. While his heart was never far from the Puerto Rican people, his legacy has been obscured because he attempted too much at a time out of time. Still, despite the limitations of his tenure, Fox's main contribution was to challenge the premise that decision-making in the church was a one-way process from the bishop down. Fox absorbed the social trends and the political language of the 1960s and introduced them into the design of chancery programs for the Spanish-speaking. He also suggested that such programs follow the mandates of the Second Vatican Council and characterize all church policies. He articulated a vision of church in which the social distance between the urban poor, suburbanites, and the clerical elite was banished. In its stead was a liberating attitude of self-discovery through concern for others.

Fox's outspokenness, his national reputation as an artisan of the renovated Catholic church after the Council, and his personal gifts for communication outweigh any criticism of his administrative deficiencies. Moreover, with the money he received from government sources, he acquired considerable independence from the control the archdiocese had traditionally used over church-related efforts at social concerns. He successfully focused upon the people of the community, because in a certain sense, he did not need the chancery's help to achieve his results.

In the five years of his tenure, which coincided with the Second Vatican Council, Fox transformed the image of what the Spanish-speaking apostolate could be. Clearly, it was a place where innovation and experimentation had taken place. The Office of Spanish Community Action had played a pioneer role in bringing the changes of the Second Vatican Council not only to the parishes where Latinos were the faithful, but also to the style of ministry by priests and religious. The emergence of a native Puerto Rican leadership throughout the city in the aftermath of the War on Poverty and the liberal Lindsay administration, however, had confused the role of the archdiocese in sustaining its influence. These Puerto Rican leaders were often divided by differing professional, political, and radical ideologies (Stevens-Arroyo and Díaz-Ramírez, 217–18). Moreover, the influx of other Hispanics, chiefly people from the Dominican Republic, required attention. Finally, the idea of an office of coordination based in the chancery had been lost in Fox's charismatic instinct for an apostolate of magical realism.

7. Deroutinization of the Church, Inc.

MINISTRO PARK: Soy representante de la Iglesia de Dios, Incorporada.
DOÑA GABRIELA: ¿Dioh incorporao? ¿Incorporao a qué?
MINISTRO PARK: No, no. Dios no está incorporado. La que está incorporada es la Iglesia.
DOÑA GABRIELA: ¿Y qué quiere desir eso?
JUANITA: Como lah sentraleh, mamá. Como lah sentraleh en Puerto Rico.
DOÑA GABRIELA: No entiendo.

MINISTRO PARK: I am a representative of the Church of God, Incorporated.
DOÑA GABRIELA: God incorporated? Incorporated to what?
MINISTRO PARK: No, no. God is not incorporated. What's incorporated is the Church.
DOÑA GABRIELA: And what does that mean?
JUANITA: Like the sugar factories, mamá. Like the sugar factories in Puerto Rico.
DOÑA GABRIELA: I don't understand.

The Oxcart, Act III

Robert L. Stern was appointed to the directorship of the Office of Spanish Community Action in the fall of 1969. He had been suggested for the position by the previous coordinator of the office, Monsignor Robert Fox, who in fact had placed the naming of Stern as a condition for abandoning his post. Stern had been among the first newly ordained group of priests from the Archdiocese of New York sent to Puerto Rico to study the Spanish language and Puerto Rican culture at the Institute of Intercultural Communication founded by Illich. According to Stern's own report, he "entered the seminary in 1953, participated in the newly established language classes there, and studied in the Ponce Program in the summer of 1959 and again the summer of 1960 as a participant in a special program of Latin American studies" (Stern 1982, 72).

Father Stern was atypical of most priests in the Spanish-speaking apostolate, because after three years of pastoral experience in a Hispanic parish, he had been sent to Rome, where he secured a degree in canon law. Study in Rome for canon law is usually preparation for a chancery post as an ecclesiastical bureaucrat and, not infrequently, a training ground for future bishops. Moreover, Stern's background is not typical of the New York Catholic family. His father is a Jew who never abandoned his beliefs, although he allowed his Irish wife to raise their children as Catholics.

Immediately following his appointment, Stern set out to bring a new direction in the apostolate among the Puerto Ricans for the archdiocese and inaugurate substantial revision of the role of the Office of Spanish Community Action within the chancery. Moreover, the Spellman years had ended, and Stern's appointment was part of the transition to the new administration under Cardinal Terence Cooke. Stern was seen as a protege of Archbishop Maguire, whom some had considered a possible successor to Spellman (interview with Stern, May 15, 1981). Stern states, "Archbishop Maguire had commended to Cardinal Spellman that the immediate Chancery staff include a Spanish-speaking priest with parish experience in the Hispanic community" (1982, 72, 73). Stern was a good choice. He would bring to the directorship of the Spanish-speaking apostolate not only a practical grass-roots experience of work in the inner city but administrative and organizational skills from his experience in the Chancery Office, as well.

Focused upon better communications with the chancery, Stern's administration began with the new name given to the office. No longer the Office of Spanish Community Action, it became the Office of the Spanish-Speaking Apostolate,[1] its head was no longer a coordinator, but director, similar to any other chancery office in the archdiocese. The word *apostolate* signaled a departure from the policy of Monsignor Fox. Ostensibly, the new title placed emphasis upon the sacramental orientation of pastoral concern, a direction that Archbishop Cooke preferred to the office's social action focus under Fox (Annual Report 1969–70, 1).

Stern's understanding of the office was at another level. Rather than a return to the sacramental limitations of pastoral care, he interpreted the word *apostolate* as an application of Fox's efforts to a new area. This is made clear in Stern's annual report of 1969–70, the first of several meticulously prepared analyses of office activities that serve as an indispensable chronicle for these years. There he described a double "mission" for the office and specified a third objective for his administration that would make it possible for the office to achieve its purposes.

> This mission of the office has a double aspect. On the one hand, it involves something personal and spiritual: the promotion of the apostolate. Here the task is to encourage those who work for the spread of the reign of God, to pattern relationships and communicate among them, and to unify and focus the tremendous dedication, experience and insights of the priests, religious, and lay leaders involved in the work of Christ.
>
> On the other hand, the mission involves something visible and institutional. Besides the need for leadership, there is need of administration and deployment of existing institutional resources. The office accordingly includes direct responsibility for all operational programs of the archdiocese concerning the Spanish-speaking and a further responsibility to collaborate with and be at the service of parishes, educational institutions, and diocesan agencies and offices in all that concerns the Spanish-speaking.
>
> Finally, it functions as a representation of the archbishop and of the archdiocese to all Spanish-speaking orientated organizations, groups and interests (Annual Report 1969–70, 1).

Stern's definition of the office's function as "mission" introduced terminology usually reserved for movements, religious orders, and ecclesiastical jurisdictions. He thus demonstrated that this view of the office transcended a merely bureaucratic function. Rather than abandon the interpersonal focus stressed by Fox, Stern "baptized" these human relationships as "spiritual." He did, however, retreat from the community orientation of Fox to emphasize that the direct area of focus for the office was upon the institutional church itself. In other words, Stern inverted the flow of Fox's activities. Instead of merely using the office as a base to provide the Puerto Rican people with church leadership drawn from the ranks of the United States clergy, he sought to engage the Puerto Ricans in the myriad of "existing institutional resources" within the church institution by their active involvement with the leadership apparatus of the church. This was to be accomplished

Figure 5

Spanish-Speaking Apostolate: Administrative Organization

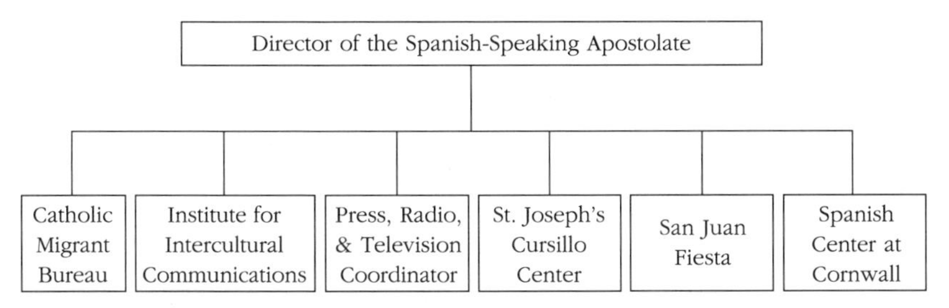

Source: Robert L. Stern's personal files.

by including Latinos and their concerns in commissions and in advisory capacities.

At the same time he sought to strengthen the role of "their" office within the archdiocese—the Office of the Spanish-Speaking Apostolate. Tiny by chancery standards, the office was housed in two rooms and its staff consisted of three persons: Stern's secretary; one assistant, Angel Pérez, who was in charge of community affairs, ecumenism, and mass media; and a clerk-typist. Stern anticipated that under his directorship the Office of the Spanish-Speaking Apostolate would address "all operational programs of the Archdiocese concerning the Spanish-speaking parishes, educational institutions, and diocesan agencies and offices" (see Figure 5).

The agenda Stern had prepared for discussion with the priests assigned to the Spanish-speaking apostolate in the archdiocese during his first fiscal year reveals the encompassing nature of Stern's vision of ministry. His holistic projection of the office's role rendered it in effect a chancery within a chancery (see Figure 6). This vision was inaugurated by a series of meetings during a ten-month period from April 1970 to February 1971. The first meeting was a three-day retreat (April 21–23, 1970) devoted to the following topics: The Archdiocese and the Hispanos, 1970; The Church's Proper Mission: Priesthood and Ministry; Pastoral Goals and Priorities, 1970; Restructuring for the Apostolate; *Pastoral de Conjunto;* Organization of the Spanish-Speaking Apostolate 1970; and Future Plans and Resolutions.

Figure 6

Spanish-Speaking Apostolate: Organization for the Apostolate

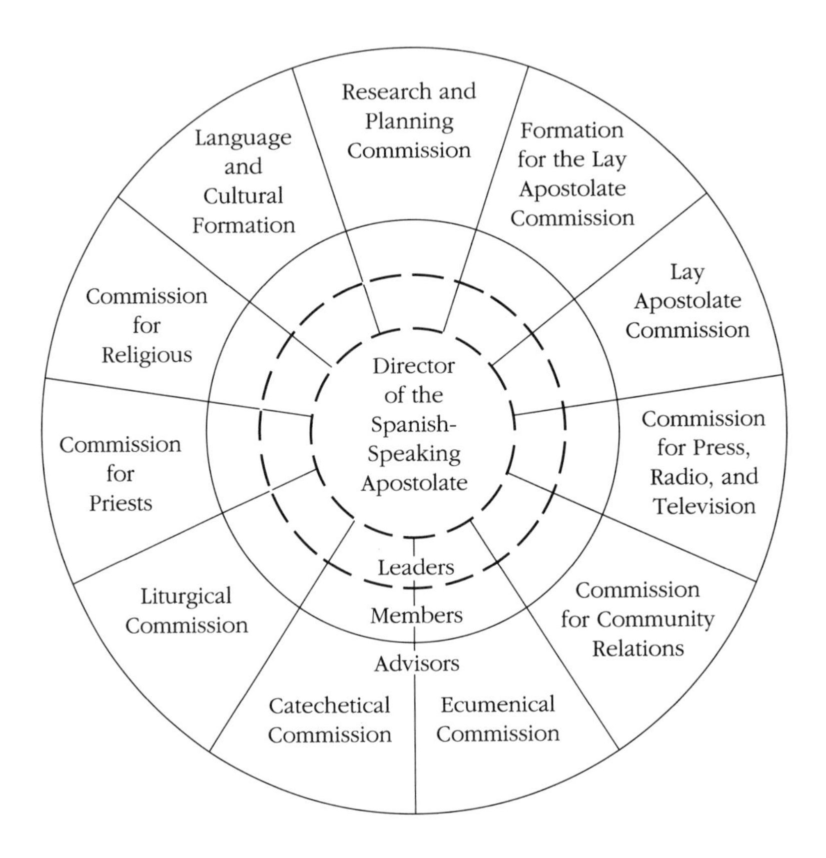

Source: Robert L. Stern's personal files.

The second was a two-day retreat (June 24–25, 1970) devoted exclusively to the Cursillo Movement. Six more one-day meetings were conducted as part of the initial phase of restructuring the apostolate. In these meetings Stern communicated with laity and the clergy alike about every aspect of church activity among Hispanics and shared with them an emerging plan for sustaining this dialogue.

As Figure 7 shows, Stern adopted a strategy of targeting the apostolate for different elements of the Hispanic community in New York. The different socio-economic, nationality, and age

Figure 7

Spanish-Speaking Apostolate of the Catholic Archdiocese of New York, Organization of the Lay Apostolate

Type of Person	Type of Program			
	Human Development (Mass Media)	Basic Religious Formation	Lay Apostolic Formation	Lay Apostolates
Child		Religious Instruction		
Youth		*Cursillos de Catequesis*	*Cursillos de Vida (Encuentros)*	*Juventud Obrera Cristiana; Juventud Estudiantil Cristiana*
Parishioner	Television, Radio, Press, Motion Pictures, Theatre	Sunday Liturgy Parish Mission Retreats		Junior Legion of Mary Senior Legion of Mary *
Adult		Instructional Class	*Cursillos de Cristiandad; Movimiento para un Mundo Mejor*	*
Married Person		*Familia de Dios*	*Encuentro Conyugales*	*Movimiento Familiar Cristiano*
Professionals			Profession Sodalities	Professional Apostolate

* Parish Societies **Social and Community Action Source: Robert L. Stern's personal files.

groups were to be addressed by church initiatives designed to meet their special needs. However, the office was at the center of all these activities (Figure 6). For the sake of his chancery superiors, Stern translated these community-based outlines into the standard organizational patterns described in Figure 5, drawing a distinction between "organization of the apostolate" (Figure 6 and 7) and "administrative organization" (Figure 5).

This twofold mode of organization—outward toward the community Fox had targeted (Figure 6 and 7) and inward toward the administrative focus of the chancery (Figure 5)—was the contribution of Stern to the office. On the one hand, he sustained the impetus of his predecessor; on the other, by expanding the charismatic experimentation of Fox his attempt threatened to set free the chancery structures to the input of the people from the base. It is in this sense that he can be said to keep company with Charles Borromeo and be called a "deroutinizer of the institutional church" (McNamara 1968, 17–18; see above, chapter 1). Stern believed that by establishing communication with the chancery, the office would officially represent the archbishop in relation to "all Spanish-speaking oriented organizations, groups and interests." By incorporating input and leadership from the community rather than merely reporting from the people to the cardinal and vice versa he believed the communication process could be expedited. The Office of the Spanish-speaking Apostolate was the voice of the people united with the support of the archdiocese. Stern went beyond Fox's notion of listening to the people and their needs so that the process of discussion under the aegis of a chancery office constituted policy (Annual Report 1969–70, 1) and gave the people a sense of contributing in a positive way to the apostolate. Certainly this had been a key concept of Fox's dynamic leadership, but now the charismatic and personal character of Fox's activism was institutionalized.

From the outset Stern thought it advisable to emphasize his official ecclesiastical role. It appears as if his emphasis upon his charge as official archdiocesan representative initially presented no threat nor did it evoke resentment among either church officials and leaders or those in the lay and civic communities. This, it is my belief, was partly due to the redefinition that had been made of the office's mission and partly due to Stern's soft-spoken and persuasive manner. It should be remembered that, in contrast,

Fox rarely had recourse to his formal titles. His magnetic personality had generally bestowed its own mystique to his leadership.

Stern's redefinition of the office necessitated new mechanisms, which he began to develop as soon as he assumed responsibility as director. In September of 1969 he sent a letter to all clergy in the archdiocese and all religious houses explaining the "redevelopment of the Spanish office." Beginning in May of 1970 a steady flow of communication with all the clergy and religious houses in the archdiocese was instituted through a newsletter, the purpose of which was "to keep them informed of activities and programs of the Spanish-speaking apostolate as well as to circulate other useful information" (Annual Report 1969–70, 3). He also circulated a series of occasional reports and studies.

These mechanisms, however, depended primarily on the time and effort of Stern and his limited office personnel. Recognizing that government funding of his chancery-based vision was unlikely, he sought collaborators. He envisioned a group of people with particular expertise who would be able and willing to complement each other's work through support and communication. He wrote that "proper structuring implies setting up an effective pattern of communication and sharing of ideas, enthusiasm and experiences. Also such a pattern must reflect a sound theology of the Church; it must be flexible and ongoing, and its dynamism must be centrifugal, not centripetal" (Annual Report 1969–70, 9).

This was the principle that Stern took to heart when projections were made for the "many distinct fields of the apostolate needing attention." The leadership for these areas would be representative of the total church community and would include experts who had recognition and acceptance in the secular community as well. In other words, they would be cross-validated, with the archdiocese conferring legitimacy upon their rising visibility with the people. "It was decided to choose eleven persons, each of whom would accept a special responsibility for some area of concern and would develop a working group to assist them composed of priests, religious, and laymen and advisors and experts as needed" (Annual Report 1969–70, 9).

The areas of concern Stern initially singled out for special attention were: 1) research and pastoral planning; 2) linguistic and cultural formation; 3) apostolate of religious; 4) apostolate of priests; 5) formation for the lay apostolate; 6) lay apostolate;

7) community relations; 8) ecumenical relations; 9) press, radio, and television; 10) liturgy; and 11) catechetics. Of the priests he invited to work in the office that year, three were of Puerto Rican origin: Antonio M. Stevens-Arroyo (Puerto Rican-Hungarian born in Philadelphia; Passionist stationed in Jamaica, New York); José McCarthy-González (Puerto Rican-Irish born in New York; Capuchin stationed in Manhattan); Peter Ensenat (Puerto Rican-Cuban born in New York; a priest of the archdiocese). Stern actively sought to invite any priests of Puerto Rican or Hispanic origin to participate with the office, even if the cleric was not actively engaged in the Spanish-speaking apostolate. Later two other Puerto Rican priests and two Dominicans were also engaged as collaborators with the office: Luis Ríos (born in New York of Puerto Rican parents; Assumptionist stationed in Manhattan); César Rámirez (a native of Puerto Rico, a priest of the San Juan Archdiocese who had served as secretary to its bishop, Luis Aponte Martínez); Porfirio Valdez and Milton Ruiz (natives of the Dominican Republic on leave to New York).

The choice of these native Latinos was not accidental. Stern recognized that one of Fox's obstacles had been the claim of Puerto Rican leaders that non-Latino clergy did not speak for them. By encouraging these clerics to be a part of his circle of collaborators Stern pulled into the apostolate virtually all the Puerto Rican and Dominican priests in New York at that time. It should be noted that these native clergy belonged, for the most part, to religious orders or to dioceses outside the United States. In all cases these priest-collaborators were under the territorial jurisdiction but not the immediate jurisdiction of the cardinal archbishop of New York; that is, they depended upon the cardinal for faculties and other priestly privileges but owed immediate obedience to their religious superiors. Moreover, of the lay people assigned to leadership responsibilities to these areas throughout Stern's administration, seven were of Puerto Rican origin (see Díaz-Ramírez 1983, 260). Thus Stern placed Puerto Ricans in a decision-making role in the restructuring of the office.

The premise that only Puerto Ricans could successfully represent Puerto Rican interests, just as only blacks could successfully represent blacks, had found some acceptance in the general liberalism of New York's civic life (Stevens-Arroyo 1980, 178–79). While it was true that Puerto Ricans still lagged behind the general population at the economic and educational levels, by 1969 they had managed to lay the basis for a city-side leadership. This emergence was symbolized by the surprisingly strong showing of Hermán Badillo in the 1969 Democratic Primary for the New York City mayoralty (Rosa Estades 1978). Afterward, the Puerto Ricans were perceived as the political leaders of a growing Hispanic population and were increasingly considered a rising force in New York politics (Glazer and Moynihan, lxiii-lxx).

Stern was conscious, as Fox had been, that since 1964 an influx of non–Puerto Ricans was occurring in New York. The office did not neglect these other Hispanic groups. When the Dominicans began to come to the city in considerable numbers, Stern sought to do for them what had been done for the Puerto Ricans in terms of the apostolate. But he took care, in the process, not to supplant "Puerto Rican" with "Hispanic." He sought to harness the institutional capabilities that up to that time had been used to respond culturally and linguistically to the Puerto Ricans in order to service all of the Spanish-speaking. In doing this he felt he was also giving the Puerto Ricans a wider representational base, because considerable numbers were being added to the city's Hispanic population, of which thus far Puetro Ricans had constituted a majority. This way, he thought, an expansion of Puerto Rican community strength could be achieved without diluting nationalistic identification. Stern thus linked the potential of the Puerto Ricans, who numbered nearly one million and who enjoyed United States citizenship by birth, to a growing population of some four hundred thousand other Hispanics in New York in 1970.[2]

The harmonization of interests among these different nationalistic groups was to be achieved through the office which, while not claiming to represent them individually, represented them all collectively as Hispanic Catholics. Thus, Stern turned a limitation of the office into an asset. He warded off criticism that the church was not allowing native Puerto Ricans and Hispanic clergy and laity in official positions. Simultaneously, he staked a claim for the church to attest to the as-yet-unexplored importance of a "Hispanic population." He did this at the pace of the groups themselves, allowing them time to discover their own common interests. Thus his plan corresponded to Padilla's diagnosis of Latino ethnic consciousness (see above, chapter 6). Stern's strategy relied upon collaboration among the different groups under the aegis of the office's programs.

The principal mechanism chosen by Stern to orchestrate collaboration in the apostolate was the Coordinating Committee, which was composed of different leaders from areas of pastoral care and had both a diversified Hispanic representation that included clergy, religious, and laity as well as all the movements, agencies, and areas of church activity among the Spanish-speaking in New York. Communication was key to Stern's notion of mission. But whereas Fox perceived church structure as inimical to interpersonal communication, Stern utilized interpersonal communication to revitalize the ecclesiastical institution.

The Coordinating Committee was democratic in its decision-making procedures, deciding most issues by majority vote (interviews with Stern, Kalbfleish, and Stevens-Arroyo, 1981–82). But while Stern wanted this group to **form** policy, he did not allow it to **decide** policy; he maintained the strictly consultative nature of the Coordinating Committee. The final decisions were made by him, more or less in parallel with the entire chancery, which could formulate policy for the cardinal but deferred to him for the final word. However, Stern frequently stressed that it would be foolish for him to oppose the majority of the committee on any issue since the effectiveness of any course of action depended upon their continued cooperation. Thus, the Coordinating Committee not only fostered unity among the diverse Hispanic nationality groups but also provided a forum for democratic decision-making within one of the chancery offices.

Stern soon recognized the power of the mass media. Initially he relied upon the efforts of Mr. Angel Pérez, a veteran from the Fox administration, who was named by Stern to continue both as a member of the office staff and chairman of the Committee on Press, Radio, and Television. Mr. Pérez was likewise able to aid Father Ignacio Lazcano, one of the Canons of the Lateran, in Ecumenical Relations. "Cara a Cara en el Mundo de la Religión," a series of twenty-four radio dialogues between a Catholic priest and a Protestant minister, were begun on WBNX radio in February of 1969 and continued throughout the succeeding months. In October of the same year a similar program began on Channel 47 as part of the television series "Tribuna Hispana" and continued on an experimental basis for four months. For Christmas of 1969 a special one-hour ecumenical program was broadcast on Channel 47, preceding the midnight mass. The ecumenical program was a festive meal in Puerto Rican style hosted jointly by the director of the Office of the Spanish-Speaking Apostolate, the chairman of Ecumenical Relations, and the president of the Fraternity of Spanish Ministers. There was table conversation on religious themes among the Catholic and Protestant clergy, religious, and laity. The dialogue was punctuated by Christmas carols and family scenes. The midnight mass was preceded by a specially taped Christmas message by Cardinal Cooke and was concelebrated by Robert L. Stern, director of the Office of the Spanish-Speaking Apostolate of the Archdiocese of New York and John O'Brien, director of the Office of the Spanish-Speaking Apostolate of the Diocese of Brooklyn. For Holy Week of 1970 thirty-four hours of radio programming were produced for the three Spanish language stations. A special four-hour ecumenical service of the Seven Last Words was broadcast live from Holy Agony Church and televised live that same day. Beginning on October 12, 1969, a mass celebrated in Spanish was broadcast weekly on Sundays over WBNX radio from St. Christopher's Chapel in Manhattan. Every week a different parish came to celebrate the mass, bringing its own celebrant, servers, lectors, and choir. On November 11, 1969, Channel 47 began to televise a Sunday liturgy at noon, which had been pretaped in their studios. Again, groups from different parishes participated regularly in the program, which was assigned to Stevens-Arroyo (Annual Report 1969–70, 15–17).

Seeking better participation, in June of 1970 the celebration at St. Christopher's was discontinued in favor of a liturgy taped in a parish church and rebroadcast later in the afternoon. According to Stern, like the radio mass, although primarily presented for shut-ins and those otherwise impeded from attending mass in a church, this televised mass had "an important function of diffusing knowledge of the new liturgy and of catechizing people for it. Further it provided a religious experience of value in itself, especially the Liturgy of the Word" (Annual Report 1969–70, 15–17). Perhaps most important, these programs had a high level of community participation.

On February 11, 1970, an eight-minute ecumenical religious news broadcast live on Channel 47, entitled "Noticiero Religioso," was begun. In addition to a selection of religious news, both local and worldwide, it offered an editorial on each broadcast. There were other occasional conferences and programs arranged throughout the year. Many of these productions embodied the seeds of the new vision of the office. The work accomplished through press, radio, and television also portrayed the office and the archdiocese as dynamic agencies concerned for the spiritual and social welfare of New York's growing Latino community.

In one year Pérez had organized for the office more Spanish-language television and radio religious broadcasting than was available to the English-speakers of the archdiocese. Moreover, this had been accomplished with only one full-time staff person assigned to communications, while the chancery office charged with this task for the English-speaking had several full-time assistants and secretaries.

The programming was directed from the office and became an effort to promote the "mission" that Stern had visualized for the office (Stern 1982, 88–90). The news, the liturgy, the music, and the sermon generally reflected both in style and content the basic pastoral commitment of the office as defined by Stern and in accord with conciliar guidelines.

Stern had begun with the premise that not all structures had to be eradicated. He believed that within the church as institution one could no sooner do away with norms, traditions, and structures of New York Catholicism, than one could do away with the language, traditions, and customs of the Puerto Rican and Hispanic religiosity. These could be blended so that the institutions of the archdiocese could be turned to service for the Spanish-speaking.

Such service would strengthen these offices by turning them away from attention only to a shrinking English-speaking community and toward the growing numbers of Latinos. In the process of dialogue it would be possible to discern which church structures required renewal and adaptation. Unlike the anti-establishment tone of Fox's work, reorganization of the apostolate on Stern's terms called for assessment and utilization of existing resources of church and people so that a Christian community could be developed in a manner that was consonant with the potential of all (Annual Report 1969–70, 74). Stern suggested that anything done to enhance the apostolate among Puerto Ricans and Hispanics would ultimately benefit the entire church community.

Stern's canonical training led him to a comprehensive outreach, transcending Fox's target upon the inner city. Thus, he made a strong effort to intensify the ministry to Hispanic migrant farm workers in rural New York State. During the year 1969 this program had consisted of a priest, a deacon, a seminarian, and three religious sisters working in Orange County during the summer months, celebrating masses in the camps and offering a program of visitations, social assistance, and recreation. Before Stern's administration the program had been conducted in relative isolation. But after an evaluation in conjunction with the program's staff and chancery officials in the fall of 1969, it was decided to completely reorganize the program (Annual Report 1969–70, 74).

Father Jesús Iriondo, another of the Basque Canons Regular of the Lateran, was assigned to St. Joseph's Parish in Middletown to direct the migrant ministry on a year-round basis. Faithful to the principle of democratization, Stern saw to it that the reorganized program worked with the assistance of an advisory board. As director of the Office of the Spanish-Speaking Apostolate, Stern was ex officio member of this board. Upon his advice, local pastors were invited to contribute counsel and financial assistance. Two seminarians, members of a summer exchange program begun by Stern in 1970 (and discussed at length further on in this chapter), were added to the program as assistants to Father Iriondo during the peak months of July and August. The response from the Hispanic farm workers that year was encouraging (Annual Report 1969–70, 3).

In the Newburgh-Beacon area of the archdiocese a group of sisters from Spain, the Oblate Sisters of the Most Holy Redeemer, had been working among the Spanish-speaking Catholics since 1964. Their base of operations was a convent complex in Cornwall, New York. The sisters' apostolate consisted of traditional aspects of pastoral care: family visitations, census-taking, language and doctrine classes, formation of church societies, promotion of the liturgy, and occasional works of charity. During the Fox administration little contact between the office and the sisters had been maintained. By August of 1969 "there was considerable dissatisfaction among the Oblate Sisters about their work in the county areas and a possibility of their mission being terminated (Annual Report 1969–70, 4, 5). Stern sought to reestablish communications with the sisters and their superior general in Spain. As a consequence, it was agreed that they not only would continue their work but expand it, and that their convent complex would be considered for formal establishment as an institute within the Archdiocese of New York.

Within a year Stern had achieved the assignment of an archdiocesan priest to coordinate the Spanish-speaking apostolate for the Dutchess-Putnam and Orange-Rockland vicariates and had reestablished the development of pastoral programs for Hispanics in the Newburgh-Beacon area through the work of the Oblate Sisters at the Spanish Center at Cornwall. Most important, these operations were coordinated from his office.

The task of restructuring church activity under the aegis of the Office of the Spanish-Speaking Apostolate was not as easily accomplished in the city itself. Programs and movements that had grown used to relative autonomy under Fox did not always welcome Stern's suggestions for a more clear role for the office. The Cursillo Movement, for example, functioned under the exclusive direction of the staff of St. Joseph's Cursillo Center on 142nd Street and a secretariat approved by the cardinal.

The Cursillo Movement had experienced two full years of complete independence from the Office of the Spanish-speaking Apostolate, when in September of 1969, Father David Arias, O.A.R., was appointed director of the center by his congregation's superiors. Serious, hard-working, and yet approachable, Arias was to become one of Stern's successors as director of the Office of the Spanish-Speaking Apostolate before being ordained auxiliary bishop of Newark. Stern seized the change in directorship of the Cursillo Movement to reclaim the role as representative of the cardinal, becoming the episcopal delegate who was officially coordinator of the movement in New York and head of the Cursillo secretariat. Whereas Fox had surrendered an effort at changing the mentality of the *cursillistas,* Stern embarked on that course by a legal restructuring. He initiated a process of redefinition of the secretariat's role and the movement's goals within the Puerto Rican and Hispanic communities of New York city. Accordingly, "a committee to study and propose a restructuring of the secretariat began work in June of 1970" (Annual Report 1969–70, 5).

The reorganization of the Cursillo began with the general two-day meeting of priests in the Spanish-speaking apostolate mentioned earlier. To prepare for the meeting, an attitudinal survey of the clergy opinion about the Cursillo Movement was prepared (Annual Report 1969–70, 6).[3]

The Cursillo Movement was at that time the largest and most extensive of all religious programs among the Puerto Rican and Hispanic peoples in New York. Its members ranged from professionals to working-class people; it included religious, clergy, and lay persons, Puerto Ricans, other Hispanics, and Spanish-speaking North Americans. However, its greatest success in terms of numbers and participation, was among the Puerto Rican working class, whose mobilization made it possible for the Cursillo Movement in 1970 to gather three to five thousand persons for an event (Annual Report 1969–70, 6).

Stern used the results of the survey to offer the Cursillo members a picture of themselves from the perspective of the parish clergy that they were supposed to serve. He used the conservative hierarchical theology of the Cursillo against the trend to view the religious at St. Joseph's Center as the sole clerical authority of *cursillistas.* Because Stern was the cardinal's representative, he—not the clergy at St. Joseph's Center—was hierarchically empowered to head the movement in New York's jurisdiction. Granted that many of the clergy had followed Fox's lead in ignoring the Cursillo Movement as a basis for a community apostolate (see above, chapter 6), still Stern's approach was effective in stimulating a change from within the movement. "The Secretariat of the movement was reorganized and its responsibilities were redefined with the positive result that there began to be a real and major assumption of responsibility for the movement by laymen in a way that had not taken place for the first several years of its life" (Stern 1982, 75).

Stern also sought to define and strengthen the relationship between the office and the Summer Institute in Ponce. Under Fox's administration the linguistic and formal educational function of the New York–based programs had been overshadowed by Summer in the City, while in Puerto Rico, the Summer Program had become virtually independent of the Office of the New York Spanish-Speaking Apostolate.

On December 18, 1969, Stern attended his first meeting of the board of directors of the Institute of Intercultural Communication; he went in his capacity as director of the Office of the

Spanish-Speaking Apostolate. At that meeting he was elected to the institute's board as vice-president. At that meeting Stern also pushed for evaluation of the criteria for recruitment of seminary students for the linguistic and cultural training of the institute. Accordingly, a meeting was held on January 6, 1970, with the rector, dean of studies, and the director of pastoral programs of St. Joseph's Seminary at Dunwoodie, New York, to discuss ways of familiarizing the students with Spanish and Latin American culture. It was decided to establish a branch of the institute at the seminary in Dunwoodie, offering a class a week and employing as instructors Spanish-speaking residents of Yonkers. Stern also urged that the program be open to all interested persons in the Yonkers area. Thus Stern projected his office into the sensitive area of seminary training and opened the door for lay people to use a facility ordinarily reserved for the exclusive preparation of seminarians and clergy.

Moreover, Stern engaged lay people of Hispanic background in the training of future clergy. In an effort to reorient seminary training along progressive lines, Stern himself taught a special seminary course. But rather than treat only the pastoral and cultural problems the future clergy would meet upon encountering the Spanish-speaking community, Stern gave the class a theological perspective. The sessions utilized functional and statistical analysis of the Archdiocese of New York and demographics of the metropolitan New York area in order to present the reasons for adopting new concepts of church and ministry. Stern compared Latin American and Spanish Catholicism to the Irish-American Catholicism of the United States through a socio-historical prism, suggesting, as Illich had before him, that Americanization was not the purpose of church ministry to the Spanish-speaking. Accordingly, the course offered alternative ecclesiastical structures to renew parish life. In a sense Stern was teaching what Illich and Fox espoused, but now the message came from within the heart of the archdiocese.

Both on the island of Puerto Rico and at Cardinal Hayes High School in the Bronx, Stern restructured the Institute of Intercultural Communication, which had drifted from the office's supervision. After a series of meetings with the new lay rector of the Catholic University of Puerto Rico, Stern reported that "a written agreement was concluded between the archdiocese and the university defining the joint sponsorship of the summer institute, the right of the university to appoint the director of the institute after consultation with the archdiocese, and the duties and responsibilities of the director" (Stern 1982, 77).

The program at Cardinal Hayes was completely reorganized by September of 1971. For the first time a layman was named director. "The old Institute of Intercultural Communication Corporation was allowed to lapse, and the program continued as the Language Institute of the Office for the Spanish-Speaking Apostolate" (Stern, 1982, 76). As has been explained, in the previous January a special brand of language-training program had been established at the seminary. Thus, by working on the premise of routine administrative procedures, Stern had unified under his office all the training programs for the Spanish-speaking ministry of the archdiocese.

Stern's effort to restructure the office according to its newly perceived mission extended its attention to the Dominicans, who had replaced the Cubans as the second most numerous Hispanic group in the archdiocese (Stern 1982, 77). Instead of merely subsuming the Dominicans under the general linguistic category of "Spanish-speaking," Stern sought to give them special attention and to repeat for them what had been previously attempted for the Puerto Ricans. Thus, the program on linguistic and cultural formation was expanded to include the Dominican experience in New York. A program of pastoral work in the Dominican Republic was initiated in addition to the usual program in Puerto Rico. This, however, was only one side of the coin.

In January of 1970 Stern visited the Dominican Republic. Through him, the Archdiocese of New York extended an invitation to major seminarians there to work in parishes of the Archdiocese of New York for the summer months in exchange for travel expenses, room, board and twenty-five dollars a week allowance. According to Stern the purpose of this effort was twofold: "To provide assistance to those parishes especially those with large numbers or recently arrived Dominicans and to familiarize candidates for the priesthood in the Dominican Republic with the particular challenge confronted by immigrants here" (Annual Report 1969–70, 8).

Of the seventy-one students that the archdiocese sent to Puerto Rico and the Dominican Republic for summer language study and pastoral work in 1970, three priests and seven sisters worked in the Dominican Republic (Annual Report 1969–70, 7). In August three more sisters were sent to the Dominican Republic for the pastoral experience alone. The seventy-one students included nine priests, three seminarians, two brothers, forty-four sisters and thirteen lay persons. Personnel working with the Spanish-speaking were also sent to Cuernavaca, Mexico, and Medellín, Columbia. The cost for the 1970 program to the archdiocese was $47,508.35.

Several parishes and the farm workers' program in Orange County received a total of sixteen seminarians from the Dominican Republic that summer. Assignments were made to Nativity, Sacred Heart, St. Elizabeth, and St. Rose of Lima parishes in Manhattan, Our Lady of Pity, St. Athanasius, and St. Simon Stock in the Bronx.

Stern's organizational skills extended to the liturgy. When Bernard Benziger, under the name of a newly founded Community Missal Publishing Company, decided to print a Sunday and holy day leaflet missal in Spanish, he sought the cooperation of the Office of the Spanish-Speaking Apostolate. Benziger represented a well-known religious publishing house that had now turned to the growing numbers of Spanish-speaking in the country as clientele. Used to dealing with the chancery, Benziger found Stern cooperative. Utilizing all of the prestige of the archdiocese, Stern made formal contacts with the hierarchy in Puerto Rico and the Dominican Republic and provided capable advisors for the project. Since the publication was national in scope, Stern invited Mexican American liturgist Father Virgilio Elizondo of the San Antonio Archdiocese in Texas as a member of the board. Other members were Stern himself; Father James Welby and Mr. Angel Pérez from the Archdiocese of New York; and Father Baltasar Hendricks, O.P., representing the Archdiocese of San Juan, Puerto Rico. Collaborators were Antonio M. Stevens-Arroyo, C.P., of Brooklyn and Jaime Reyes, O.S.B., from Puerto Rico. Benziger was receptive to these steps, since it gave his project a publication distribution potential among the numerous Spanish-speaking Catholic populations in the Southwest and California. This initial collaboration was to serve as a harbinger of a most important coalescence of all the Spanish-speaking in the United States around common church concerns (Stevens-Arroyo 1980, 175–79). Moreover, it followed Padilla's description of a true Latino consciousness (Padilla 1985, 60–83).

In 1970 this committee petitioned the National Bishops' Liturgical Commission to allow the use of *ustedes* instead of *vosotros* in church rites in the United States. Equivalent to the substitution of *you* for thou, which had already been approved for the English-speaking, this change represented a departure from a manner of speech that was common only in parts of Spain. The advisory committee also requested acceptance of the New York Bible Society's Spanish version of the New Testament, *Dios Llega al Hombre,* because the liturgical readings offered in this translation were closer to the spoken Spanish of the Puerto Ricans and other Hispanics residing in the United States. Eventually music in native Puerto Rican, Mexican, Cuban, and other Latin American rhythms was to prove as important to the success of the liturgical publication as the texts. In a sense, just as Lutherans sang themselves into a reformation, Latinos sang themselves into an *encuentro* ("encounter").

This was the first known collaboration effort of church leaders in the United States to represent all Hispanics before the hierarchy. Moreover, as stated above, two priests from the island of Puerto Rico were also included in this effort. The response of the Bishops' Commission was that it had no episcopal members with the expertise to judge the usefulness of the request or the advantages of the translation. With that admission the Bishops' Commission indirectly confessed that no member of the episcopacy in the United States was a native Hispanic and that the bishops were therefore incapable of making a pastoral judgment about a substantial and growing segment of the United States Catholic population. Eventually, permission on the local level was granted as an experiment to the Mexican American Cultural Center in San Antonio, Texas, which was directed by Father Elizondo.

In restructuring the office Stern did not neglect the oldest of its functions, the San Juan Fiesta. Growing dissatisfaction among members of the Puerto Rican community leadership with Fox's innovations had resulted in a rather tense atmosphere:

> During the last few years there was a growing discontent among many of the lay leaders in the Spanish-speaking community who usually worked to develop the Fiesta. They felt that their views and assistance were not solicited or valued. The accuracy of the complaints notwithstanding, a public protest was made in the Spanish press which led to a series of public meetings about the Fiesta (Annual Report 1969–70, 8).

The outcome of these meetings was the revival of the Committee of Fiesta Presidents. The election of a new president was made in an open, democratic process. However, the Department of Parks refused to allow the celebration of the fiesta on a Sunday afternoon because of problems the previous year. The reason given by the Department of Parks was "excessive crowding of the Island," but the restriction may have been the result of political favors to the Puerto Rican Day Parade, which was anxious to preserve its advantage in popularity. It was decided to limit the fiesta observance for June of 1970 to a vigil mass the night before, beginning at 8 o'clock and ending at 2 o'clock in the morning.

Undaunted, Stern made a firm commitment to return to the traditional style. Civic pressure was put on city officials, and Stern appointed a Puerto Rican priest, Father Luis Ríos, A.A., to work year-round on the preparations for the fiesta. These measures proved successful in restoring the traditional style of celebration, but not, unfortunately, with the same numbers as in the previous decade. For the reasons offered above (chapter 6) it appears that with the conciliar changes the format of the patronal feast was no longer viable on a grand scale (Díaz-Stevens 1990).

The director of the Office of the Spanish-Speaking Apostolate also entered into the delicate area of clergy assignments. Two issues were of special concern: the incardination of priests from other dioceses who wished to become full-fledged members of the Archdiocese of New York, and formal contracts with others who wished to remain temporarily (Annual Report 1969–70, 19).

Stern took upon himself the task of establishing and maintaining contact with the local or provincial superiors of religious orders of priests working within the archdiocese in the Spanish-speaking apostolate. He consciously projected the authority of the cardinal in these meetings with the heads of religious orders. Without the cardinal's permission, they could not continue to function in the archdiocese, and Stern wanted their integration into his overall vision.

It was much more difficult, however, to achieve the same influence in the personnel assignments of the archdiocese. Each priest's designation to serve in a parish or office is issued by the authority of his bishop. Such assignments are generally interpreted as promotions or demotions, and to disobey such an assignment is a serious lapse of protocol. In the New York Archdiocese, a group of chancery officials explores the qualities and record of each priest—often discussing personal matters that are confidential—before making the final recommendations to the cardinal. Participation in this process offers direct influence with the cardinal and power over the lives and careers of fellow priests.

Stern's desire to belong to this process by virtue of his position was a departure from the policies of previous directors. Nonetheless, he believed this was a most important area in the development of any overall pastoral planning for the Spanish-speaking apostolate. "In May of 1970 for the first time, a formal review of assignments was made with the Archdiocesan Personnel Board, and from time to time recommendations were submitted in particular instances. There is a need to develop an effective pattern of collaboration in personnel matters" (Annual Report 1969–70, 20).

Stern initiated a dialogue with those priests working in the Spanish-speaking apostolate who belonged neither to religious orders nor to the New York Archdiocese. These *extern priests* usually came from Spain or Latin America for personal reasons. Among New York pastors they had a reputation for shallow commitment and were not among the most sought-after of the Spanish-speaking clergy. Stern began a process of dialogue with these priests and simultaneous negotiations with chancery officials in order to protect these clergymen from the sometimes unreasonable demands of local pastors. He did not neglect to protect the interests of the archdiocese, however, and suggested careful scrutiny of these priests before assignment. With the clergymen he stressed his familiar message of the new pastoral and theological dimensions of the apostolate and simultaneously expounded the reasons for including all new projects under the supervision of his office.

In summary, it can be stated that in his effort to restructure the office, Stern enlarged its scope considerably. His sense of mission was basic to all his activities, so that any invitation from Stern to communicate and find spiritual support was always accompanied with a specific proposal to institutionalize relationships under the aegis of the Office for the Spanish-Speaking Apostolate. Finally, Stern's conscious projection of his role as official representative of the cardinal made it difficult to refuse his invitations to dialogue or his proposals for institutionalization. In a sense, he tried to restructure the institutional church around new values. In this, his goals were similar to those of Illich and Fox, both of whom deemphasized the Americanizing or assimilating dimension of the apostolate among the Puerto Ricans in order to stress the church's need for openness and adaptation in a pluralistic world. But, unlike these other leaders, Stern focused much of his efforts upon the institutional order of authority.

In this way Stern "routinized the charisma" of Fox and Illich (McNamara, 60–61, 155–61, 168–73.) Stern's attention to ecclesiastical structure was satisfying to his chancery superiors at first because it appeared to be compatible with their own and a departure from the charismatic style of Illich and Fox. The emphasis upon control and coordination of all aspects of church activity among the Puerto Ricans and Hispanics helped to insulate Stern from criticism. His role as a chancery official gave him a platform from which to institute needed changes as long as he maintained the cardinal's support and the credibility as his representative before the people.

In a whirlwind first year Stern reorganized the office and established so many committees responsible to him that for his "chancery within the chancery" to function, it required more resources. It should not be inferred that Stern sought control and power for himself. The premise underlying the scope of the Office of the Spanish-Speaking Apostolate was a coordinated pastoral effort. In this way he routinized the outreach to Puerto Ricans without at the same time stultifying the apostolate with the weight of bureaucracy. In the process, the chancery bureaucracy was threatened with being deroutinized by the injecting of a Latino voice. Stern's "chancery within a chancery" was the antidote to the "island within an island" that had resulted from the social distance between Puerto Rican and North American Catholics. He preserved the egalitarian social relationships advocated by Illich and Fox, but elevated the Puerto Rican and other Latino members of his committees to the level of chancery office staff. Thus, a bespectacled and gentle canon lawyer created the most revolutionary of chancery offices in the archdiocese. The effects of this gargantuan effort will be analyzed in the next chapter.

8. *The Humpty Dumpty Syndrome*

Humpty Dumpty sat on a wall;
Humpty Dumpty had a great fall;
And all the king's horses
And all the king's men
Couldn't put Humpty together again.
—Mother Goose Nursery Rhyme

The reorganization of the church and its ministries in New York was paralleled after the Council by changes in the United States Catholic Conference. In 1970 the National Bishops' Committee for the Spanish-Speaking, which had primarily focused its ministries on Mexican-American farm workers, was directed to include all the nation's Hispanics. Mr. Antonio Tinajero, out-going director of this office, met with Robert Stern in New York, apprising him of impending changes in the thrust of the national agency. He asked Stern for advice in how to include Puerto Ricans, since the archdiocese was generally seen as the most experienced in organizing the apostolate among them.

The new agency was opened in Washington in 1971, directly under the USCC Department of Social Development and World Peace. Tinajero, the social worker, was replaced with Pablo Sedillo, the executive administrator (Sandoval 1990, 71). Sedillo also turned to Stern for help in finding a Puerto Rican person as a staff member. Stern suggested Encarnación Padilla de Armas, a Puerto Rican laywoman who had been influential with Cardinal Spellman in the initial stages of the New York apostolate to the Puerto Ricans (see above, chapter 3). Puerto Rican by birth, Padilla de Armas had earned a degree in political science from the pre-revolution University of Havana. Besides her own civic and political work with the Liberal Party of New York, she had worked in journalism, social services in the city, and was widely known in community affairs. Moreover, she had traveled extensively in the

United States and abroad. After working in the Southwest for the Bishops' Committee for the Spanish-Speaking in the United States, she had been the first administrator of CIDOC, Illich's center at Cuernavaca, Mexico. Thus Padilla de Armas enjoyed a working relationship with the Mexican and Mexican-American reality as well as with the Cuban and Puerto Rican experience in New York.

At an age when many would have been looking forward to retirement, Encarnación Padilla de Armas enthusiastically assumed the challenge of working in a new national office. Besides the gifts she brought to the USCC office in Washington, her appointment gave the New York Archdiocese and Stern's office a direct voice in the conduct of national policies toward the Spanish-speaking.

Stern did not neglect the Northeast in his zeal for using official bureaucracy to a pastoral purpose. He invited directors and coordinators of the Spanish-speaking apostolates in other dioceses. By 1971 an Interdiocesan Coordinating Committee for the Spanish-Speaking Apostolate had been formed and was functioning as an institutionalized version of the 1955 conference in Puerto Rico, which had been organized by Gildea, Fitzpatrick and Illich (chapter 5). The Interdiocesan Coordinating Committee consisted of the directors of the Spanish-speaking apostolates in Bridgeport, Brooklyn, Newark, New York, Paterson, Rockville Centre, and Trenton. Boston, Camden, and Hartford also participated in its monthly meetings (Memoranda, Weekly Reports, and Minutes, 1971). Stern recognized that such extra-diocesan organizations enhanced the prestige and efficiency of his office, lending his policies wider application. His aggressive approach also gave Puerto Ricans a greater visibility at the national level of church authority, making the New York office and the Puerto Rican Catholics virtually identifiable before the national Catholic church and its agencies as the leaders of the entire northeastern part of the United States.

Stern's ambition to institutionalize a charismatic form of church reform encountered resistance from both conservatives and progressives. On the one hand, the democratic policy formation with the Spanish-speaking laity was a radical break with chancery policy in the archdiocese at the time. The laity invited to participate had generally been wealthy benefactors of the church, who did not seek an active pastoral role. In the Office of the

Spanish-Speaking Apostolate, on the other hand, persons of ordinary professional credentials—or none at all—were participating in forming church policy on the basis of deep apostolic involvement with the people. Those who objected to this mixing of ecclesiastical power and community input, both Hispanics and non-Hispanics alike, cast a wary eye on Stern's ever-increasing administrative scope. He seemed constantly to expand his compass to include virtually every facet of archdiocesan activity. With his search for Hispanic participation, he was like the Socratic "gadfly" pictured by O'Dea (1962, 23). And because his effort was couched in the bureaucratic and jurisdictional language of other canon lawyers in the chancery, it was not easily ignored. Resistance came primarily after 1970, as Stern tried to prepare a budget for his office. By controlling his funds, a short leash was put on his administrative outreach (Díaz-Ramírez, in Stevens-Arroyo 1980, 208–13).

Progressives, particularly those closely allied with Monsignor Fox, questioned whether Stern would ever be able to reform the chancery. They became skeptical of the endless meetings, which produced written plans ultimately dependent upon Cardinal Cooke's authorization. Some felt that sooner or later Stern would have to choose between the system and the people (see Stevens-Arroyo 1980, 175–79).

That confrontation came in the case of the St. Brigid's Parish experiment. The parish experiment had been designed as a trial initiation of Illich's ideas for a new kind of clergy. But the open-house atmosphere of the parish rectory and the lax manner with which priests, religious, and laity mingled made it controversial. Matters were complicated when one of the priests there was called to respond to matters of a personal nature.

Since Stern lived in St. Brigid's Parish, Cooke asked him to give an evaluation of the parish experiment. When disciplinary action was taken by the archdiocese, Fox was among those supporting the local priests; Stern was among those choosing not to support them (interview with Stern, 1981). Stern left St. Brigid's standing on the opposite side from Monsignor Fox and others who supported the experiment at St. Brigid's despite its problems.

If these frictions weakened Stern's clout among the clergy and with chancery officials, they did not dampen his outreach to the leaders working on his committees. In September of 1971 the office sponsored two workshops, one for priests and the other for the Coordinating Committee and other lay leaders. The inspiration for these workshops had come from a chance meeting by Stern with Father Edgar Beltrán, a Colombian priest who provided a window on the emerging theology of Latin America at the 1970 CICOOP convention held in Washington, D. C. Beltrán had been with the pastoral department of CELAM, the Episcopal Conference of Latin America, and served as director of the Instituto Pastoral Latinoamericano. A participant in the preparations and successful conduct of the Medellín Conference held in 1967 and 1968, he described to Stern the integration of spirituality, theology, and social analysis that had been used in Colombia to fuse together pastoral care with social concerns for the Latin American episcopacy. The experiences of Beltrán in convincing the Latin American bishops of these new ideas appealed to Stern. He saw it as an opportunity to strengthen his thrust at the institutionalization of these innovations by adding a theological legitimation.

The agenda for this meeting anticipated in the United States what was to become known as "Pastoral Encounters" (Stevens-Arroyo 1980, 146–50; 180–207; 313–33; Deck, 147–53).

> Three main themes were agreed upon for the two encuentros: ecclesiology, anthropology, and pastoral directions.... For the first one, every parish with pastoral services for Spanish-speaking was asked to send at least one priest representative; clergy from nearby dioceses in the Northeast were also invited. The workshop was attended by 94 priests and religious. It was not only successful as an enterprise for pastoral planning in the Archdiocese of New York, but it gave a stimulus to pastoral planning and collaboration on a Northeast and even national scale.
>
> It was clear that the plan would have to arise from the interest, need, and experience of local lay leaders and priests. It was decided to have two workshops to reflect on pastoral theology, planning, and goals, one for priests and another for selected lay leaders of parishes and apostolic movements (Stern 1982, 94, 95).

Forty-seven selected lay leaders participated in the second Archdiocesan Encuentro, as these workshops came to be known. The participants came chiefly from the leadership of the Cursillo, Christian Family Movement, and the Youth Movement under Fr. McCarthy González, which was the strongest movement for social justice within the apostolate at that time.

> At the conclusion of the workshop there was considerable enthusiasm about the prospect of continuing this new experience of collaboration among the various lay leaders. They decided to set apart a weekend every six months to conduct seminars for lay leaders and priests together, to request the Coordinating Committee to add the principal lay leaders of each archdiocesan movement to its membership, and to request a personal meeting of lay leaders with the Cardinal to discuss the Spanish-speaking apostolate. To implement this last decision, a special committee of eighteen persons was elected (Stern 1982, 96).

This was the first extensive involvement of grass-roots Hispanic laity in the United States with the pastoral process of Medellín that has come to be known as the theology of liberation (Stevens-Arroyo 1980, 145–50; Stevens-Arroyo and Díaz-Ramírez 1980). Although Stern was primarily interested in the New York Archdiocese, Beltrán urged him and those attending the priests' workshop to link their own vision to the needs of all the Hispanics in the United States. The value of this idea was recognized, and subsequently it was recommended to the Interdiocesan Coordinating Committee for endorsement.

The idea of a national *encuentro* took on greater impetus when the National Congress of Religious Educators, meeting in Miami that same year, stressed the need for 1) proper formation of personnel working among the Hispanic communities; 2) more Hispanic representation in the hierarchy and decision-making positions; and 3) a forum for Catholic leaders in the Hispanic communities.

In December, after consultation with Padilla de Armas, Father Stern and Father John O'Brien of the Spanish apostolate of the Brooklyn Diocese, in the name of the Interdiocesan Coordinating Committee, proposed to Paul Sedillo that a national *encuentro* be held (*Primer Encuentro Conclusions,* A. 1). In January of 1972, joining this request from the Northeast with that of the Miami congress, Sedillo forwarded the recommendation to the general secretary of the United States Catholic Conference, Bishop Joseph Bernadin. With his endorsement, the preparations for the *encuentro* were underway. A planning committee was named, holding its first meeting on February 9–10, 1972, in Chicago, which had been projected as the site for the first national assembly of Hispanic Catholics in the United States. Subsequently, it was decided to hold the *encuentro* in Washington, D. C., from June 19 to 22, 1972. Through the help of Padilla de Armas, the facilities of Trinity College in Washington, D. C., were secured (Stern 1982, 94–96).

Stern's advice and participation were instrumental throughout the process of the *encuentro.* The imprint of his experience in the New York Office of the Spanish-Speaking Apostolate and his vision of the mission of church clearly is shown in the documents that reflect the purpose, planning, and conclusions of the *encuentro.* The general thrust of the national assembly was identical with the *encuentros* that had been celebrated so successfully in New York. "The Encuentro is not a conference, but an extended workshop; its style will be participatory. Its specific purpose is to analyze the present pastoral situation in the Hispanic community and to discuss possible solutions to the many problems that exist" (*Primer Encuentro Conclusions,* B. 1).

Stern's focus upon planning for all aspects of the apostolate is reflected in the general organization of the national meeting. Each of seven workshops was to "be initiated by the presentation of a working document by a qualified and experienced person in that field." Perhaps most important, the approbation of the bishops was carefully sought, and it was clearly stated that the deliberations of the *encuentro* would be "made available to the National Conference of Catholic Bishops and local dioceses for their consideration and implementation" (*Primer Encuentro Conclusions,* B. 1).

One of the results of the lay leadership *encuentro* of September 1971 in the archdiocese was a decision to request a meeting with Cardinal Cooke. Stern knew that such a meeting with the lay leadership could not easily be refused by the cardinal and that the matters discussed would have to go beyond a mere repetition of administrative details. Stern had frequently been hindered in his efforts to expand services and hire staff by the restrictions of budgetary decisions imposed by chancery officials. A meeting between the cardinal and the lay leaders would offer direct communication with the head of the archdiocese, so that any favorable decisions about policy would implicitly carry with them the authorization for funds to implement the plans (Díaz-Ramírez, in Stevens-Arroyo 1980, 208–13; Stern 1982, 104–14). The apostolate leaders hoped that the dialogue with the cardinal would articulate the theological goals they had developed in the archdiocesan *encuentro.*

Beltrán imparted a sense of urgency to the formulation of the requests for pastoral participation and imbued the elected delegates with a keen perception of their responsibility fraternally to call the cardinal's attention to the unfulfilled needs of the Puerto Rican and Hispanic people. A letter detailing all these issues was sent on March 13, 1972, requesting an interview, which was granted on Wednesday of Holy Week, March 29, 1972. The letter began by pointing out to the cardinal that although "the overwhelming majority of the Spanish-speaking migrants here arrive in New York as Catholics," many subsequently turned to Protestantism because the Protestant churches seem better equipped and willing to serve "the Spanish community with their own Spanish-speaking pastor" (letter to Cardinal Cooke, March 13, 1972). The letter continued by giving an assessment of the archdiocesan apostolate:

> In our archdiocese at this time approximately one half of the Catholics are Spanish-speaking. Of the 407 parishes of the archdiocese, 97 provide services in Spanish. Among the over 1,100 diocesan priests, 134 speak some Spanish and for 4 of them, it is their native language. In parishes staffed by religious orders there are 88 Spanish-speaking priests, 16 of them native speakers. In addition there are 76 native Spanish-speaking priests working in our parishes, although for the most part, they are considered visitors to the archdiocese.

According to the letter the problem was not only that there were relatively few priests to care for the Hispanic Catholics of the archdiocese, but also that when it came to decision-making positions they were even less proportionately represented:

> Of the 7 bishops who are actively serving the archdiocese, none speaks Spanish fluently. The Vicar General does not speak Spanish, nor do any of the Episcopal Vicars; only one of the heads of an administrative department is fluent in Spanish. Of the 49 priests who comprise your Senate, 9 are Spanish-speaking, none is of Hispanic origin. In parishes, there are only 39 Spanish-speaking pastors, 3 of whom are of Hispanic origin and belong to religious communities as well.

The letter draws two conclusions: 1) "Pastoral care of our people is overwhelmingly in the hands of associate pastors and visiting and extra-diocesan priests . . . the latter being almost totally without voice and suffering many forms of discrimination within the clergy"; and 2) "It is evident that in our Archdiocese the major resources of manpower, money and service are in favor of what is numerically becoming the minority population in our local Church, the non-Hispanic Catholic" (letter to Cardinal Cooke, 1972).

The letter also engaged in its own interpretation of the historical process of immigration and church response:

> Our migration to New York is the first great non-European migration and the first to come unaccompanied by a native clergy. Historically in former migrations, that clergy assumed a role of leadership for the migrant community, not only with regards to the religious ministry, but in the whole process of the development of the migrant. The present structures of the New York Church were developed in response to the needs of a particular people and in the past served well that people. Our presence in New York without our own clergy has presented a new challenge to this Church, one that to date has not been adequately responded to. We are Hispano-Americans and we are Catholics. We believe that, although what has been done is insufficient, it is possible to mobilize the resources of the Church in the city to further the development of our people as human beings and as children of God (letter to Cardinal Cooke, 1972).

What follows is a list of petitions that were proposed as "a first step towards achieving this goal and as a sign of hope and leadership":

1. That an Episcopal Vicar for the Spanish-speaking be appointed with the consultation of the Coordinating Committee of the Spanish-Speaking Apostolate and that the person chosen be Spanish-speaking, totally identified with the Spanish people and their culture, and have all those faculties expressed and implied by such a position in accordance with Canon Law.
2. That on the next occasion of appointment of a Vicar General, a Spanish-speaking priest be named.
3. That the Vicar General and the Episcopal Vicar for the Spanish-speaking consult and work closely with the Coordinating Committee of the Spanish-Speaking Apostolate in all matters affecting the Spanish-speaking community of the Archdiocese.
4. That on the next occasion of appointment of new Auxiliary Bishops in recognition of the Spanish-speaking community at least one of them be of Hispanic origin and experienced in pastoral work in New York and that this appointment be made

> with the consultation of the Spanish-speaking community through the Coordinating Committee of the Spanish-Speaking Apostolate (letter to Cardinal Cooke, 1972).

This was the letter that brought the commission of eleven persons to the meeting with the cardinal which took place on March 29, 1972, and lasted two and one-half hours (Fontánez 1972a). Besides the four points specified in the letter, the participants discussed the role of the Office of the Spanish-Speaking Apostolate; the participation of Hispanics in decision- and policy-making; the further development of Hispanic leaders; the need for accommodating the diaconate program to the situation of Hispanics; the preparation of seminarians for the Spanish-speaking apostolate; the need for Hispanic religious vocations and the reasons for the lack of them; and the educational needs of Hispanics in Catholic schools. Two other topics of interest were discrimination from pastors toward Hispanic clergy and laity and the availability of the cardinal for communication and consultation (Stern 1982, 102, 103).

Ten years later Stern put forth a most optimistic interpretation of the meeting:

> The meeting was a very positive one. For the first time the Archbishop of New York heard directly from the leaders of New York's Hispanic Catholics and heard both their gratitude for the archdiocese's pastoral, educational, and charitable services to them and their desire to share greater responsibility for the Church in New York and to participate in making decisions about it. The meeting symbolized a coming of age and, in that sense, the fulfillment of Cardinal Cooke's mandate to develop lay leaders. The Hispanic Catholics of the Church of New York wished to exercise leadership, not just be a client population; in the words of the Gospel, they wished not to be served, but to serve! (Stern 1982, 102, 103).

On the surface the recommendations made by the Hispanics to the cardinal may seem predominantly of an administrative nature. The process by which they were formulated and presented to the cardinal, and the projections for future decision-making, however, contained a distinct theological vision—one that Illich had begun to articulate in the 1950s. This vision called for collegiality, not only among members of the clergy, but included lay leaders and grass-roots communities. Responsibility for the decision-making process of the church was to be shared at all membership levels. The political and social awareness of Fox was also there. However, the focus upon canonical authority, so that Hispanics had the power to replace traditional policy and decision-making structures with new ones, came from Stern. Thus, while Illich and Fox had to work with policies of coexistence with ecclesiastical institutions far from the direct reach of the laity, under Stern's administration the Hispanic laity had "come of age" and in a sense surpassed its non-Hispanic or Anglo counterpart by directly approaching the cardinal and asking for direct and real participation in the decisions henceforth to be made involving Hispanic lives within the church.

If the Cardinal had granted the Hispanics these requests through the Office of the Spanish-Speaking Apostolate and its Coordinating Committee, it might have given them the legitimacy to ask for a far greater share of responsibility in the archdiocesan decision-making process than ever afforded any group within the church. This would have also meant a shift of services and concerns, since a more proportional redistribution of personnel, funds, and overall resources would have been the logical consequence. Moreover, as the NCCB's 1976 Call to Action Conference in Detroit and the Bicentennial Hearings that preceded it later demonstrated, what was happening with the Hispanics could easily set the norm for all the faithful (Stevens-Arroyo, 1990; cf. Varacalli). In other words, the cardinal's response to the Hispanics' requests in New York (which shortly afterward would be mirrored in the conclusions of the First National Hispanic Encounter) could have far-reaching consequences beyond the archdiocese and the Catholic Hispanic community. But while Hispanics and non-Hispanics alike were asking for a greater voice in their church, it was the Hispanics who had initiated the process and set the tone. In the hierarchy's mind perhaps this was part of the "problem."

Much was at stake, and the meeting was charged with tension, producing anxiety among all the participants, including the cardinal. Stern states:

> In the course of the meeting it became clear that there were different expectations about its purposes and mutual suspicions about motivations among its participants, but they were success-

> fully brought to light and discussed. On the part of the delegation, because of the long and till then inconclusive study of reorganization of the Spanish apostolate by the Vicar General, there were some suspicions about the sincerity and good will of the archdiocesan authorities. As far as the Cardinal was concerned, although the background and preparations for the meeting had been reported in the minutes of the monthly meeting of the Coordinating Committee, the weekly memoranda giving a report on the Spanish-Speaking Apostolate to the administrative staff heads of the Archdiocese, and the monthly newsletter of the Spanish Office as well as discussed personally beforehand with the Vicar General, he appeared suspicious of the motives of the letter and of the delegation and, occasionally, annoyed at the points of view raised (Stern 1982, 102; also see Fontánez 1972).

No immediate response to the requests was given, and as the date for the national *encuentro* in Washington approached, both sides saw prudence in awaiting the outcome of the Washington assembly before turning attention once again to the archdiocesan matter. In a sense, the meeting had produced a stalemate. Stern and the commission members believed that if Hispanics nationwide articulated similar demands, the archdiocese would be forced into going along with the commission's petition at the local level. Those around Cardinal Cooke, on the other hand, felt that Stern had gone too far in presenting not a petition, but a list of demands.

It proved particularly unsettling to those around the cardinal that the social distance between clergy and the laity had been compromised, so that the frankness of the leaders during the meeting seemed an affront to the dignity of the cardinal and of his clerical assistants. The politics of confrontation of minority groups against "the white establishment" was being introduced within the bosom of the archdiocese in the chancery. Unacquainted with how well the pastoral and theological development of the laity in the Coordinating Committee had succeeded, it was hard for those around the cardinal to believe that the letter or the arguments presented orally were spontaneous. It must have appeared to them that the committee had been rehearsed for the meeting by Stern. Moreover, it is likely that the request for a Spanish-speaking auxiliary bishop (which was not the same as a request for a *native* Hispanic) seemed part of a campaign to make

Stern a bishop for the Spanish-speaking. There were others close to Cooke who desired that role.[1] It seemed advisable for the chancery to send its own representatives to the *encuentro* as a means of defusing the threat.

It should have surprised no one that the national *encuentro,* which had taken so much of its impetus from Stern's vision and Beltrán's workshop, reflected in its conclusions the basic requests presented by the archdiocesan commission to the cardinal. The same thrust, officially sanctioned by a national assembly, gave legitimation to the programs of Stern's office (Stevens-Arroyo 1980, 197–201). The conclusions called for "a reorganization of the structure of the United States Catholic Conference and of the National Conference of Catholic Bishops and the creation of several new national institutions." A plea for cultural sensitivity and an integrated pastoral plan was also made and Stern's focus on authority repeated.

> A pastoral plan for Spanish-speaking Catholics is necessarily concerned with the structures and institutions of the Church at the national, regional, diocesan and local level; with the recruitment, development and coordination of Christian and apostolic leadership; with the quality of prayer, celebration and formation and schooling; and with particular social and economic challenges faced by our Spanish-speaking people (*Primer Encuentro Conclusions,* J. 3).

The *encuentro* departed from the institutional arguments of Stern to introduce language borrowed from PADRES, the national association of Mexican-American priests. The focus upon secular and political struggles for leadership was extended to the authority structures of the Catholic church. The addresses given at the *encuentro* and the conclusions stated that those best suited for ministry to Hispanics are Hispanics themselves. When they are not available, then candidates who can identify with the Hispanic culture and community must be sought. In all cases it is imperative that Hispanic culture and community should have representation in proportion to their numbers so that their voice may be heard within the church (*Primer Encuentro Conclusions,* J. 3.; also see Stevens-Arroyo 1980, 178–79).[2]

> A first priority of the American hierarchy should be the recruitment and ordination of Spanish-speaking bishops in such numbers

> that the percentage of Spanish-speaking ordinaries in the Catholic Church in the United States is in proportion to the percentage of the Spanish-speaking Catholics in the American Church (*Primer Encuentro Conclusions,* J. 4).

Moreover, the church was expected to take the Hispanic questions seriously enough so that "a special and major portion of the funds, facilities and properties of the United States Catholic Conference and the National Conference of Catholic Bishops should be deployed in the services of the Spanish-speaking" (*Primer Encuentro Conclusions,* J. 4). It was recommended that the Division for the Spanish-Speaking be elevated in status so that it would be placed directly under the general secretary of the conference "with the mission of assisting him to promote and coordinate attention to Spanish-Speaking Catholics in all the departments, divisions, programs and institutions of the United States Catholic Conference." Finally, the National Bishops' Committee for the Spanish-Speaking was to have a bishop of Hispanic origin named as its chairman with the task of making "the entire hierarchy more aware of and concerned with the needs of the Spanish-speaking Catholics" (*Primer Encuentro Conclusions,* J. 3).

A national training center was sought, which would in turn engender regional centers for pastoral research and study; for the linguistic, cultural and pastoral formation of ministers; and for the diffusion of information about pastoral theology, methods, resources, and experiences. The legacy of Illich, Fitzpatrick, and Fox was evident in the centrality afforded Hispanic culture as a positive value.

> In education and formation, a harmonious and organic development of each person demands a respect for, understanding of, and realization of the potentialities of the culture and society in which he lives and from which he has sprung. The right development of Spanish-speaking Christian leadership necessitates appropriate institutional forms. This criterion is not separatist but unifying. True integration is achieved when diverse groups are at positions of relatively equal strength and prestige and have mutual respect. Attempted integration of minorities into majorities prematurely results in an undesirable assimilation, not integration. Such assimilation means cultural absorption or, from the other point of view, cultural domination and replaces the mutual enrichment which is the fruit of true integration (*Primer Encuentro Conclusions,* J. 1).

Local pastors and priests were cautioned not to disregard or show disrespect for "the linguistic, cultural, and religious expressions of the Spanish-speaking . . . for . . . integration should not be confused with assimilation" (*Primer Encuentro Conclusions,* J. 6). Furthermore, the democratization of decision-making through committees, regional *encuentros,* and mixed teams or *equipos* of clergy, religious, and laity was suggested as the controlling authority for the apostolate at all levels.

These recommendations were clearly even more ambitious than the four recommendations that had been made to Cardinal Cooke in March. Implementation of the conclusions was essential to Stern's administration of the office. And if what the national *encuentro* had recommended was implemented, the parallel requests of the commission at the archdiocesan level could not be ignored. Unlike Illich and Fox, who were accustomed to carry on the achievement of their vision outside archdiocesan structures, Stern had made internal change an essential part of his apostolate.

Conflict developed between Stern and chancery officials over the *encuentro* conclusions. On the grounds that the conclusions were not official until reviewed by a special committee of the national conference, Stern was prohibited from publishing the text of the *encuentro* documents. This position was a use of canon law to torpedo the momentum given to Stern's efforts by the generally favorable response nationwide to the *encuentro.*

Stern, and others like him, on the other hand, believed that the voice of the people was a share in ecclesiastical authority: *Vox populi, vox Dei.* The National Conference eventually did respond, and its decisions were included as part of the proceedings of the national *encuentro*—but the long wait for the document to clear official channels delayed any action on the requests of the archdiocesan commission.

Despite these looming difficulties, Stern's ambitious two-year effort at restructuring the Office of the Spanish-Speaking Apostolate was virtually complete and had been extremely productive. Looked at from today's perspectives, Stern had made the Coordinating Committee and the archdiocesan commission that sprang from it into a tightly knit ecclesial community, an archdiocesan *comunidad de base.*

The successes of the group's members in gradually coming to grips with their diversity and the need for communal action followed the prescriptions of Gramsci for his "modern prince" (see chapter 5). Each Hispanic member of the committee was an organic leader, tied by work and experience to the parishes and the movements within the Spanish-speaking community of New York. Stern had not told them what to say or what to think, but he had created the opportunity for the members to recognize that an alternative society and church were possible.

The Coordinating Committee had realized Gramsci's democratic centralism, which "requires an organic unity between theory and practice, between intellectual strata and popular masses, between rulers and ruled" (Gramsci, 190). Gramsci's description of a successful movement seems applicable to the Coordinating Committee after the meeting with the cardinal and the triumph of the national *encuentro*.

> This leadership was not "abstract"; it neither consisted in mechanically repeating scientific or theoretical formulae, nor did it confuse politics, real action, with theoretical disquisition. It applied itself to real men, formed in specific historical relations, with specific feelings, outlooks, fragmentary conceptions of the world, etc., which are the result of "spontaneous" combinations . . . of disparate social elements. This element of "spontaneity" was not neglected and even less despised. It was educated, directed, purged of extraneous contaminations; the aim was to bring it into line with modern theory—but in a living and historically effective manner. The leaders themselves spoke of the "spontaneity" of the movement, and rightly so. This assertion was a stimulus, a tonic, an element of unification in depth; above all it denied that the movement was arbitrary, a cooked-up venture, and stressed its historical necessity. It gave the masses a "theoretical" consciousness of being creators of historical and institutional values, of being founders (Gramsci, 198).

Stern's superiors decided to counteract the deroutinizing reforms he had slipped into the chancery under the guise of better administration of the apostolate. They adopted strategies not unlike those described by Dworkin and Dworkin (see above, chapter 1) for a majority's control of a minority. They began by reinterpreting the conclusions in order to divide the Coordinating Committee. The divisions among *cursillistas* and progressives, between secular and religious order clergy, the ethnic differences among Puerto Ricans, Cubans, Dominicans, and Spaniards had been remedied in part by the positive experiences of the Coordinating Committee. But the potential to reawaken these differences remained. Moreover, since most members were representatives of movements, appointing new leaders who had not experienced the process would undercut the cohesiveness Stern had accomplished so dramatically.

Time and delay have always been on the side of bureaucracies, and Stern was asked for more and more reports, thus distracting him and dissipating his energies. When James P. Mahoney was named vicar general of the archdiocese in the late spring of 1971, he required Father Stern to review and revise the plans for the office. This resulted in a plethora of inconclusive meetings and exchanged memoranda for the next year and a half (Stern 1982, 104–16). Budget battles continued unabated, causing an endless shuffle of papers. The "chancery within the chancery" was required to compete bureaucratically against the whole institution, which possessed much greater resources. And this took place against the "ticking clock" of Stern's appointment as director, which was due to end after three years—in September of 1972.

The final strategy was to reduce the staff of the Office of the Spanish-Speaking Apostolate. For example, the vicar general of the Archdiocese of New York transferred the staff members of Stern's communications division to the Office of Communications of the archdiocese. This move was ostensibly to strengthen the Hispanic role in the communications operations of the archdiocese, as suggested in the *encuentro* conclusions. But such a transfer served to dilute the ability of the office to coordinate activities (Díaz-Ramírez, in Stevens-Arroyo 1980, 212; Stern 1982, 113–16). An Office of Pastoral Planning was created under Father Philip Murnion, who had a following with the progressive priests and religious close to Fox. Thus Stern was outflanked by the same organizational strategy he had used to challenge the chancery.

When appointments were made to archdiocesan posts, Hispanics and Spanish-speaking priests who had not participated directly in Stern's reorganization efforts were chosen; some indeed, had no previous record of leadership among the Hispanic community. Thus, while some of the changes sought by Stern were made, the personnel chosen were not his collaborators. Instead of providing greater cohesiveness to the implementation of a comprehensive vision of apostolate, these appointments only served to dilute further the office functions. Appointments to the liturgical committee and the naming of a vicar for Hispanic affairs without consulting or informing Stern or the Coordinating Committee may be considered in this light. Such administrative steps altered the flow of communication between the Hispanic people and the office, creating new agencies and personalities that rivaled the organic approach to mission Stern had initiated.

The archdiocese delegitimated the organic leadership by using ethnic identity against the community's petitions. This is the so-called Simmons Law whereby "The bureaucracy tends to reward those Hispanics who are most like themselves in ideas and Action patterns" (see Stevens-Arroyo 1980, 97). The claim of ethnic identity became a negative tool against the needs of the community in a process of co-optation of leadership (see Stevens-Arroyo 1980, 197–201).

With the fragmentation of the responsibilities of the office and the creation of rival groups and personalities for claims to represent the Hispanics, Stern began to lose the clout as administrator that had supplemented his non-charismatic leadership. Stern's word was no longer seen as that of the cardinal. Traditionalists, such as some of the Spanish priests in the *Asociación de Sacerdotes Hispanos* (ASH), focused only on those *encuentro* conclusions that coincided with their interests, while downplaying others that gave a role to lay leadership. For instance, the association opposed the creation of a permanent diaconate in the archdiocese (conversation with Father Luis Alvarez of ASH, December 1973).

More progressive or liberal Catholics, such as those in the Youth Movement, wanted stronger action from Stern to bring about the implementation of the *encuentro* conclusions. But at the same time, the Dominicans who dominated the Central Team that directed the youth movement, *Equipos Unidos,* began to quarrel among themselves over an outreach toward Puerto Rican youth. This dispute introduced into the Coordinating Committee friction between Dominicans and Puerto Ricans.

The majority of lay persons, mostly Puerto Rican members of the Cursillo Movement, tended to wait for the cardinal to call a second meeting with the delegation of March 1972, a meeting which was never held. In the meantime, the vicar general, Monsignor James P. Mahoney, informed Father Stern that all the deliberations of the previous year had been reversed in favor of a new approach.

> He [Monsignor Mahoney] now envisaged two distinct positions: one, a vice-chancellor with responsibility for matters concerning parishes, clergy and canonical affairs; the other, a coordinator of programs of apostolic formation. He suggested that Fr. Stern take the latter position, which was a complete reversal of the plans made to date (Stern 1982, 115).

Stern was offered a pastorate, which he refused. Then, on August 24, the vicar general told Stern that the training of the laity would be taken over by the seminary. Finally, on August 30, 1972, Cardinal Cooke informed Father Stern that he would be reappointed as director of the Office for the Spanish-Speaking Apostolate for another three years (Stern 1982, 116). Yet this was a Pyhrric victory, because three months later the chancery dismissed the official translator of the archdiocese. The transfer of this woman from Father Stern's office, where she had been his administrative coordinator, to the Office of Communications was supposed to represent the commitment of the archdiocese to putting persons of Hispanic background into every agency and department of the chancery. It was on this premise that Stern had acquiesced to the dismemberment of his office. Now the director of the Office of Communications argued that there were insufficient materials to be translated into Spanish in the archdiocese to justify a full-time translator (Stern 1982, 117 n. 160). Moreover, the dismissal was to take effect on December 8, without severance pay or the customary Christmas bonus.

Stern (1982, 116–19) details the fallout from this dismissal.[3] The Coordinating Committee objected in the most strenuous terms and the matter was finally taken to the Pastoral Renewal Committee of the Archdiocesan Priests' Senate, where the translation policy of the chancery was called into question. The humiliation of the dismissal, however, was only the culmination of the process of undoing what Stern had created. I have summarized the process in another place, and it bears repeating here.

> Father Stern wanted to expand the office; his budget was not approved. Father Stern gave the services of his secretary, administrator, and translator to the Communications Office at the insistence of Monsignor Mahoney, and the Communications Office dismissed

> her without consulting either her or Father Stern about the cause of the dismissal. Father Stern began a special program in Dunwoodie Seminary in language, culture and pastoral ministry to Hispanos, and the seminary was put in charge of it even though nobody at the seminary was prepared for such a task. Father Stern tried to employ Puerto Rican priests, and he as well as they met with a lot of difficulties; as a result neither Father Stern nor the four Puerto Rican priests presently work in the office. Father Stern tried to coordinate the Institute of Intercultural Communication more effectively; the Cardinal insisted that the institute was not the responsibility of the office and passed it over to the supervision of the Catholic University of Puerto Rico. Father Stern tried to improve the Migrant Ministry, seeking the naming of a diocesan priest to this post and a new religious congregation to help him; but in the first months, the Archdiocese irresponsibly did not pay either the priest or the religious, forcing them to beg for voluntary contributions (Díaz-Ramírez, in Stevens-Arroyo 1980, 211–12).

With a decreasing staff and funds, with a divided constituency and antagonistic rivals, and the effort to destroy his credibility, Stern recognized it was impossible to continue working as head of the office and resigned in February of 1973, convinced "that he had outstayed his usefulness in the post and lacked that confidence of his superiors that he felt necessary to his continuance" (Stern 1982, 118–19; see Anson, 29–33).

The Office for the Spanish-Speaking Apostolate continued after Stern's departure, but it was substantially reduced in scope. With the foundation of the Northeast Pastoral Office in 1974, the regional and national stature of the office was subsumed. The naming of bishops McCarrick and Garmendia in 1977, neither of whom had been a part of the Coordinating Committee, dissipated the plea for episcopal representation. *Equipos Unidos,* the archdiocesan youth movement, was disbanded, and a new movement allied to the Cursillo was founded. Finally, a sociological survey was ordered to set a pastoral plan based on scientific data about the Spanish-speaking in the archdiocese. By that time the organic leadership function of the Coordinating Committee was totally destroyed and virtually all of its original members were gone.

These administrative changes completely undid the work of Stern, and in a sense, of Fox and Illich before him. Like Humpty-Dumpty, it is unlikely that any subsequent effort can ever repair the damage done to the office. Yet in a deeper sense, what happened to the office harmed the archdiocese as well. It lost prestige and influence at a time when the apostolate to Latinos was growing in importance. Indeed, it is estimated that by the year 2000, half of the Catholics in the United States will be of Hispanic origin (González 1988, 9–12; Stevens-Arroyo 1990).

Instead of standing among the vanguard of such an important ministry, the archdiocese surrendered the leadership Stern had brought by his administration of Illich's and Fox's ideas. Like the cane-worker impaired in the plantations of my homeland, the archdiocese had severed its index finger—the one pointing the way to a new path. And like the fingerless *jíbaro,* the New York church must bear the scars of its decision. In the concluding chapter I will attempt to explain sociologically the factors that led the institution to so wound itself.

9. Escape from Experimentation: Conciliar Reform as an Institutional Process

Cambió la gente, cambió el mar, cambió el aire. . . . ¿Tú ves? Si un cambio así viniera de golpe una se asustaría y le daría tiempo pa huir. Pero cuando el cambio viene poquito a poco, una se acostumbra, una también cambia, y entonseh no hay manera de escapar.

The people changed, the sea changed, the air changed. . . . You see? If a change like that had come all of a sudden you would have been startled and it would have given you time to escape. But when the change comes little by little, you get used to it, you yourself change and then there is no way to escape.

—Doña Isa in Act II

In 1970 noted sociologist of religion Robert Bellah wrote, "Systematic analysis [of religious institutions] is still in its infancy. I have relatively little to contribute on this point" (Bellah, 272). Nearly a decade later the late Barbara Hargrove was able to include an entire chapter on study of the institutional churches in her important study, *The Sociology of Religion* (251–68). She noted that the parameters of this study were undergoing rapid and radical revision.

> In recent years new perspectives have emerged in the sociology of religion that reflect both a greater recognition of the organizational nature of religious institutions and a growing sophistication of the discipline in the study of organizations of all kinds. Questions have been raised concerning the utility of such complex and relatively static concepts as those of "church," "sect," and "cult." Instead, some developments have begun that would bring into the sociology of religion insights from other areas, particularly those that

> would study religious organizations on the basis of "open-systems" models (Hargrove, 251).

She frames her survey of the literature by citing James Beckford's (1973) four important variables: social environment, resources, processes, and structures.

Most of the studies cited by Hargrove focus upon parish studies, thus reducing the institution in question to the smallest of church units. She does highlight McNamara's work upon the role of clerical leadership on behalf of the apostolate among the Mexican-Americans (Hargrove, 258) in substantiating Beckford's finding that "religious groups that make strenuous attempts to maximize their recruitment or to produce major changes in the outside world are highly susceptible to environmental influence" (Hargrove, 251). In the case of the priests among the Mexican-American farm workers, their relatively low position in the organizational structure of Catholicism greatly limited their effort at change.

My own focus, it should be clear, is not upon the parish but upon the complex institutional process within the New York Catholic Archdiocese that fosters, thwarts, experiments with, or rejects adaptations to the social environment. The most satisfying of studies that address Catholicism at this level are typological studies of Latin America and Europe. Before constructing my own model of institutional change to explain the impact of the Puerto Rican migration upon the New York Archdiocese, I would like to review three important contributions that have shaped my own thinking. Initially, I had hoped to find among them one that would adequately explain the historical data and the social processes that took place during the period 1950 to 1972 in the Catholic Archdiocese of New York. But for reasons that I will explain, it was necessary to devise a new model.

The first typology considered was that of Ivan Vallier as developed in his book *Catholicism, Social Control and Modernization in Latin America*, published in 1970. This study opened up to sociologists of religion the richness of Latin American Catholicism from a cross-cultural and institutional perspective. While many will agree that the last twenty years have seen an improvement on Vallier's method, they will equally be in accord that his conceptual approach to the study of competing clerical elites, institutional goals, and evolving socio-economic conditions provided an important advance to the field of sociology of religion and that of institutions and processes. Not only has Vallier's study benefited cross-national analysis of Catholicism in Latin America, but it has also been applied to the Dutch Catholic church.

Vallier's typology (Figure 8) offers five stages of development in the Latin American church. The first stage, *Monopoly,* characterized by the clergy's role as civil bureaucrats or employees of the state, is a situation not applicable in the United States. At this stage the church's base of control and influence is dependent upon the clergy's relationship to upper-status individuals whose interests are represented by the government.

In the second stage, *Political,* the church assumes a posture of defense in alliance with the conservative elites when its formal guarantees and monopoly position are threatened. The infringement upon its privileges is seen as an attack on the religious system. Thus, the energies of church elites are concentrated on political activity directly connected to Catholic interests.

The third stage is *Missionary.* This mode insulates Catholics from secular forces by providing an outward but supervised missionary emphasis where sponsorship of trade unions, mutual benefit associations, youth programs, professional societies, and schools is provided. A subculture develops in which the clergy's role is diminished and the expansion of Catholic values is given as charge to a nuclear group of lay persons trained in a variety of specifically Catholic solutions to social, economic, and political problems. A major problem is the threat of "contamination" of the membership by secular values and a weakening of the importance of sacramental life.

The fourth stage, *Social Development,* is marked by the church's effort to gain generalized visibility as it leaves behind particularistic political ties and appeals to underprivileged groups. Working for secular social change to benefit the poor, it frees itself from conservative groups and identifies with universal values acceptable to all modern groups. Society's rather than the church's interests are sought, and the clergy are active agents in achieving change.

The fifth stage, *Cultural-Pastoral,* is characterized by advocacy in society for a higher moral order. This call is issued at a cultural level, which emphasizes the contemporary needs of all

Figure 8

Vallier's Church Types and Influence Systems Paradigm

Type	STAGE I "Monopoly"	STAGE II "Political"	STAGE III "Missionary"	STAGE IV "Social Development"	STAGE V "Cultural-Pastoral"
1. Level of ambition	high	high	high	high	high
2. Church-society relationship	structural fusion	opposition and dependency	separation and controlled contact	public involvement	integrated autonomy
3. Major basis of influence	total institutional complex	coalitions with traditional elite	differentiated Catholic organizations	social action programs among marginal strata	socio-ethical leadership
4. Secondary base of influence	ritual monopoly	clerical threats; withholding of sacraments	ideological formation	mass media	local church
5. Target group	total population	aristocracy	workers and middle-class	*campesinos* and urban poor	"other person"
6. Dominant Ideology	territorial expansion and consolidation	defeat political opposition	block or overcome secularization	provide religious basis for change	pluralist participation
7. Religious action principle	diffuse control	defense of privilege	penetration of strategic secular sphere	solution of social problems	secular involvement
8. Priest's primary roles	ritual agent and civil servant	patron and/or politician	missionary and militan organizer	program developer and agent of change	pastor and spiritual leader
9. Organizational mode	segmental	coalitional	grass-roots missions	mobilization	national unity; co-ordinated microunits
10. Layman's role	ritual client	faithful follower	hierarchical auxiliary	participating colleague	Christian-citizen

Source: Ivan Vallier, *Catholocism, Social Control and Modernization in Latin America* (Englewood Cliffs, N.J.: Prentice-Hall. 1970), p. 72.

persons, whether Catholic or not. At the institutional level this approach sponsors programs of public assistance and social development in spheres not handled by the government. Vallier cross-tabulates these five stages with ten factors: 1) level of church ambition; 2) church-society relationship; 3) major basis of influence; 4) secondary basis of influence; 5) target group; 6) dominant ideology; 7) religious action principles; 8) priest's primary roles; 9) organizational mode; and 10) layman's role (Figure 8 above).

Vallier's five types describe the perceptions of Roman Catholicism in action rather than the theoretical possibilities in an institution undergoing change. For this reason Vallier was unable to predict the impact that the theology of liberation would have in Latin America subsequent to his study, predicting instead that it would not be of great consequence (Vallier 1970, 156–59).

John Coleman's work, *The Evolution of Dutch Catholicism, 1958–1974,* adapts Vallier's work to study the church in the Netherlands (Figure 9). Coleman is successful in describing the events and forces that expanded the power potential of the Dutch church and made it so important to the conciliar period. He dovetails the social variables that affect the background of key episcopal leaders with the forces of change in Dutch society during the postwar prosperity, and thus attempts to emphasize a dynamism in church policy that a definition of ideal types based on theology alone would not have accomplished.

Coleman employs a theoretical perspective in sociology that views collectivities as problem-solving entities similar to individuals who usually do not search for problems, but when confronted with one that persists, are forced first to recognize it and then seek out a solution (Coleman, 4). Thus, most solutions are found by trial and error through collective experimenting. At the beginning the problem is at the "prosaic, pragmatic level of adaptive behavior," so that old solutions are applied until it is realized that a failure to find a better solution threatens the cores of the institution itself. However, when an adequate solution is found "they tend to lock onto it and generalize and perpetuate it as long as it works." Due to the dialectic nature of social life, "any collective solution to a problem," says Coleman, "has built into it potential new strains, conflicts and problems" (Coleman, 4). The resisting, conservative nature of collectivism justifies fundamen-

Figure 9

Pre-Vatican and Post-Vatican Structure

Factors	Missionary Strategy	Cultural-Pastoral Strategy
1. Level of church ambition	High	High
2. Church-society relationship	Separation and controlled contact	Integrated autonomy
3. Major base of influence	Differentiated Catholic organizations	Socio-ethical leadership
4. Secondary base of influence	Ideological formation	Local congregation
5. Target group	Workers and middle-class within Catholic population; converts	Intellectuals and youth within Catholic population; general "other person" within society
6. Dominant ideology	Block or overcome secularization	Pluralist participation
7. Religious action principle	Penetration of strategic secular spheres *en bloc*	Secular involvement
8. Priest's primary role	Missionary and militant organizer, political middleman for Catholic economic minority	Pastor and spiritual leader
9. Organizational mode	Grassroots missions and Catholic action cells coupled with decentralized pastoral units	National unit and coordinated micro-units at congregational level
10. Layman's role	Hierarchical auxiliary; agent of the bishop	Christian citizen

Source: John A. Colemen, *The Evolution of Dutch Catholicism, 1958–1974* (Berkeley: University of California Press, 1978), p. 12.

tal redefinition of the social structure only when change seems imperative and any attempt to restrict its extent brings about mounting pressure resulting in persistent and increasing threat.

This concern for problem-solving within an institution led Coleman to include in his study of Dutch Catholicism Smelser's understanding of differentiation in the study of social movements (Smelser, 79). There a sevenfold sequence of change is proposed, which Coleman adapts for his own study (Figure 10). Accordingly, in stage one detection of the problem, symptoms of dissatisfaction with the performance of incumbents or with the organization of roles within the institution arises. In stage two symptoms of disturbance, protest, or calls for change are made evident. In stage three the problem is held at bay by handling and channeling the symptoms of disturbance. In other words, the first line of defense of agencies of control is a kind of holding action. According to Smelser and Coleman, the institution attempts to contain the disturbances caused by dissatisfaction.

At stage four, however, the problem is analyzed. The collectivity finally encourages the new ideas that purport to deal with the problem. At stage five a proposal is made, that is, the collectivity attempts to specify the institutional forms that will ease the dissatisfaction. At the level of essay and evaluation, stage six, the collectivity attempts to establish new institutional forms. Stage seven calls for locking-in, and consensus becomes apparent. Here the new forms of collective action are consolidated within the institution as permanent features.

With this addition of Smelser's model, Coleman's typology is not only able to label the differences and changes taking place within the institution, but also shed some light on how they are treated at diverse levels of institutional authority. He also suggests that problems, when solved, become part of the structural response of institutions. What his model does not provide (and Coleman admits to this) is a clue as to why the structural changes take the particular content and direction they do.

Another limitation is that while Coleman's typology well describes the institutional process, it offers no linkage between existing conflict and its theological expression. In the case of the Archdiocese of New York and the Puerto Rican community, Coleman's typology is not useful in demonstrating that not only the institution's mode of action was altered by the Puerto Rican

Figure 10

Sequence of Change in Institutions or Organizations

Stage One:	Symptoms of dissatisfaction with the performance of incumbents of an institutionalized role or with the organization of the roles themselves.	detection of the problem
Stage Two:	Symptoms of disturbance, protest, or calls for change, reflecting this dissatisfaction.	communication of the problem
Stage Three:	Handling and channeling the symptoms of disturbance. The first line of defense of agencies of control is a kind of holding action in attempts to contain the results of dissatisfaction.	holding the problem at bay
Stage Four:	The collectivity encourages the new ideas which purport to deal with the supposed source of dissatisfaction.	analysis of the problem
Stage Five:	The collectivity attempts to specify the institutional forms that will ease the supposed sources of dissatisfaction.	proposal
Stage Six:	The collectivity attempts to establish new institutional forms.	essay and evaluation
Stage Seven:	The new institutional forms are consolidated as permanent features.	locking-in and consensus

Sources: John A. Coleman, *The Evolution of Dutch Catholicism 1958–1974* (Berkeley: University of California Press, 1978), p. 7; as adapted from Neil J. Smelser's seven-sequence model.

migration, but the institution's mode of conceptualizing itself was also at stake. Coleman proposes to avoid an evolutionary schema while maintaining dynamism in his typology. But he falls short, as his effort does not make for a clear presentation of theological definitions, which are also in flux; that is, the conflict and resolution process he describes for the institution is not focused upon defining theological concepts. And since these concepts acquire different meanings in their implementation and influence behavior, exclusion of these theological processes renders Coleman's typology devoid of a dimension vital to a full understanding of church response.

A third typology considered in the present study was developed by Daniel Levine in *Religion and Politics in Latin America* (1981). Levine evaluates the applicability of a typological model in the study of Roman Catholicism in Venezuela and Colombia. He concludes that Vallier's typology has to be modified and reinterpreted in order adequately to interpret Latin American Catholicism in these two countries.

Levine proposes "not one typology, but several, distinguishing religious from sociopolitical dimensions of action" (Levine, 141), in order to trace analytical and empirical relations between types and establish patterns in the way religion and sociopolitical perspectives come together. He is interested in how ideas are crystallized in regular patterns of action and how institutions develop characteristic styles of action ultimately shaping the activities of their members in the general social context.

Among the typologies Levine examines there is one contained in an early work on religious elites by Vallier (in Lipset and Solari). As explained in an earlier chapter, according to this typology, the differences that set groups apart in contemporary Latin American Catholicism involve two major dimensions of analytical importance: 1) the choice of sphere (internal—its organizations and rituals—or external—involvement with secular groups and events from which the Church is to gain its major source of influence), and 2) the organizing principle of religious-social relationship, which is termed "hierarchical" and "cooperative" (see chapter 1). Levine argues that classifications employed ought not to be static since the reality they attempt to portray emerges from a continuous dialectic "between social and religious positions, or between substance and style" (Levine, 138).

Hence, an individual's vision of the church or his or her views of the world do not, by themselves, account for that person's behavior; rather, they work together in what Levine calls "an elective affinity," each one "providing for the other and [making] it more likely" (Levine, 138). This affinity seems to be present also at the collective level, so that the church influences social and political behavior and is, in turn, influenced by these. While the church's goals go beyond those of other secular institutions to include an escatological dimension, it is recognized that as an entity existing in concrete historical situations its positions "inevitably have temporal consequences and temporal problems have an impact upon the lives of believers," who are also social actors (Levine, 13).

The broad socio-political orientations Levine offer refer not so much to ideology, according to his own critique, but to the style and form of action deemed appropriate for the church; that is, "the way elites see the proper role of the church (however they define it) in dealing with social problems" (Levine, 139).

In Levine's schema, then, it is not necessary to classify the *liberationist* as less concerned with religious values than the *pastoralists,* nor the *pastoralists* as less committed to social change than the *liberationists* (Stevens-Arroyo 1980, 178). Those who seek a traditional solution to social problems by separating pastoral care from social concern are not denied a compassionate involvement with the material well-being of the people. This would seem a better description of this position than Vallier's label as *politician* (Vallier 1970, 72).

The variations possible within the same religious sphere category are formulated on a premise of dynamic, dialectical interaction between religious values and socio-political trends. "Such sensitivity," comments Levine, "to the mutual influence between ideas and models from each sphere, makes possible a more adequate response to the central issues" (Levine, 140).

Levine's central issue of how ideas take form or crystallize in regular patterns of action and his concern to identify a typology that is capable of adequately giving an answer to this question are a major part of my subject. His combination of religious and socio-political spheres in the typology for the church's religious control system is applicable here. But the difficulty in simply importing his model to a study of the New York Archdiocese lies in the monopoly over religious culture that Catholicism exercises in Latin America. As was stressed in chapter 3, the adaptation of Catholicism to the United States has accepted religious pluralism in ways that are not found in Columbia or Venezuela, countries that Levine studied. He presumed a connection between church policy and the total society (Levine, 285) that is not operable in the United States. Moreover, my subject deals with the pluralism of cultural Catholicism—Oxcart Catholicism and the adapted Catholicism of New York's second and third generations—in addition to the ideological and theological differences encompassed within Levine's framework.

In summary, none of the typologies reviewed in this study is entirely satisfactory in application to an analysis of the encounter of New York Catholicism with that of the Puerto Rican migration. My principal dissatisfaction with these typologies is twofold: 1) with the exception of that of Levine, they seem to lack sufficient dynamism; and 2) none accounts for a reciprocal chain interaction between groups that have different racial composition, national origins, and economic status, peculiar to the United States.

In my own analysis of the New York Archdiocese I offer a new paradigm (Figure 11) in order to examine the attitude and diverse roles religious elites may assume in the institutional church's response to a crisis situation or to a particular need that may arise. This typology incorporates categories or factors defined by Vallier and repeated by Coleman, which are listed as the bases and focus of influence. However, in accordance with Levine's combination of the two spheres, they are divided into three sets:

1) *self-contained,* that is, internal to the church's structures—such a description details what McNamara (1969 5–34 et passim) offers in his use of the "priest" category in his important study of Catholic leadership among Mexican-Americans;
2) *integrating,* which includes the social class factors and material resources of the Church and its membership; and
3) *transitional,* that is, an area of decision-making and setting priorities, which includes the categories of target group and organizational mode.

As can be seen, the ten factors Vallier defines have been reduced to eight and modified to form three groupings generally conform-

Figure 11

A Proposed Paradigm for Understanding the Role of Elites in the Institutional Church Response*

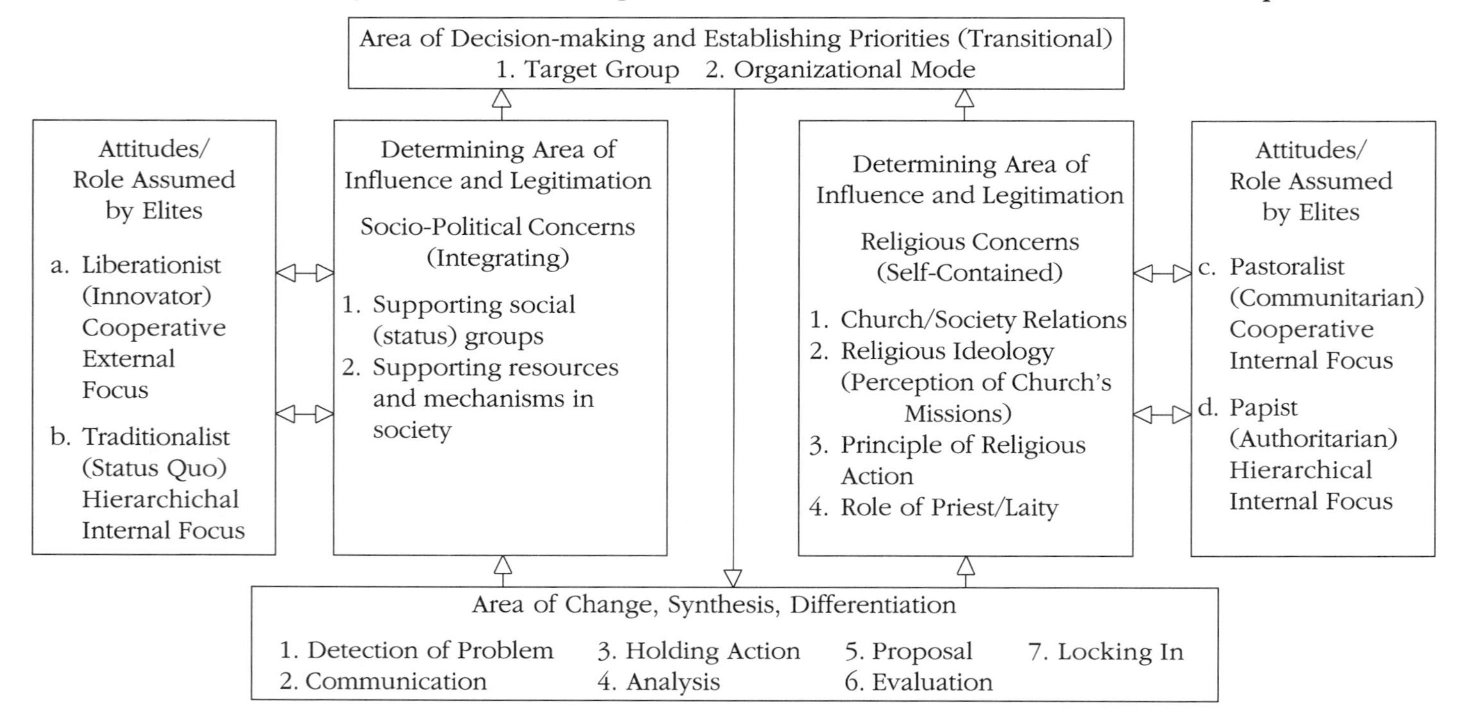

*This "paradigm" suggests the key variables a sociologist would take in account in presenting a comprehensive picture of social change.

ing to Levine's conceptualization. Thus, the determining orders of influence and legitimation are given to well-defined areas roughly corresponding to the internal-external dichotomy, but allowing for a dynamic, intermediate area that is transitional.

While utilizing Vallier's factors, the typology substitutes for vertical and non-dynamic types of missionary, cultural pastoral, and so on. Instead, the religious elites are categorized in accordance to a religious ideology dimension and a socio-political one. Thus, it is possible to describe elites' attitudes and assumed roles as combining a pastoralist type in religious ideology and either a liberationist or traditionalist one in the socio-political area. In the paradigm pastoralists and papists have been placed closest to the religious concerns sphere and the liberationists and traditionalists to that of the social political concerns. My graph, however, would be better presented on a cylinder in order to show the non-dichotomous nature of these categories. The two-dimensional sheet of paper unfortunately distorts this concept.

The interchange, articulation, and differentiation of these roles or attitudes occur in the transitional area of setting priorities. In the paradigm this is indicated by one-directional arrows between the two areas of influence and legitimation and that of decision-making.

The process of deciding on a target group and an organizational mode for church activity engages the types of religious elites in a dialectic. This process is described by the steps of institutional response offered by Smelser and Coleman, which may or may not occur in exact sequence. This is indicated in the paradigm by a one-directional arrow leading directly from the area of decision-making to that of change and synthesis.

Eventually, however, the analysis, proposal, and evaluation of the institution's response requires the elites to bring their own religious ideology and socio-political conceptualizations into the interchange. Thus, the arrows lead from the area of change and synthesis back to the determining areas of influence and legitimation and from there, eventually back to the clerical elites who originated the ideas for change in policies. For this reason, the arrows between the elites and the determining areas of influence and legitimation are shown as a two-directional ones.

The introduction of more permanent values into the assessment of a heretofore transitional activity is even more acute in the case of locking in or institutionalization of the policy. Such a final step would have the virtual effect of making a transitional or temporary policy part of the permanent dimensions of religious ideology and socio-political activity.

The interchange on such an issue may well create losers and winners, in terms of policy decision, but the entire institution experiences the challenge to its permanent values. Even if institutional policy may be assessed in terms of approval or rejection, the impact of the interchange may penetrate to all spheres of church awareness. The impact may vary—polarization when the elites drift further apart or synthesis when they compromise—but in either case the typology describes the process in terms of its major elements.

The suggested paradigm lends a dynamic interpretation to the process of change within the institution and is useful in explaining some of the historical events that created the institution of the Roman Catholic church in New York. The following phenomena include changes within the Archdiocese of New York that involved the clerical elites in a process of recognition, response, and evaluation of problems that confronted the church institution.

Beyond personality traits, which often condition individual behavior, the dynamic model derived from analysis of the typologies studied here introduces the factors of a transitional mode and theological worldviews. Thus, it is possible to analyze individual behavior against the backdrop of sociological and institutional forces as well as the elements that explain institutional response and structural change, especially in a crisis situation.

For instance, the authoritarian centralization of Archbishop Hughes produced less conflict among the clergy than the polices of his eventual successor, Archbishop Corrigan, who, among other serious problems, had an unfortunate confrontation with Father Edward McGlynn. It might be expected that by reason of his strong personality and forceful initiatives of change, Hughes would have been a more likely target of opposition than Corrigan, who faithfully served Cardinal McCloskey before assuming the responsibilities as ordinary himself. This apparent anomaly may be explained in part by use of the paradigm.

Hughes defined a target group and an organizational mode for a diocese that had previously responded largely as a loose collection of urban ethnic villages. Hughes rose to a power position in the church at a time of crisis when anti-Catholic bigots threatened Catholic immigrants. By skillfully dealing with an outside threat, Hughes was able to lend greater cohesiveness to the Irish immigrants, who made up the bulk of New York's Catholics. This unity in the face of a crisis focused church resources upon these incoming Irish immigrants and provided the bishop with a reason to centralize the institutions of New York Catholicism. Hughes successfully transformed the church into an urban institution with authority and finance structures paralleling those of the urban political machines that simultaneously emerged in nineteenth-century New York to incorporate these immigrants into the city's life.

When it came to non-Irish groups, especially the German and Italian Catholics, however, Hughes adopted another structure. The national parish was not as centralized as the territorial parish, which was administered by the diocesan clergy and resembled the urban ethnic village that was otherwise in the process of being replaced. These divergent policies were appropriate for a rapidly expanding church to the extent that the clerical elites did not compete for the same resources. The suspension of the Italian cleric who, without Hughes's approbation, sought private donations for an Italian chapel was one of the instances cited in this study as an example of how Hughes replaced clerical initiative with his own policy. As described above, Hughes's episcopacy saw the replacement of priestly activity focused upon service to individual clients by one that stressed the building of institutional resources—the contrast between a Father Félix Varela and a brick-and-mortar pastor. The result was to impede clergy participation in the process of evaluation. It also prevented the locking in of these transitional policies. In effect, all of Hughes's programs for the Archdiocese of New York were in this transitional mode, because although he institutionalized many structures in governance and finance during his tenure as bishop, he did not simultaneously develop a structure for widening clerical leadership. By concentrating authority in his own hands, Hughes prevented the growth of a clerical elite, which might have grown at the same pace as the expansion of the physical resources of the archdiocese. Moreover, his divergent policies toward the non-Irish national parishes virtually segregated the ministry in New York by ethnic group.[1]

But although Hughes's personal style of centralized authority generally prohibited the emergence of any clerical leadership differing from his own, it also maintained a rigorous unity of purpose within the archdiocese. Hughes's controversial policies did not result in major conflict within the structures of archdiocesan leadership. However, his successor, Archbishop Corrigan, faced more than one such serious problem. Religious leaders, like Mother Frances Cabrini, who worked with the Italian immigrants, and Father Edward McGlynn, who developed an apostolate of social justice by advocating the political alternative of Henry George, had emerged as part of the clerical and religious elites of the archdiocese. This emergence was aided in part by the interest of Rome in seeing greater attention given to the non-Irish Catholics in the United States. These forces, and others such as those generated by the Cahensly dispute and the condemnation of Americanism (see above, chapter 3) strengthened the diversity of opinion within the archdiocese and lent legitimacy to clerical elites who differed with Archbishop Corrigan.

Policy shifts by Corrigan, such as those regarding the pastoral care of Italians, were unable to keep pace with the growing diversity of problems within New York Catholicism. Thus, in the McGlynn affair, the attempt of Corrigan to deprive his fellow priest of legitimacy by suspension is the same step Hughes took against the Italian cleric. Corrigan, however, was forced to withdraw the suspension, whereas Hughes had been successful in maintaining his control. The determining areas of influence and legitimation described in the paradigm under the headings of socio-political and religious concerns had become increasingly diverse due to the emergence or rival formulations of external and internal ideologies for church policy. Of course, the description of these ideologies, that is, *papist, politician, liberationist*, and *pastoralist,* do not directly apply to the historical period of the nineteenth century. But it may be suggested that Corrigan's use of Hughes's measures failed because the bishop alone was no longer able to define the areas of decision-making and setting priorities for the archdiocese. The more flexible approach adopted by Cardinal Farley and his successors, on the other hand, allowed for the flow of ideas and exchange among clerical elites suggested in the paradigm as the model operative during the period of the Spanish-speaking apostolate under study.

In terms of the New York Catholic archdiocesan response to the Puerto Ricans, the early years of activity inspired by such intellectuals as Kelly, Illich, and Fitzpatrick may be characterized as belonging to the transitional order. Cardinal Spellman perceived the need for decisions and establishing priorities in the effort to target a response to the Puerto Rican migrants and provide the archdiocese with a mode of organization that could cope with the problem. At his invitation, Kelly, Illich, Fitzpatrick, and others initiated a process of analysis and proposal that flowed from their own religious ideology and socio-political vision, but which did not threaten these aspects of Cardinal Spellman's worldview or theology. Only later on, under Fox and Stern, would there be an effort to evaluate the policies toward the Spanish-speaking and, in the case of Stern, to institutionalize them. These two heads of the apostolate office were required to act in a leadership role. Fitzpatrick, on the other hand, continued as the classic intellectual; as a university professor he influences by research and study. His recommendations refer to specific aspects of institutional responses of the church to the Hispanics and are generally designed to analyze pastoral problems.

Fox and Illich, on the other hand, focused their thought and activity upon the socio-political dimension, relating the apostolate to Puerto Rican community needs. This emphasis of Fox and Illich gradually removed them from that process of interchange with the hierarchy and other religious elites, thus reducing their institutional impact.

One may even suggest that Fox's Summer in the City did not belong to the transitional area of church activity but formed part of a permanent apparatus for religious control outside of the archdiocesan structures. This would explain why the innovative programs of Fox were less threatening to established authority within the church than the institutional renovations of Robert L. Stern. Summer in the City did not engage religious elites in a debate over religious ideology. The efforts of Stern, on the other hand, sought to lock in an organizational mode and emphasis upon the Spanish-speaking as a target group that proved to be more radical. Stern, rather than Fox, forced a reformulation of issues such as church-society relation, the definition of the church's mission in a concrete cultural and historical situation, the principle of religious action, and a change in the role of priests and laity. Fox, as explained earlier, faced the constraints imposed by federal funding and nonsectarianism. These impeded any locking in of Summer in the City to the church institutions, since these innovations were perceived as belonging to an order external to the church. Moreover, as explained before, Fox did not have a strong interest in such an institutionalization.

The typology also helps conceptualize the crux of Stern's problem. He attempted to lock the programs, which up to that time had been of a temporary or transitional nature, into a religious ideology that was permanently legitimized. He was the "deroutinizer of the first order" (Stark, 207; see above, chapters 1 and 7). By inserting what had been considered extraneous or experimental to the ordinary business of the chancery, Stern had destabilized the status quo more than his predecessors.

The importance of the Second Vatican Council should not be underestimated. Precisely because it forced the conservative ecclesiastical mentality to confront new theological values and reformulate a traditionalist vision of church in the world, it intensified and multiplied the number of issues that were pushed into the transitional arena of decision-making and prioritizing.

In the New York Archdiocese, not only outreach to the Spanish-speaking, but also liturgy, ecclesiology, concepts of authority, selection of bishops, the nature of parish life, and the role of the laity were matters for debate, reformulation, and experimentation. Stern incorporated values that represented innovation in a plethora of theological areas so that an institutionalization of his programs for the Spanish-speaking apostolate would have implicitly approved of lay involvement in the selection of bishops, the formulation of archdiocesan policy, and possibly, a principle of ethnic representation in the episcopate ever afterward. Despite the eventual rejection of these innovations by the archdiocese, the process of interchange and issue differentiation did provide permanent changes in the archdiocesan vision of itself and its apostolate among the Spanish-speaking.

These changes may be summarized by citing the objectives of the 1982 Pastoral Study of Hispanics. In the foreword Cardinal Cooke confessed, "There have been failures in our efforts to serve our Hispanic brothers and sisters." I believe the "our" refers to the clerical elites of the archdiocese, particularly in the chancery, and while the cardinal probably did not wish to exclude from the admitted "failures" the decisions by Fox and Stern, neither did he exclude himself. This is the first achievement of the process that I have described until Father Stern's dismissal in 1973: the admission of failure on the part of decision-making by the archdiocese. This is occasioned, I believe, by the loss of prestige that New York has suffered while other regions, notably the Southwestern United States, have become the Catholic paradigms for the Spanish-speaking ministries.

The Pastoral Study of Hispanics was intended as a search for scientifically generated data about Hispanics (Doyle, et al., 1). Included in the scope of information were religio-cultural attitudes on the part of people (what I have called for Puerto Ricans "Ox-cart Catholicism") and indications of religious practice according to the norms of United States Catholicism. The applications of the data included:

> to identify new directions for ministry; to involve the Hispanic Community more fully in the parish life of the Church; to develop a plan for evangelization to the Hispanics; to identify new directions for fostering vocations; to disseminate information concerning the Hispanic Community; and to make the Church of New York even more aware of the full dimensions of the Hispanic presence (Doyle, et al., 1).

I interpret these applications as attempts to reduce the social distance between Hispanic Catholicism and United States Catholic institutions, particularly the parishes. The study establishes a sort of halfway point: the archdiocese will appreciate Hispanics more if they, on their part, integrate themselves into parish life. This goal is described by Fitzpatrick (1987, 118–21) as "inculturation." Included in the list is a hierarchical notion of ministry focused on the search for more vocations, but this is balanced by the call for "new directions," which involves lay roles.

By calling for a "plan for evangelization" the agenda implicitly rejects all previous plans, including those of Connolly, Fox, and Stern. Moreover, there is a conspicuous absence of any social or political perspective. The study seems content to "disseminate information" and to produce more awareness, both of which fall far short of social action. Even when one adds the detailed "Statement of Concern" articulated by a representative group of clergy and academics (Doyle, et al., 213–24), it appears that, except for the issue of abortion, the archdiocese has retreated from an apostolate of social concerns. The principal goals are directed against conversion to "Pentecostal sects," which are perceived (unfairly, I think) as beyond the reach of ecumenism (220), and concern for the assimilation of young people into United States culture (219). Interestingly, an archdiocese that had originally attempted to "mainstream" Puerto Ricans and other Latinos now perceives part of its task as preserving traditional culture and its values to some degree.

Since 1972 there has been a shift in control of the ministry at the archdiocesan level to native Hispanics, both clerical and lay. This is principally true of movements such as the Cursillo. Moreover, the principle of inclusion of Hispanic representation has meant that few if any appointed commissions or committees of the archdiocese lack at least one native Hispanic member. In a sense Hispanics have achieved acceptance as one of the "ethnic groups" of the archdiocese. Still, it should be clear that the archdiocese has blurred purposely the nationality differences among Puerto Ricans, Dominicans, and Central Americans. There never was a clear political meaning to the emphasis upon Puerto Ricans when they constituted nearly 80 percent of all the Spanish-speaking in the city, but there is even less now that they are 65 percent (Doyle, et al., 5).

The non-Hispanic archdiocesan clergy has lost visibility, but not necessarily importance in the Spanish-speaking apostolate. These clerics, most of whom speak Spanish well and were trained in Puerto Rico, exercise leadership principally at the regional level of vicariates and the various pastoral centers. Such centers are involved in inter-parochial religious education of the laity, particularly for specific parish roles such as lectors, catechists, and parish council members. These pastoral centers work in concert with the priests and religious of their respective vicariates, which often adopt political strategies for social change at the local level.

Without a further study that would exceed the scope of this book it would be difficult to assess further the impact of the changes upon the process of decision-making for the Spanish-speaking apostolate since the dismissal of Father Stern. But I believe the following the most salient.

- Loss of prestige by the Archdiocese of New York as an innovator and leader in the ministry to the Spanish-speaking.
- Fragmentation of responsibilities from one chancery-based office among movements, national organizations, and local pastoral centers.
- Acceptance of a role in cultural preservation and partial rejection of Hispanic assimilation as a goal of ministry.
- Dispersal of responsibility for social concerns to local pastoral groups.
- Enhanced visibility of native Hispanics in official posts, although not necessarily in decision-making ones.
- Inclusion of native Hispanics as integral members of the ethnic groups of the archdiocese.
- Exclusion of a social concerns apostolate on behalf of the Spanish-speaking from the archdiocesan agenda.
- Aggregation of all nationality Latin American groups under the one cultural grouping of Hispanic.

All represent positive or negative responses to the initiatives taken by Fox and especially by Stern. The last one was initiated during Fox's tenure, redefined under Stern to highlight all commonalities without deemphasizing particularities, and finally gained wide acceptance after Stern's departure. But the dispersal of power among various constituent groups has totally subverted the meaning of a single office for coordination. Furthermore, pastoral care and social concerns are not knit together by a visionary theology. Despite Murnion's theopolitan vision, the office he left behind is, as its name indicates, a Pastoral Research Office, focused upon the collection and interpretation of data rather than upon advocacy for the apostolate. At best, it serves in a consultative capacity with no power invested in it for actual policy-making on behalf of the Puerto Ricans and Latino groups.

The compartmentalizing of responsibilities allows for more local initiative, but less overall impact upon archdiocesan priorities. In fact, the practical result of the rejection of Stern's institutional reforms is a double-tiered apostolate. The "official" office of the archdiocese is focused almost entirely upon maintaining standards of direction for movements like the Cursillo and providing a point of contact when a native Spanish-speaker is desirable. The local apostolate is centered in the parish and coordinated by the respective pastoral center, which can initiate some experimentation, formation of native leadership, and socio-political activity.

The adoption of "Hispanic" as a cultural ethnicity within the church may be more effective in the future than it was in the time of Fox (see above, chapter 6) because there is a secular political movement toward "Latino identity" (Calitri et al.). However, this tends to be most successful when it is based on a clear group identity (Padilla 1985, 72–83), and this does not seem to be seriously considered in the present structure of the apostolate or in the data sought by the Pastoral Study of Hispanics.

The use of a systems model to understand the process of change and adaptation of the Archdiocese of New York contributes to a clearer understanding of the impact the Puerto Rican Great Migration made upon the institutional church and its processes. Moreover, it offers several advantages to a better idea of the universality of Catholicism.

First, the policy innovations suggested for Puerto Ricans by the clerical elite associated with the Office for the Spanish-Speaking Apostolate in New York must be related to conciliar changes. Policies of the Spanish-speaking apostolate anticipated the mandates of Vatican II, while the conciliar directives widened the applicability of positive results toward the Spanish-speaking ministry. What worked with the Puerto Ricans acquired the aura of a paradigm for what the entire church should become. The Spanish-speaking apostolate has thus been a key factor in the modifications of internal archdiocesan structures.

Second, the institutional changes in the New York Archdiocese during the period under study are comparable to the changes in Catholicism in Latin America and Holland. Internal theological premises and external social changes combine to alter the policy formulation of clerical elites, and these processes are found in New York as well as in other parts of the world. The typological approach makes it possible to assemble a considerable amount of data for cross-national comparison. And although I am not prepared to begin such a comparison here, it may well constitute an area for further study.

Third, in my use of the typological approach I have emphasized the relationship between socio-political factors, theological premises, and pastoral policies in the New York Archdiocese. The effort of the church to incorporate Puerto Ricans into its activities was premised upon its nature as an urban institution and past successes in assimilating immigrants to a new form of Catholicism and life in the United States. If the Archdiocese of New York had failed in the 1950s to initiate a process of integration for the Puerto Ricans, it would have been unlikely to maintain the primacy of Catholicism as the city's largest denomination.

As Glazer and Moynihan have pointed out, this hegemony of Catholicism in New York now has been lost (1970, lviiff.). However, inefficacy toward the Puerto Ricans or their lack of upward social mobility were only partial factors in the replacement of institutionalized Catholic influence. The systems model allows for analysis of the dynamics of church response, not only to social and political changes but also to the reforms of the Council. The Council permitted a variety of theological premises and pastoral policies to compete for legitimation, which resulted in fragmentation of Catholic leadership and resources. The typology allows for an overview of how the church functions both as an urban institution and an organization that collectively represents believers, with mutually interacting results. Both are important to a proper understanding of Catholicism, for the church is neither merely a social institution like all others nor a body of abstract theological doctrines divorced from the world and concrete historical change.

Fourth, the synthesizing typology introduced in this brief presentation provides a mode of analyzing the institutional processes of a Catholic religious organization. According to the typology, clerical elite attitudes can be classified into three spheres:

1) the self-contained theological premises and policies of pastoral care;
2) the socio-political concerns for the material well-being of church membership and for the allocation of resources independently of specifically religious production; and
3) a transitional area of decision-making and setting priorities, dependent upon both internal needs and continuity with theological premises.

The analysis of the response of the Archdiocese of New York to the Puerto Rican presence, 1950–73, suggested that despite differences in their attitudes toward the self-contained and the socio-political dimensions, clerical elites can agree on transitional policies directed toward a target group that needs a new organizational mode in order to be incorporated into church activity. However, when these policies attempt to achieve permanence, the process is liable to evoke conflicts. Seldom are such conflicts articulated in consciously political language, although they are related to differing conceptualizations of church relation with sociopolitical forces. Instead, the conflict is expressed in theological language and/or practical administrative procedures.

In this regard I believe my typology may be used to analyze not only the Puerto Ricans and the New York Archdiocese, but other groups and other dioceses as well. I have already traced a similar process in Comerío, Puerto Rico (Díaz-Stevens 1988). A future study may examine another situation to test the typology and the hypothesis of transitional agreements becoming conflictive as they are made permanent.

Finally, by exploring the concept of organic intellectuals and differing modes of leadership, I hope to have provided a perspective with which to judge the importance of connecting ethnic identity with common interests. When Robert Stern created a sort of *comunidad de base* with the Coordinating Committee of his office, he realized the alternative form of church organization that his predecessors had essayed. But his changes came so quickly that the institution had time to escape Stern's projections by jettisoning much of the office. But although his recommendations were not acceptable as such by the chancery, they survive with differing degrees of success in progressive parishes and movements, incubating the promise of a more radically altered Catholicism. In this sense the dismemberment of Stern's office serves as anticipation for a Vatican-directed process against much of the Latin American Church since the Puebla Conference (Leroux).

Yet the refusal to lock in upon the innovations of Stern, including the elimination of social distance between clergy and laity, between Hispanic and non-Hispanic, between practitioner of the gospel and pastoral theologian was only that, a locking out. The exclusion from official status in the chancery structure is not the same as annihilation of an ideal or of the need for reforms. There is much vitality within the Archdiocese of New York at the local level of the parishes.

Thus, the trek of Oxcart Catholicism to Fifth Avenue is important because it is one history among many that constitute the journey of the People of God toward a realization of the kingdom. The dismemberment of an office is like the amputation of a finger by the simple cane-cutter in the village of my Puerto Rican homeland. Carrying the scars of a mistake, we nonetheless move on to a new opportunity for life.

NOTES

1. The Stone and the Pitcher

1. For a description of the difficulties in estimating the Puerto Rican migration into the United States, see Fitzpatrick (1971, 10–13), and Rodríguez (1989, 6–8).

2. The complex question of racial and/or ethnic perception of Puerto Ricans is extensively analyzed by Rodríguez (1989, 49–84). The description of Fitzpatrick (1971, 101–14) is also useful.

3. For these residential patterns in 1950 see C. Wright Mills, et al. (218–24) and Fitzpatrick (1971, 53–57), where he summarizes the work of Lawrence Chenault. Lankevich and Furer (265) highlight the importance of Oscar Handlin's *The Newcomers,* which appeared as part of a larger study.

4. Studies during the 1950s produced by non–Puerto Rican scholars generally talk of Catholicism in cultural terms, neglecting institutional and faith issues. Works by Puerto Ricans during the 1970s have been silent on the issue of religion, with the notable exception of Antonio M. Stevens-Arroyo. The Centro de Estudios Puertorriqueños, despite its exhaustive studies of the Puerto Rican experience in New York, has never considered these religious associations of Puerto Ricans in its published analyses. Nor are they mentioned except in passing by Sánchez Korrol (1983) in her study of the Pioneer Migration. Happily, this trend seems to be changing. Sánchez Korrol has prepared "In Search of Non-Traditional Women: Histories of Puerto Rican Women Preachers before Mid-Century" (1985), a paper presented at the meeting of the American Historical Association. Rodríguez (1989, 111–12) also laments the absence of data on religious organizations. In 1989–90, the Inter University Program, of which the Centro is a member, funded an exploratory conference, "Project for Analysis of Religion Among Latinos." In 1991 the Lily Endowment awarded the newly constituted program $257,000 to conduct a nationwide comprehensive study on Latino religiosity.

5. I have chosen not to analyze any religious institution other than Catholicism in this book. The work of mainline Protestant churches

among Puerto Ricans in New York has met with limited success in terms of numbers; the impact of Pentecostalism and Evangelical churches, on the other hand, has been remarkable (see Wakefield 1959). The prediction of Poblete (1960), that after resolving anomie Puerto Ricans would return to Catholicism, does not seem to have been evidenced (see Doyle et al., 2:26–27).

6. This term is adapted from the important study of the Centro de Estudios Puertorriqueños. It should be noted, however, that the numbers of migrants from Puerto Rico rose steadily throughout the 1980s, approximating the average number of those arriving during the Great Migration. Despite the lack of return migrants—or perhaps, until their next manifestation—the social changes on the island and in the United States argue for maintaining a different name for this phase of the Puerto Rican phenomenon than that of the Great Migration.

7. These figures are based on findings of the study by the Office of Pastoral Research of the Archdiocese of New York, 1982. Curiously, they do not appear in the report. They were secured from Ruth Doyle, head of the Center, by telephone.

2. ISLAND WITHIN THE ISLAND

1. Information contained in this chapter also appears in my article "Social Distance and Religious Conflict in the Pre-Vatican Catholicism of Puerto Rico," MACLAS *Latin American Essays* 4 (1991), 291–301.

2. A well established point that requires little elaboration here is that the Puerto Rican was a Catholic migration unaccompanied by a native clergy. It was not apathy or lack of apostolic zeal on the part of Puerto Rican priests that gave rise to this situation. According to Cardinal Spellman, "their priests do not come with them only because they cannot come with them. There are not enough priests in Puerto Rico to care for those remaining there." See William Ferrée, Ivan Illich, and Joseph P. Fitzpatrick, eds., *Spiritual Care of Puerto Rican Migrants* (Cuernavaca, Mexico: CIDOC, 1970); reprint ed. (New York: Arno Press, 1980), p. 0/7. Also see Joseph P. Fitzpatrick, *Puerto Rican Americans: The Meaning of Migration to the Mainland* (Englewood Cliffs, N.J.: Prentice-Hall, 1971), p. 2.

3. *Compadrazgo* is described as "ritual kinship" by Mintz in Steward, 386–91.

4. Picó, 141. Sts. Peter and Paul (June 29), Our Lady of Mt. Carmel (July 16), St. James the Apostle (August 15), St. Rose (August 30), the Assumption (August 15), Our Lady of Monserrate (September 8), and in the case of Utuado, St. Michael (September 29), patron saint of the town, were important feast days. The entire month of October was dedicated

to Our Lady of the Rosary; in November the feast of All Saints was second in importance to the day dedicated to the dead and the souls in purgatory; and finally, at the end of the year, two other Marian feasts—the Immaculate Conception (December 8) and Our Lady of Guadalupe (December 12) were celebrated (Píco, 143).

5. The fact that Monserrate is the patroness of Catalonia, Spain, and that she is often depicted there also as a black madonna does not detract from this perception on the part of Puerto Ricans, who see their African experience reflected on her. Notice also that in the Puerto Rican imagery she is accompanied by a *jíbaro* and either a charging or kneeling bull.

6. The only dissenting voice was that of Bishop Blenck, who came to advocate independence in 1913 after having left the see. His position was quickly repudiated by the rest of the hierarchy (Julián de Nieves, 125).

7. The Redemptorists, the Sisters of St. Joseph from Brentwood, Long Island, and the Amityville Dominicans came from the New York provinces. The Philadelphia groups included the Holy Ghost Fathers (now Fathers of the Holy Spirit) of Conwall Heights and the Trinitarians, which included both men and women religious.

8. Two Redemptorist bishops of the Ponce diocese were Aloysius J. Willinger (1929–47) and James McManus (1947–63).

9. The question of whether the missionaries were "right" or "wrong" in their teaching and practice is not addressed here. The facts are merely stated, and value judgments are left to others more educated in these matters. Perhaps the documents of the Second Vatican Council and those of Medellín and Puebla (especially those on the subject of culture and religion, and the religion of the people), may be both of help and interest. For example, the *Constitution on the Sacred Liturgy* states:

> Even in the liturgy, the Church has no wish to impose a rigid uniformity in matters which do not involve the faith or the good of the whole community. Rather she respects and fosters the spiritual adornments and gifts of the various races and peoples. Anything in their way of life that is not indissolubly bound with superstition and error she studies with sympathy and, if possible, preserves intact. Sometimes in fact she admits such things into the liturgy itself, as long as they harmonize with its true authentic spirit.

3. From Village Parishes to Cosmopolitan Archdiocese

1. See Michael A. Corrigan, "Register of the Clergy Laboring in the Archdiocese of New York from Early Missionary Times to 1885," *Historical Records and Studies* 5 (November 1907): 398. According to Cor-

rigan, the ascetic appearance of Varela and his devotion to the poor and sick overshadowed any traces of business acumen. However, the qualities of the "brick-and-mortar priest" were the ones to be emphasized when history recorded the pastorate of Varela's Irish-born successor, Father Thomas Treanor. The renovation and expansion of the church and the construction of a belfry are mentioned as Treanor's most memorable achievements. The brick-and-mortar tradition took such a hold that in 1899 William Strang wrote a *Business Guide for Priests,* which was published in New York. George W. Potter writes that when a priest of the brick-and-mortar tradition died, the eulogy focused on his building accomplishments, *To the Golden Door* (Boston: n. p., 1960), p. 362. Thus, he was remembered not only as a good, zealous, and faithful priest but also as a man of excellent business habits. A fate similar to that of Father Varela awaited St. John Neumann, CSSR, Bishop of Philadelphia (see Colman J. Barry, *The Catholic Church and German Americans* [Milwaukee: The Bruce Publishing Co., 1953), p. 13.

2. For the opposing point of view, see John Lancaster Spalding, *The Religious Mission of the Irish People and Catholic Colonization* (New York, n.p., 1880). See also Hennesey, 1981a, 128–35, passim.

3. Casita María is presently located in the Bronx, New York (928 Simpson Street) in the Parish of St. Athanasius. It should not be confused with Centro or Casa María run by the Spanish congregation, Daughters of Mary Immaculate in Manhattan (251 West 14th Street).

4. In the case of the Puerto Ricans, I have been unable to secure any documentation voicing either approval or disapproval for such a proposal, or that the question was even considered. An important survey of the period reported only that there was a reluctance on the part of some church personnel to deal with Puerto Ricans. See George A. Kelly, "Catholic Survey of the Puerto Rican Population in the Archdiocese of New York" (1955), mimeographed. The plans of the island administration under Luis Muñoz Marín did assist Puerto Ricans to migrate to rural areas as farm labor (Centro, 244–48), but that differs substantially from Maynard's proposal.

4. THE MISSIONARY IMPULSE AND THE BASEMENT CHURCHES

1. When Monsignor Cornelius J. Drew set out to raise a million dollars for a community center for citizenship classes and adult education, Cardinal Spellman presented the first check for ten thousand dollars and, referring to newspaper reports that the national office of the Communist Party had been moved to Harlem, declared: "This was no surprise since we have been warned again and again that the Communist

Party line for 1952 would concentrate on the Negroes, and for years the Communists have been playing on their emotions in the hope of stirring up race hatred and mob violence." The check was given in the confidence "that this new project [the community center] will help to make Harlem healthier and happier and that the young and old will be benefited and assisted to be better citizens of our beloved country and of the Kingdom of God" (Gannon, 270). If Cardinal Spellman was so concerned that blacks would not fall victim to Communist propaganda, he would likely have been equally concerned with the fate of Puerto Ricans. For a detailed account about Marcantonio's social and political involvement in causes that earned him a reputation as a Communist sympathizer, see Gerald Meyer (1989). Meyer gives ample evidence of Marcantonio's support of the Puerto Rican community and independence for their homeland and shows, likewise, how he was accepted by the Puerto Ricans as capable and trustworthy to champion their cause.

2. Most of the information regarding the Cursillo Movement is based on personal experience, conversations with a a a number of *cursillistas,* a series of in-depth conversations with Stevens-Arroyo, and Stevens-Arroyo's writings quoted in the text. For a satisfying description of the Spanish origins and the type of spirituality promoted by the Cursillo, see Vidal.

3. See the commentary in *Social Justice* 58: 2 (May 1965): 59. Other relevant sources for understanding the impact of the Cursillo at this time include *America* 116: 17 (19 April 1967): 616ff.; and O'Flannery, *American Catholic* 22: 3 (Fall 1961): 195–206.

4. This description is based upon my personal life experience and the life experiences of my family.

5. THE INTELLECTUALIZATION OF AN EXPERIMENT

1. Gramsci, born in Sardina in 1891, became one of the founders of the Italian Communist Party in 1921 and its Secretary General in 1924. He was imprisoned by Mussolini in 1926 and released only six months before his death in 1937. His most important work, *The Prison Notebooks,* was written while in jail (Entwistle, 1–10).

2. Data in this description of the *fiestas patronales* is amplified in Ana Mária Díaz-Stevens, "From Puerto Rican to Hispanic: The Politics of the Fiestas Patronales in New York," *Latino Studies Journal* 1 (January 1990) 1:28–47.

3. The impact of the Cuban migration was principally upon the Archdiocese of Miami, Florida. In New York significant contributions were made by various Cuban priests, notably the late Monsignor Raúl del

Valle, and Catholic laity, such as Dr. William Romagosa (now ordained a deacon) and Serafín and Hilda Villariño, who helped organize the Catholic Family Movement for the Spanish-speaking. There is a Cuban-American Catholic presence, with annual masses and other activities, but the scale in New York does not rival the Cuban impact in Miami, parts of the Newark Archdiocese, or even in the Diocese of Brooklyn.

4. The article was eventually published in the June-July 1967 issue of *The Critic,* and again in 1970 in a publication of the Urban Training Center Press under the general title of *The Church, Change and Development,* (ed. Eychaner, 1970: 61–68).

6. Culture as a Sacrament

1. For a description of the changes in such laws see Moore and Pachón, 54–56. An overview of Caribbean migration is provided by Sutton and Chaney, with excellent articles on Dominicans (235–306). See also Virginia R. Dominguez, *From Neighbor to Stranger: The Dilemma of Caribbean Peoples in the United States,* Antilles Research Program, Occasional Paper n. 5, Yale University, New Haven (1975), which contains a plethora of immigration charts and statistics.

2. The literature on Feire's ideas is extensive. See his own *Pedagogy of the Oppressed,* trans. Myra Bergman Ramos (New York: Seabury Press, 1973). For the relationship to liberation theology see Denis Goulet, *A New Moral Order* (Maryknoll, New York: Orbis Books, 1974).

3. This was part of the bitter conflict between Father Louis Gigante and Councilman Ramón Vélez five years later. See John Darnton, "Gigante and Vélez in Ring of Slum Politics," *The New York Times,* November 19, 1973, pp. 37–40.

7. Deroutinization of the Church, Inc.

1. Note that Stern uses the term *Spanish-speaking* to define a person of any nationality, Hispanic or non-Hispanic in origin, who speaks the Spanish language. He refers to people of Hispanic origin as "native Spanish-speakers."

2. Compare Bureau of the Census, *Persons of Spanish Origin,* Government Printing Office, Washington, D.C., 1970, with Romeo F. Saldigloria, "Religious Problems of the Hispanos in the City of New York," in *Prophets Denied Honor,* ed. Antonio Stevens-Arroyo (Maryknoll, N.Y.: Orbis Books, 1980), p. 166.

3. Stern kept a copy of most of the reports, memoranda, and conclusions of conferences, but the data resulting from this survey is not in his archives. The Office of the Spanish-Speaking Apostolate was not able to locate any record of the survey in 1982.

8. THE HUMPTY DUMPTY SYNDROME

1. Theodore McCarrick, former vice-rector at the Catholic University in Puerto Rico, spoke Spanish very well. He was to return to the archdiocese as Cardinal Cooke's personal secretary. Later named an auxiliary Bishop, he was then given the newly created see of Metuchen, New Jersey, before being ordained Archbishop of Newark.

2. For a comparison of the conclusions of the First National Hispano Pastoral Encounter with the Lucerne Memorial of 1891 (see above, chapter 2), see Anthony M. Stevens-Arroyo, "Cahensly Revisited?: The National Pastoral Encounter of America's Hispanic Catholics," *Migration World* 15:3 (Fall 1987), 16–19.

3. I have used Stern's original manuscript of the history of the office and of this dismissal because the version published as part of the 1982 archdiocesan study was edited to remove aspects of the conflicts that developed after the dismissal. The editing was done by Friar Roberto O. González, O.F.M. without consulting Stern (Interview with Stern, January 1982). Subsequently, González was ordained Auxiliary Bishop of Boston. In Stern's original manuscript reference is made to Ms. Díaz. For the sake of clarification, please note that the author of this book, Ms. Díaz, Ana María Díaz-Ramírez and Ana María Díaz-Stevens is one and the same person.

9. ESCAPE FROM EXPERIMENTATION

1. While segregating the ministry, one of the results of the national parish was to act as a base for integration with the greater community. See Fitzpatrick (1987, 108–18) where he calls attention to the critical role of community not only as a basis for solidarity but also as a basis for political power and influence. The national (ethnic) parish played a major role in community among these earlier immigrants. The absence of the national parish for Puerto Ricans, however, left them in a situation where the creation of community through the church was more difficult.

GLOSSARY

Preface

Luis Muñoz Marín: First elected governor of Puerto Rico, 1948–64.

Partido Popular Democrático: Popular Democratic Party, founded by Luis Muñoz Marín, first elected governor of Puerto Rico under the U.S. domination.

Populares: Members of the Partido Popular Democrático.

Jíbaro, jibarito: A Puerto Rican peasant or mountain dweller. (Notice that in Spanish "ito," or "ita" is used to form the diminutive of a word.)

Cafetal: Coffee plantation.

Barriadas, barrios: A designation for a rural grouping of homesteads without legal status as a village. Used interchangeably for "urban ghetto," marginalized communities of Latinos living in a city neighborhood.

El Barrio, El Barrio Hispano: Name commonly used among Puerto Ricans and other Latinos to refer to a section in Manhattan also known as Spanish Harlem.

Comadre: Literally, co-mother; used to name the person who is either the mother of one's godchild or the godmother of one's child.

Compadre: Literally, co-father; used to name the person who is either the father of one's godchild or the godfather of one's child.

El Norte: Literally, the North; used in reference to the United States.

La Carreta, The Oxcart: A play by Puerto Rican playwright René Marqués about a Puerto Rican rural family's trials and tribulations as its members experience the migration process from the hinterland to an urban ghetto in San Juan, and from there to a metropolitan ghetto in New York.

René Marqués: Puerto Rican essayist and playwright, author of *La Carreta*, later translated as *The Oxcart.*

Virgilio Dávila: Early twentieth-century Puerto Rican poet; native values, traditions and patriotism are among his themes.

Máquina: Machine; machinery; industrial equipment; technological advancements.

La Patria: The Motherland; the Fatherland.

Criollo, criollismo: Creole; used to denote a mixture of cultures and/or races, and/or the process of adaptation and acculturation that takes place when various peoples come together in a specific geographic location.

Comadrona: Literally, co-mother; midwife; among other Latinos, especially Mexican-Americans, the word *partera* is commonly used to mean the same thing. *Partera* refers more specifically to *parto,* thus, the one who helps in birthing, or delivery of a child.

Paso fino: A special breed of horse common to Puerto Rico; noted for its fine gait.

Rubio: Blondish or red-haired; name used for an animal, in this case, a horse.

Santo catequista: Saintly catechist; one who teaches the foundations of Christian doctrine to others, especially to young ones.

El cura: The curé or priest.

Predicadores: Preachers.

Madrina: Literally, little mother; godmother.

Padrino: Literally, little father; godfather.

La Candelaria: When written in lower case, "*candelaria*" literally means fire or bonfire; in upper case Candlemas or Feast of the Purification, February 2. This coincides with the beginning of the agricultural cycle when the land is made ready for planting, oftentimes by a slash-and-burn technique. Devotion to Our Lady of the Purification was brought to Puerto Rico by settlers from the Canary Islands, where the cult prospered early in their colonization period.

Camino recto y seguro para subir al cielo: Literally, straight and secured path to attain heaven; the title of an old book of prayers found in Puerto Rican households in the 1940s and 1950s.

Santos de palo: Wooden statues of saints; in Puerto Rico this folk art was cultivated by a select number of families, and handed down from generation to generation. The endeavor of the Puerto Rican *santeros* (not to be confused with the Afro-Cuban practice of *Santería*) is considered a special religious calling and their production is highly valued, especially pieces dating from the Spanish colonization period.

Santa Teresita: St. Thérèse, the Little Flower of Lessieux, not to be confused with the Spanish mystic *Santa Teresa de Avila,* reformer of the Carmelites and Doctor of the Church.

Rezador, rezadora: Prayerful person; the one leading the people in communal prayer; a special role conferred upon a person on account of his or her wisdom and piety. Oftentimes the *rezador(a)* was also a *cantador(a),* since this person was called upon to lead in such religious communal celebrations as the *rosarios cantados* (sung rosaries), *rosarios de cruz* (for the Feast of the Exaltation of the Cross during the month of May), and *bakinés* (sung prayers for a child's wake).

Cantador, cantadora: In the same tradition as the *rezador* or *rezadora,* this person is called upon to sing at special celebrations. The *cantador* or *cantadora* may also be an *improvisador* or *improvisadora,* composing and singing the songs on the spur of the moment.

Parrandas (parrandas navideñas): This Puerto Rican tradition, which is connected to Christmas (lasting approximately from late November to the second week after January 6, the Epiphany) should not to be confused with *asaltos navideños*, which take place at the same time but are of a more spontaneous nature. *Asaltos* is a form of merrymaking where a group of relatives or friends on the spur of the moment "assault" or "crash" into a home without previous invitation. Including a religious component, and oftentimes dedicated to a particular saint (particularly the sacred family and the three kings), the *parrandas* are more organized and serious in nature. In older times, in the rural communities, everyone knew who would "take out *parrandas*" and the approximate date and itinerary for each *parranda* of the season. This Puerto Rican Christmas tradition of going from house to house, singing, sharing food and hospitality, asking for gifts and good cheer in actual fact anticipates, prepares, and celebrates in a communal fashion Christ's manifestation to the gentiles. From each household persons are recruited to accompany the group on its journey to the other houses. Most of the songs used for this celebration are improvised, and in them the *cantadores* talk about the need to share in imitation of the three wise men's generosity toward the Christ Child. Thus, the word *aguinaldo* is used both for the song and the gift received. Although more secular in nature, this tradition is similar to the Mexican *posadas.* Unlike in México or among people of Mexican extraction, however, the word *parranda* in Puerto Rico and among Puerto Ricans does not have a pejorative meaning.

Rosarios de cruz: Because these festivities are celebrated during the month of May, they are also referred to as *Fiestas de la Santa Cruz* or *Fiestas de la Cruz de Mayo.* The community comes together at one of the homes to sing a special rosary before an altar prepared beforehand to honor the holy cross upon which Jesus was crucified. After the prayers, partaking of foods and socializing is common.

Bakiné: A child's *velorio* or wake, called a *bakiné* or *florón,* is celebrated with special sung prayers. In earlier times, the deceased child was surrounded by flowers, placed on a table made to look like an altar, in the middle of the room. A famous painting, "*El velorio,*" by Puerto Rican painter Francisco Oller, immortalized this tradition.

Velorios: Wakes, where relatives and friends come together to say the final farewell to the deceased member of the community, to reminisce, to console the family of the deceased, to make preparations for the burial, and to celebrate the person's passage to a new life.

Congregación de Las Hijas de María: Congregation of the Children of Mary, comparable to Marian Sodalities in the United States.

Esencias y colorines: Literally, perfumes and rouge; toiletries or make-up.

Público: Literally, public; in Puerto Rico the word is used for "taxi."

Curandera: One who cures or heals; a faith healer. Sometimes the name *yerbatera* is used since the healer often uses *hierbas curativas,* curative plants. Also *santigüera* or *santiguadora,* from the verb *santiguar,* meaning to mark with the sign of the cross as part of the healing process.

Maryknoll Sisters of St. Dominic: The first native United States missionary religious congregation, founded in 1912 by Mary Rogers and Bishop J. Walsh and Father T. Price in Ossining, New York. At the same time a community of secular priests and religious brothers was founded, also under the name of Maryknoll. Maryknoll has been very active in Central and South America and for some years worked among the Puerto Ricans in the Bronx and Chicago areas.

Congregación Dominica de las Hermanas de Fátima: Dominican Congregation of the Daughters of Fátima, a native Puerto Rican congregation for religious women founded around 1948 in Yauco, Puerto Rico, by Sister María Dominga Guzmán of the Amityville Sisters of St. Dominic. The congregation is dedicated to the family apostolate.

Nuestra Señora de la Monserrate: Our Lady of Monserrate, a madonna originally from Cataluña, Spain. The original statue, from which the devotion sprang, had been discolored by time, hence the attribute as a "black" madonna (*la virgen negra*). In Puerto Rico devotion to this madonna spread, especially in the interior of the island, and at least two miracles were attributed to her intervention in the mountain town of Hormigueros, where a sanctuary in her honor has existed since the eighteenth century. Also referred to as Our Lady of Hormigueros.

The Oxcart: See *La Carreta.*

Gracias: Literally, graces; thank you.

1. THE STONE AND THE PITCHER

Operation Bootstrap: An economic plan geared to the rapid industrialization and urbanization of Puerto Rico launched in the 1950s during the administration of Luis Muñoz Marín.

The Puerto Rican Great Migration: Also referred to as the Great Puerto Rican Migration in other writings; one of three categories employed in a periodization model of Puerto Rican migration to the United States devised by Stevens-Arroyo and Díaz-Stevens. The Great Migration includes the years 1946–1964, when close to a million Puerto Ricans left the island for the northeastern United States. This periodization first appeared in *The Minority Report* edited by Gary and Rosalind Dworkin in 1982 and has been repeated by other authors such as Clara Rodríguez in *Puerto Ricans Born in the U.S.A.,* 1989.

The Pioneer Migration: The first period of Puerto Rican migration to the United States from 1902 to 1945.

The Revolving Door Migration: The third period of Puerto Rican migration, from 1965 to the present; this period is characterized by back-and-forth movement between the island and the mainland.

Brain drain: Term used in the social sciences to refer to the loss, usually through migration, of a highly skilled portion of the population.

The Commonwealth of Puerto Rico: The accepted English translation of *Estado Libre Asociado,* which names the official relationship of Puerto Rico to the United States. This designation was also used for the present Office of Puerto Rican Community Affairs housed in New York.

Autonomic Charter of 1897: Through this charter Puerto Rico received its autonomy from Spain. It guaranteed the island and its people greater freedom of action and rights than they have enjoyed under U. S. rule. This autonomy was short-lived, since the United States claimed Puerto Rico as war booty following what today we know as the Spanish-American War (the Cuban War of Independence from Spain). It is important to note that Puerto Rico was not involved in this conflict, and since the Charter of 1897 guaranteed consultation with the Puerto Rican people prior to any measure affecting their autonomy, many have described the United States take-over as an invasion and an illegal act.

Public Law 600: The legislation signed by President Harry S. Truman in 1950 that authorized the drafting by Puerto Ricans of their own constitution. It became the legal foundation of the present commonwealth status in 1952.

Deroutinizer: A term based on the methods of Max Weber and used by sociologist Rodney Stark to refer to a person who introduces charismatic goals to an institution, in this case the church, and thus changes the mode in which pastoral care is delivered.

Cursillistas: Those who have made the Cursillo, a three-day retreat devoted to intense mini-course on theology; a classification by Stevens-Arroyo in *Prophets Denied Honor* (1980) to define Vallier's "Papists" category (1972). See *El Cursillo.*

Second Vatican Council: The second of two major assemblies of bishops in the entire history of the Catholic church; this gathering, called by Pope John XXII, took place during the years 1962–65. The purpose was to assess the church and to plan for a response consonant with the needs of the time.

Post-Conciliar, Post-Vatican: Taking place after the Second Vatican Council, usually in response to the Council's mandates.

2. Island within the Island

Alonso Manso: Arriving on the Isla de San Juan Bautista de Puerto Rico in 1511, Manso was the first bishop of the island as well as the first bishop and inquisitor in the New World.

Taíno: From *Nitaíno,* the name for the indigenous people of Puerto Rico and the Dominican Republic.

Compadrazgo: The relationship established between individuals who are the parents and godparents of a child.

Peleita monga: A Puerto Rican *jíbaro* way of behaving, which psychologists translated as circumventive aggression.

Negrito: Literally, blackish or little black one; in Puerto Rico used as a term of endearment meaning "loved one" or "darling."

Blanquitos: Literally, whitey or little white one; in Puerto Rico used pejoratively to mean the opposite of negrito; thus, one not to be trusted.

Ermitas: Wayside chapels; hermitages; shrines.

Tiempo muerto: Literally, "dead time." In Puerto Rico, a period of low agricultural activity, thus low economic income.

Hacendados: Those who own the *haciendas* or large tracks of cultivated lands; the lords of the land.

Ex-votos: Charms, usually made of silver or gold, representing the part of the body cured by heavenly intercession.

La virgen negra: See *Nuestra Señora de la Monserrate.*

La morenita: Literally, the little dark girl, women or lady; in México, Our Lady of Guadalupe.

El gíbaro: Book written by Manuel Alonso when he was studying medicine in Spain, later published in his native Puerto Rico in 1849. Written in the idiom of the mountain dwelers, it immortalizes Puerto Rican customs and traditions. (The spelling is different from today's *jíbaro,* but the pronunciation is the same).

Pueblo: A town; also a people or nation.

Misa de (del) gallo: Literally, the rooster's mass; Christmas midnight mass.

El ideal católico: A weekly publication founded by a Spanish Vincentian in Puerto Rico in the early twentieth century.

Los Hermanos Cheos: Laymen missionary institute founded in the early twentieth century in Puerto Rico to combat Protestantization of the countryside.

Fondos de Fábrica: Literally, building funds; centralized banking and finance system established by Bishop Ambrose Jones in Puerto Rico under United States occupation to replace the Spanish government's funding for institutional Catholicism.

Cabildo: A board composed of leading citizens under Spanish rule who could set economic regulations and sometimes influence policies.

Our Lady of Hormigueros: See *Nuestra Señora de la Monserrate.*

Campesinos: Peasants or rural dwellers; often equated with the lower classes and humble origins.

Isla, La Isla: The island, short for Isla de San Juan Bautista de Puerto Rico, the official name of that Caribbean island during Spanish domination.

Juan Alejo Arizmendi: The first Puerto Rican elevated to the office of bishop (1803–14). He was persecuted by Spanish officials for his identification with Puerto Rican nationalism. After Arizmendi no other native Puerto Rican was named as bishop until the second half of this century when Monseñor Luis Aponte Martínez was elevated to the see of San Juan.

Bohíos: Originally, thatched huts of the Taínos Indians of the Greater Antilles. Today the term is used to refer to a country cottage.

Propaganda Fidei: A Vatican Office for the Propagation of the Catholic Faith. There are branches all over the world.

Blenck, James Humbert: A Bavarian-born, naturalized U.S. citizen, Blenck was named by the Holy See as the first bishop of Puerto Rico under U.S. rule.

Catholic Standard and Times: An official publication of the Philadelphia Roman Catholic Archdiocese at the turn of the century.

3. From Village Parishes to Cosmopolitan Archdiocese

The Chancery Office: The curia or central office of a local Roman Catholic Church.

Jose Martí: Cuban patriot and nineteenth-century revolutionary leader who died in the conflict between Spain and Cuba, which later turned into the Spanish-American War. He cautioned against U.S. intervention in the Cuban struggle for independence and is credited with the famous phrase: "I lived in the belly of the monster and thus know its entrails." Martí was also a *modernista* writer. Among his poems are the well-known *"Versos Sencillos,"* from which the popular song "Guantanamera" is derived.

El Centro Obrero Español: The Spanish Workers' Center, a self-help worker movement in New York during the first part of the twentieth century, following the Masonic Lodge; for the most part secularist and even somewhat anti-clerical.

El Congreso de los Pueblos de Habla Española: The Congress for Spanish-speaking Peoples, part of the Marxist wing of the Congress of Industrial Organizations and of the political power base of the East Harlem Congressman, Vito Marcantonio.

Puertorriqueño: Puerto Rican; a native of the island of Puerto Rico or a child of parents born in Puerto Rico. For the latter, the words "Neo-Rican" or "Nuyorican" are sometimes employed, but not favored. *"Boricua," "borinqueño"* (from the Indian name of the island, *Burenké* or *Borinquen*) and *"riqueño"* are other words meaning Puerto Rican.

4. The Missionary Impulse and the Basement Churches

Puerto Rican Nationalist Party: Founded by Pedro Albizu Campos, *El Partido Nacionalista Puertorriqueño* regards armed struggle as a feasible and justifiable option in the island's quest for political and economic independence from the United States.

Pedro Albizu Campos: Founder of the Puerto Rican Nationalist Party, who was imprisoned for armed insurrection. Died under house arrest. He is held in high esteem and considered by Puerto Ricans of diverse political persuasions as a patriot and a martyr for the cause of Puerto Rican independence.

Partido Independentista Puertorriqueño: Like the *nacionalistas,* the Puerto Rican Independence Party seeks the eventual separation of Puerto Rico from the United States, but peaceful negotiations are emphasized by the *independentistas.*

Fiesta: A feast or celebration.

Fiestas patronales: Patron feastdays; derived from European medieval Christendom, these week-long celebrations allow each town in Puerto Rico to make the liturgical commemoration of the saint under whose protection the town has been placed into an occasion for reaffirmation of the communality of belief. The celebrations, however, transcend the religious observances to include carnival-like festivities in the town plaza.

La Fiesta de San Juan Bautista: The Puerto Rican *fiesta patronal* par excellence. The national Puerto Rican feast day in honor of St. John the Baptist is celebrated on June 24. Originally the name of the island was Isla de San Juan Bautista de Puerto Rico. Today the capital port city bears the original name of the island, and the island bears the name of the port.

La fiesta de la comunidad hispana: In New York, the San Juan Fiesta was transformed in the 1960s into a feast day for all Latinos and came to be known as the Hispanic Community Feastday. It is celebrated on the closest Sunday to June 24.

La Gran Misión: In the late 1950s and early 1960s the Spanish Jesuit preacher Saturnino Junquera strove to introduce devotion among Puerto Ricans to Our Lady of Providence (*Nuestra Señora de la Providencia*), who later would be enthroned as patroness of the island. In New York Junquera engaged in an itinerary preaching program, "The Grand Mission," at parishes with large Puerto Rican and Latino communities.

El Cursillo: The Cursillo Movement, first established in Spain, came to New York in the 1960s and gained great popularity among the Puerto Ricans. It is a three-day intensive mini-course in theology geared at educating lay persons in the Catholic faith so that they may assume leadership positions in the local church and community. Although the directorship of the movement is ultimately in the hands of the clergy, the lay leaders assume much of the responsibility for giving the *rollos* or lectures during the three-day retreat and other activities connected with the Cursillo afterward.

Caballeros del Santo Nombre: The Knights of the Holy Name, comparable to the Holy Name Society.

Las Damas del Sagrado Corazón de Jesús: A laywomen congregation dedicated to spreading devotion to the Sacred Heart of Jesus.

Ultreyas, Cursillo Ultreyas: City-wide cursillo meetings, gathering members from all parishes throughout the archdiocese.

Misas de sótano: Masses for the Puerto Rican and Latino congregations celebrated in the lower or basement churches.

5. THE INTELLECTUALIZATION OF AN EXPERIMENT

Cuartitos: Boarding rooms in the homes of Puerto Rican families, common during the Great Migration period.

Piñata: A papier mache container, usually in the form of an animal, which is filled with candy and suspended by a rope. A blindfolded child is urged to strike the moving container with a bat, eventually breaking it and causing the candy to spill to the ground where other children await anxiously to partake of the spoils.

Doña Felisa Rincón de Gautier: Served as mayor of San Juan, Puerto Rico, for twenty-two years, from 1946 to 1968. An early supporter of Muñoz Marín, she was noted for populist style of government and social concerns despite her upper-class orientation.

San Juan Medal: An award bestowed upon a Catholic lay person during the annual celebration of the San Juan Fiesta in recognition for that person's services to the community.

La Fortaleza: Literally, the Fortress; Puerto Rican Governor's Residence.

Nueva York Hispano: A Spanish monthly magazine, begun in 1964 by Rev. Marcelino Pando. Until its demise the magazine carried news about Cursillo events and other activities in the Hispanic Catholic community of the Northeast.

The Knights of San Juan, Caballeros de San Juan: Fashioned somewhat along the lines of the Knights of Columbus, this Puerto Rican organization in the Archdiocese of Chicago enlisted large numbers of lay leaders in its outreach, social help, and pastoral care efforts. In New York a similar attempt was not successful.

National Council of Catholic Bishops: The official national body of Catholic Bishops in the United States; headquarters are in Washington, D.C.

6. CULTURE AS A SACRAMENT

Aspira: Now a national organization with headquarters in Washington, D.C., Aspira was first established in New York City through the efforts of Puerto Rican educator Antonia Pantojas. Today it has regional offices in Puerto Rico, Chicago, Philadelphia, Newark, New York City, Florida, and Puerto Rico and continues to its advocacy role on behalf of better education for Puerto Ricans and Latinos.

Summer in the City: A community-based program, approximately from 1965 to 1969, financed from the Johnson's Administration War on Poverty funds and sponsored and staffed by the Spanish Community Action Office of the Archdiocese of New York under the leadership of Monsignor Robert Fox.

War on Poverty: An economic program launched during President Johnson's administration; its purpose was to combat urban poverty by emphasizing community organization and self-help projects.

The Puerto Rican Day Parade: Also known as *El Desfile Puertorriqueño,* this parade down Fifth Avenue is usually celebrated during the summer, close to *La Fiesta de San Juan.* Attended by the general public as well as dignitaries from Puerto Rico and the United States, it offers an additional forum where Puerto Ricans celebrated among themselves and before others their Puerto Rican national pride and identity.

Puerto Rican hometown clubs: These clubs originated in New York at the beginning of the century with the influx of Puerto Rican migration. The purpose of the clubs was to nourish Puerto Rican cultural identity and to offer a place for mutual support and celebration. The name of each club reveals the particular place of origin of its membership, since each club is named for a town in Puerto Rico. To the name of the town the word *ausente* (absent) is usually added; for example, *Club San Germeños Ausentes,* for those originating in San Germán, Puerto Rico. A curious phenomenon is the existence of a club in Puerto Rico fashioned after these home-town clubs called *Neo-Ricans Ausentes.*

Puerto Rican Community Development Project (PRCDP): This project was an effort to shape a city-wide poverty agency for Puerto Ricans during the first administration of New York Mayor, John Lindsey (1965-1969). It would have utilized poverty funds on the basis of ethnicity, rather than on territoriality. This aspect of the plan was rejected, although the PRCDP was funded at a lesser scale and became an agency to train community workers.

Puerto Rican Forum: A New York city organization of Puerto Rican professionals in government and business who addressed the need for a single, coordinated plan for addressing the needs of Puerto Ricans. Founded in the mid-1950s, the Puerto Rican Forum generally sought to influence the awarding of government funds to Puerto Rican agencies and to foster the naming of Puerto Ricans to administrative positions.

The Young Lords: A Puerto Rican militant organization of the late 1960s. Founded in Chicago as a street gang, the Young Lords assumed an identity and an ideology in New York inspired by the Black Panthers. The Lords gained visibility when they took over church facilities and advocated political and economic change. Later its members constituted themselves into The Puerto Rican Workers Revolutionary Party, a Maoist organization. Although the Young Lords no longer exist as an organization, many of its members are still active in such professions as education and journalism.

Full Circle Associates: An incorporated agency founded by Monsignor Robert Fox; its main purpose was the empowerment of people at grass-root levels.

Rosarios de Cruz: An annual tradition in Puerto Rico that celebrates the building of home altars. The feast coincides with the former liturgical observance in May of the finding of the Holy Cross and was brought to Puerto Rico by settlers from Tenerife in the Canary Islands. The Holy Cross is enthroned amid flowers and candles, and the people come together every night to sing the rosary, a Marian devotion consisting of the recitation of the doxology, Hail Marys, and Our Fathers. The *rosarios de cruz* also feature special hymns and prayers, which date back to Spanish colonial times.

Latino: Used interchangeably with Hispanic and Hispano; used to name people from the Spanish-speaking Caribbean, Central and South America, and their children born in the United States.

7. DEROUTINIZATION OF THE CHURCH, INC.

Pastoral de Conjunto: An approach toward ministry, generated by the Second Vatican Council, that calls for greater cooperation among lay members of the local communities, clerics, and other religious personnel working at different levels.

"*Cara a Cara en el Mundo de la Religión*": Under the directorship of Angel Pérez this series of twenty-four radio dialogues between a Catholic priest and a Protestant minister began transmission on WBNX radio in February 1969. It was also produced on an experimental basis on "Tribuna Hispana" on Channel 47 for four months beginning in October 1969.

Noticiero Religioso: An eight-minute ecumenical religious news program broadcast live from Channel 47; it began on February 1970 and included local and worldwide religious news and an editorial.

Dios Llega al Hombre: New York Bible Society's Spanish version of the New Testament.

Encuentro, also Encuentros, Encuentros Nacionales, National Encuentro, Primer Encuentro, Segundo Encuentro: Literally, encounter. There have been three National Hispanic Encounters in the United States and countless regional and diocesan encounters as well. The *encuentros* were introduced during the 1970s. Edgar Beltrán, a priest who had been active at the meetings at Medellín and Puebla, was instrumental in the construction of these national meetings of

Latinos with church personnel, as was the Puerto Rican laywoman Encarnación Padilla de Armas and Robert L. Stern, the priest director of the Office of the Spanish-Speaking Apostolate for the Archdiocese of New York.

8. THE HUMPTY DUMPTY SYNDROME

CIDOC (Centro de Información y Documentación): Founded by Ivan Illich in Cuernavaca, Mexico, this center provided training for progressive church leaders and gathered documents relating to the church in Latin America.

USCC (United States Catholic Conference): The administrative agency of the National Council of Catholic Bishops. Originally instituted during the Spanish-American War to counter the characterization of Catholics as against the conflict, the agency gradually assumed the role of a social welfare agency under the name National Catholic Welfare Council (NCWC), before reorganization for a wider scope of administrative activities.

Institute of Intercultural Communication: This cultural and language training center was located at Larraín Institute in the Catholic University of Ponce. It was created around 1956, when Ivan Illich was vice-rector of the university, and its purpose was to train priests and other religious personnel working with Puerto Ricans in the Northeast, particularly in New York, in the Spanish language and Puerto Rican culture.

Bishops Committee for the Spanish-Speaking: Also known as the National Bishops' Committee for the Spanish-Speaking, this entity was set up primarily to respond to the spiritual needs of the Mexican-Americans of the Southwest. Later it became truly national in scope, addressing itself to the needs of other Latinos throughout the United States. Ultimately, in the early 1970s, a secretariat for Spanish-speaking affairs was opened as part of the USCC in Washington, D.C. with a Chicano and a Puerto Rican woman sharing responsibilities.

Medellín: The first meeting of Latin American bishops in their role as an episcopal conference with powers delegated to rule on liturgy and internal organization as authorized by the Second Vatican Council. Held in Medellín, Colombia, in two sessions (1967–1968), the conference drafted progressive documents on ways to implement the Council's mandates in Latin America.

Puebla: The second meeting of Latin American bishops at Puebla, México (1979). The first important episcopal conference under the pontificate of John Paul II, the Puebla conference evaluated the results of activities and policies set at Medellín and planned for the future of the Catholic church in Latin America.

CICOP (Catholic Inter-American Cooperation Program): A program of the Latin American Bureau of the NCWC (now USCC), which began in January 1964 a series of annual meetings and exchanges among Catholics of North and South America.

Comunidades eclesiales de base: Grass-root Christian base communities (CEBs) originating in Latin America. Their purpose was to aid local members of the Christian community to assess their lives and to seek ways to integrate the Christian message in the workings of everyday life, with the purpose of causing a positive impact upon the structures of society.

Interdiocesan Coordinating Committee: A committee initiated by Robert L. Stern through the Archdiocesan Office of the Spanish-Speaking Apostolate to bring together in collaborative effort the diocesan directors of the apostolate among Latinos and other leadership personnel in the Northeast area.

NCCB (National Council of Catholic Bishops): The national organization of Catholic bishops in the United States; located in Washington, D.C., its task is to make and oversee policies for the Catholic church at a national level.

CELAM (Concilio Episcopal Latinoamericano): An organization of Catholic bishops for all of Latin America, including Puerto Rico. Its task is to make and oversee policies for the Catholic church in that region as a regional episcopal conference established by the Second Vatican Council.

ICLA (Instituto Catequístico Latinoamericano): The Latin American Catechetical Institute; founded as a response to the Second Vatican Council mandates to train catechists for Latin American and the Spanish-speaking Caribbean. Dioceses in the United States with heavy concentrations of Latinos also sent their candidates there for training.

Equipos Unidos: Literally, united teams; an early 1970s Latino youth organization in the Roman Catholic Archdiocese of New York connected to the Office for the Spanish-Speaking Apostolate. *Equipos Unidos* worked with Puerto Rican and Dominican youths and was made possible through funding from the National Council of Catholic Bishops in Washington, D.C.

IPLA (Instituto Pastoral Latinoamericano): The Latin American Pastoral Institute, founded as a response to the Second Vatican Council mandates, trained religious personnel for Latin America and the Spanish-speaking Caribbean. Dioceses in the United States with heavy concentrations of Latinos, such as New York, took advantage of *IPLA*'s services, as well.

PADRES: Literally, fathers; this acronym for *Padres Asociados Para por Derechos Educacionales y Sociales* (Fathers Associated for Educational and Social Rights) was originally an association for Mexican-American priests working in the Southwest. Eventually, they joined ASH to form one national organization.

Las Hermanas: Literally, the sisters; an association for Latina women religious serving the Latino community, originating in the Southwest. Eventually it became national in scope and incorporated members from diverse Hispanic nationalities, religious and laywomen alike. *Las Hermanas* is still active today.

ASH (Asociación de Sacerdotes Hispanos): This association of Hispanic priests was to the Northeast what *PADRES* was to the Southwest. But unlike *PADRES,* ASH was always open to members from the diverse Hispanic nationalities.

BIBLIOGRAPHY

Official Documents

Abbot, Walter M., ed. *The Documents of Vatican II.* New York: Herder and Herder, 1966.

Connolly, Joseph F. "Plan of Coordination of Spanish Catholic Action for the Archdiocese of New York." Monsignor Robert L. Stern's Personal Files. The Catholic Center, New York.

Fontánez, Luis. "Report on the Meeting of March 29, 1972, with Cardinal Cooke." Record Retention Center of the Archdiocese of New York. Box 3396. 1972a.

———. "Results of the Meeting of March 29, 1972, with Cardinal Cooke." Record Retention Center of the Archdiocese of New York. Box 3390. 1972b.

"Hispanic Leaders' Letter to Cardinal Cooke, March 13, 1972." Monsignor Robert L. Stern's Personal Files. The Catholic Center, New York.

National Hispano Pastoral Encuentro Conclusions. Washington, D.C.: Division for the Spanish-Speaking, United States Catholic Conference, 1972.

Kelly, George A. "Catholic Survey of the Puerto Rican Population in the Archdiocese of New York," 1955. Monsignor Robert L. Stern's Personal Files. The Catholic Center, New York.

"Summer in the City: Information for Center Directors and Board Members." Record Retention Center of the Archdiocese of New York, Box 99.9. Spanish-Speaking Apostolate Office of the Catholic Archdiocese of New York. "Annual Report: September 1, 1969–August 31, 1970." Monsignor Robert L. Stern's Personal Files. The Catholic Center, New York.

United States Commission on Civil Rights. "Puerto Ricans in the Continental United States: An Uncertain Future." Washington, D.C.: Government Printing Office, 1976.

Books and Articles

Abbad y Lasierra, Iñigo. *Historia geográfica, civil y natural de la isla de San Juan Bautista de Puerto Rico.* (1789) Río Piedras, Puerto Rico: Editorial Universitaria, 1959.

Abell, Aaron I. *American Catholicism and Social Action.* New York: Hanover House, 1969.

Adriance, Madeline. *Opting for the Poor: Brazilian Catholicism in Transition.* Kansas City, Mo.: Sheed & Ward, 1986.

Albion, Robert G. *The Rise of New York Port: 1815–1869.* New York: Scribner's, 1939.

Albizu Miranda, Carlos, and Héctor Marty Torres. "Atisbos de la personalidad puertorriqueña," *Revista de ciencias sociales* 2, no. 3 (1958).

Alers Montalvo, Manuel. *The Puerto Rican Migrants of New York City: A Study of Anomie.* New York: AMS Press, 1985.

Alonso, Manuel. *El gíbaro: cuadro de costumbres de la Isla de Puerto Rico.* (1849) Edición facsímil. San Juan de Puerto Rico: Instituto de Cultura Puertorriqueña, 1967.

Alvarez, David J., ed. *An American Church: Essays on the Americanization of the Catholic Church.* Moraga, Calif.: St. Mary's College, 1979.

Anson, Robert Sam. "The Irish Connection." *New Times,* May 17, 1974: 29–33.

Babín, María Teresa. *Panorama de la cultura puertorriqueña.* New York: Las Américas, 1958.

Barger, R. N. In *An American Church: Essays on the Americanization of the Catholic Church,* edited by David J. Alvarez, 53–62. Moraga, Calif.: St. Mary's College, 1979.

Barry, Colman. *The Catholic Church and German Americans.* Milwaukee: Bruce, 1953.

Bates, Margaret, ed. *Lay Apostolate in Latin America Today.* Washington, D.C.: Catholic University of America Press, 1960.

Beckford, James. "Religious Organization." *Current Sociology* 21, no. 2 (1973): 34–92.

Beirne, Charles J. *The Problem of Americanization in the Catholic Schools of Puerto Rico.* Río Piedras, Puerto Rico: Editorial Universitaria, 1975.

Bell, Stephen. *Rebel Priest and Prophet: A Biography of Edward McGlynn.* New York: n.p., 1937.

Bellah, Robert. *Beyond Belief: Essays on Religion in a Post-Traditional World.* New York: Harper and Row, 1970.

Benedi, Claudio F. "The Reformist Vision of Félix Varela." *Americas* 29, no. 4 (Apr. 1979): 9–12.

Berbusse, Edward J. *The United States in Puerto Rico.* Chapel Hill: University of North Carolina Press, 1966.

Bergard, Laird. *Coffee and the Growth of Agrarian Capitalism in Nineteenth-Century Puerto Rico.* Princeton, N.J.: Princeton University Press, 1983.

Besalga, Edward, S.J. "Cultural Change and Protestantism in Puerto Rico: 1945–1966." Ph.D. diss., New York University, 1970.

Bloomfield, Richard J., ed. *Puerto Rico: The Search for a National Policy.* Boulder, Colo.: Westview Press, 1985.

Bonilla, Frank, and Ricardo Campos. "A Wealth of Poor: Puerto Ricans in the New Economic Order." *Daedalus: Journal of the American Academy of Arts and Sciences* 110, no. 2 (Spring 1981): 133–76.

Brooke, Christopher. *Europe in the Central Middle Ages, 962–1154.* New York: New York University Press, 1982.

Brown, Henry J. "Archbishop Hughes and Western Colonization." *Catholic Historical Review* 36 (Oct. 1950): 257–85.

Brown, Jack. "Subcultures of Isolation in Rural Puerto Rico." Ithaca, N.Y.: Department of Anthropology, Cornell University (mimeographed), 1964.

Brown, Thomas T. *Irish American Nationalism.* Philadelphia, Pa.: n.p., 1966.

Cadena, Gilbert R. "Chicanos and the Catholic Church: Liberation Theology as a Form of Empowerment." Ph. D. diss., University of California, Riverside, 1987.

Calitri, Ronald, Angelo Falcón, Harry Rodríguez Reyes, Juan Moreno, and José Sánchez. *Latino Voter Registration in New York City.* New York: Institute for Puerto Rican Policy, 1982.

Caro, Robert A. *The Power Broker.* New York: Vintage Books, 1975.

Carrillo, Alberto. "Towards a National Hispano Church." In *Prophets Denied Honor: An Anthology on the Hispanic Church in the United States,* edited by Antonio M. Stevens-Arroyo, 154–57. Maryknoll, N.Y.: Orbis Books, 1980.

Centro de Estudios Puertorriqueños. *Labor Migration under Capitalism: The Puerto Rican Experience.* New York: Monthly Review Press, 1979.

Chenault, Lawrence. *The Puerto Rican Migrant in New York City.* New York: Columbia University Press, 1938.

Christian, William A., Jr. *Local Religion in Sixteenth-Century Spain.* Princeton, N.J.: Princeton University Press, 1981.

Cloward, Richard A., and Frances Fox Piven. *Poor People's Movements.* New York: Vintage Books, 1979.

Cole, Mary. *Summer in the City.* New York: Kenedy, 1968.

Coleman, John A. *The Evolution of Dutch Catholicism, 1958–1974.* Berkeley: University of California Press, 1978.

Colonnese, Louis M., ed. *Human Rights and the Liberation of Man in the Americas.* Notre Dame, Ind.: University of Notre Dame Press, 1970.

Cordasco, Francesco, and Eugene Bucchioni. *The Puerto Rican Experience: A Sociological Sourcebook.* Totowa, N.J.: Littlefield, Adams, 1973.

Corretger, Juan Antonio. *Albizu Campos.* Montevideo, Uruguay: Siglo Ilustrado, 1969.

Corrigan, Michael A. "Register of the Clergy Laboring in the Archdiocese of New York from Early Missionary Times to 1885." *Historical Records and Studies* 5 (Nov. 1907): 398.

Coser, Louis A. *Masters of Sociological Thought: Ideas in Historical and Social Context.* New York: Harcourt Brace Jovanovich, 1971.

Curbelo de Díaz, Irene. *Santos de Puerto Rico.* San Juan, Puerto Rico: Museo de Santos, 1970.

Curran, Robert Emmett. *Michael Augustine Corrigan and the Shaping of Conservative Catholicism in America, 1878–1902.* New York: Arno Press, 1978.

Curran, Thomas J. "The Immigrant Influence of the Roman Catholic Church: New York—A Test Case." In *An American Church: Essays on the Americanization of the Catholic Church,* edited by David J. Alvarez, 26–50. Moraga, Calif.: St Mary's College, 1979.

Darnton, John. "Gigante and Vélez in Ring of Slum Politics." *New York Times,* Nov. 19, 1973: 37–40.

Dávila, Arturo. "Notas sobre el arte sacro en el pontificado del ilustrísimo señor de Arizmendi (1803–1814)." *Revista del Instituto de Cultura Puertorriqueña* 3, no. 9 (Oct.–Dec. 1960): 46–51.

Deck, Allan Figueroa, S.J. *The Second Wave: Hispanic Ministry and the Evangelization of Cultures.* Mahwah, N.J.: Paulist Press, 1989.

———. "The Crisis of Hispanic Ministry: Multiculturalism as an Ideology." *America* 163, no. 2 (July 14–21, 1990): 33–36.

Díaz-Ramírez, Ana María. "Puerto Rican Peoplehood and the Pastoral Practices of the New York Catholic Church." M.A. thesis, New York University, 1978.

———. "The Passion, Death and Resurrection of the Spanish-Speaking Apostolate." In *Prophets Denied Honor: An Anthology on the Hispanic Church in the United States,* edited by Antonio M. Stevens-Arroyo, 208–13. Maryknoll, N.Y.: Orbis Books, 1980.

———. "The Roman Catholic Archdiocese of New York and the Puerto Rican Migration, 1950–1973: A Sociological and Historical Analysis." Ph.D. diss., Fordham University, 1983.

Díaz-Soler, Luis. *Historia de la esclavitud en Puerto Rico.* Río Piedras, Puerto Rico: Editorial Universitaria, 1970.

Díaz-Stevens, Ana María. "A Concept of Mission: The National Parish and Francis Cardinal Spellman." *Migration World* 15, no. 1 (1987): 22–26.

———. "From Puerto Rican to Hispanic: The Politics of the Fiestas Patronales in New York." *Latino Journal* 1, no. 1 (Jan. 1990): 28–47.

———. "Social Distance and Religious Conflict in the Pre-Vatican Catholicism of Puerto Rico." *MACLAS Essays: Journal of the Middle Atlantic Council for Latin American Studies* 4 (1991): 291–99.

Dietz, James L. *Economic History of Puerto Rico.* Princeton, N.J.: Princeton University Press, 1986.

Dohen, Dorothy. *Nationalism and American Catholicism.* New York: Sheed & Ward, 1967.

Dolan, Jay P. "A Critical Period in American Catholicism." *Review of Politics* 35 (Oct. 1973): 523–36

———. *The Immigrant Church: New York's Irish and German Catholics, 1815–1865.* Baltimore: Johns Hopkins University Press, 1975; reprint Notre Dame, Ind.: University of Notre Dame Press, 1983.

———. *Catholic Revivalism.* Notre Dame, Ind.: University of Notre Dame Press, 1978.

Domínguez, Virginia R. *From Neighbor to Stranger.* New Haven, Conn.: Yale University Antilles Research Program, 1975.

Doyle, Ruth, Olga Scarpetta, Thomas M. McDonald, and Norman Simmons. *Hispanics in New York: Religious, Cultural and Social Experiences.* 2 vols. New York: Office of Pastoral Research, Roman Catholic Archdiocese of New York, 1982.

Durkheim, Emile. *The Elementary Forms of the Religious Life.* New York: Free Press, 1965.

Dworkin, Gary, and Rosalind Dworkin, eds. *The Minority Report.* 2nd ed. New York: Rinehart and Winston, 1982.

Ehrlich, Paul R., Loy Bilderback, and Anne H. Ehrlich. *The Golden Door: International Migration, Mexico and the United States.* New York: Ballantine Books, 1979.

Elizondo, Virgilio. *Mestizaje: The Dialectic of Cultural Birth and the Gospel.* San Antonio, N.M.: Mexican American Cultural Center, 1978.

Ellis, John Tracy. *American Catholicism.* Chicago: University of Chicago Press, 1956.

Entwistle, Harold. *Antonio Gramsci: Conservative Schooling for Radical Politics.* London: Routledge & Kegan Paul, 1979.

Estades, Rosa. *Patrones de participación política de los puertorriqueños en la ciudad de Nueva York.* Río Piedras: Editorial Universitaria, 1978.

———. "Symbolic Unity: The Puerto Rican Day Parade." In *The Puerto Rican Struggle: Essays on Survival in the U.S*, 82–89. New York: Puerto Rican Migration Research Consortium, 1980.

Feagin, Joe R. *Subordinating the Poor: Welfare and American Beliefs.* Englewood Cliffs, N.J.: Prentice-Hall, 1975.

Fenton, John H. *The Catholic Vote.* New Orleans: Hauser Press, 1960.

Fernández Méndez, Eugenio. *Historia cultural de Puerto Rico, 1493–1968.* San Juan: Ediciones el Cemí, 1970.

Fernández Retamar, Roberto, ed. *Cuba, Nuestra América y Los Estados Unidos.* Mexico, D.F.: Siglo XXI, 1973.

———. *Calibán: Apuntes sobre la cultura en nuestra América.* 2nd. ed. Mexico, D.F.: Editorial Diogenes, 1974.

Ferrée, William, Ivan Illich, and Joseph P. Fitzpatrick, S.J. *Spiritual Care of Puerto Rican Migrants.* Cuernavaca, México: Centro Intercultural de Documentación, 1970; reprint ed., New York: Arno Press, 1980.

Fichter, Joseph H., S.J. *Dynamics of a City Church: Southern Parish.* Vol. 1. Chicago: University of Chicago Press, 1951.

Figueroa, Loida. *History of Puerto Rico: From the Beginning to 1892.* New York: Anaya, 1972.

Finn, Brendan A. *Twenty-Four American Cardinals.* Boston: n.p., 1947.

Fitzpatrick, Joseph P., S.J. "Intermarriage of Puerto Ricans in New York City." *American Journal of Sociology* 71, no. 4 (1966): 395–406.

———. "What Illich Is Getting at." *America* 116, no. 16 (Jan. 1967).

———. *Puerto Rican Americans: The Meaning of Migration to the Mainland.* Englewood Cliffs, N.J.: Prentice-Hall, 1971.

———. *One Faith: Many Cultures.* Kansas City, Mo.: Sheed & Ward, 1987.

Freire, Paulo. *Pedagogy of the Oppressed.* Translated by Myra Bergman Ramos. New York: Seabury Press, 1973.

Gannon, Robert Ignatius. *The Cardinal Spellman Story.* Garden City, N.Y.: Doubleday, 1962.

Garrido, Pablo. *Esotería y fervor populares de Puerto Rico.* Madrid: Cultural Hispánica, 1952.

Gleason, Philip. "The Crisis of Americanization." In *Contemporary Catholicism in the United States,* edited by Philip Gleason. Notre Dame, Ind.: University of Notre Dame Press, 1969.

———, ed. *Catholicism in America.* New York: Harper & Row, 1970.

——— and David Salvaterra. "Ethnicity, Immigration and American Catholic History." *Social Thought* 4 (Summer 1978): 3–28.

Glazer, Nathan, and Daniel P. Moynihan. *Beyond the Melting Pot.* 2nd ed. Cambridge, Mass.: Harvard–M.I.T. Press, 1970.

González, José Luis. *El país de cuatro pisos.* Río Piedras, Puerto Rico: Ediciones Huracán, 1980.

González, Justo. *The Theological Education of Hispanics.* New York: Fund for Theological Education, 1988.

Gordon, Milton. *Assimilation in American Life: The Role of Race, Religion and National Origins.* New York: Oxford University Press, 1974.

Goulet, Denis. *A New Moral Order.* Maryknoll, N.Y.: Orbis Books, 1974.

Gramsci, Antonio. *Selections from the Prison Notebooks.* Edited and translated by Quintin Hoare and Geoffrey Nowell Smith. New York: International Publishers, 1971.

Grasso, Philip A. *Under Two Flags.* Dubuque, Iowa: n.p. 1958.

Gray, Francine Du Plessix. "The Rules of the Game." *The New Yorker,* Apr. 25, 1970: 40–92.

Grebler, Leo, Joan Moore, and Ralph Guzmán, eds. *The Mexican American People.* New York: Free Press, 1970.

Greeley, Andrew. *The Denominational Society: A Sociological Approach to Religion in America.* Glenview, Ill.: Scott, Foresman, 1972a.

———. *That Most Distressful Nation: The Taming of the American Irish.* Chicago: Quadrangle Books, 1972b.

———. *The American Catholic: A Social Portrait.* New York: Basic Books, 1977.

Gross, Susan Hill, and Marjorie Wall Bingham. *Women in Latin America.* Vol. 1. St. Louis Park, Minn.: Glenhurst Publications, 1985.

Gurevich, A. J. *Categories of Medieval Culture.* London: Routledge & Kegan Paul, 1972.

Gutiérrez, Gustavo. *A Theology of Liberation.* Maryknoll, N.Y.: Orbis Books, 1973.

Gutiérrez del Arroyo, Isabel. "Juan Alejo Arizmendi, primer obispo puertorriqueño (1803–1814)." *Revista del Instituto de Cultura Puertorriqueña* 3, no. 9 (Oct.-Dec. 1960): 36–39.

———. "Itinerario de la segunda visita pastoral de su Ilma. el Dr. D. Juan Alejo de Arizmendi (1803–1814)." Ibid., pp. 40–45.

Halsey, William M. *The Survival of American Innocence.* Notre Dame, Ind.: University of Notre Dame Press, 1980.

Handlin, Oscar. *The Newcomers: Negroes and Puerto Ricans in a Changing Metropolis.* Cambridge, Mass.: Harvard University Press, 1969.

Hargrove, Barbara. *The Sociology of Religion: Classical and Contemporary Approaches.* Arlington Heights, Ill.: AHM Publishing, 1979.

Harrington, Michael. *Fragments of a Century.* New York: Saturday Review Press, 1973.

Haveman, Robert H., ed. *A Decade of Federal Antipoverty Programs.* New York: Academic Press, 1977.

Hennesey, James. *American Catholics: A History of the Roman Catholic Community in the United States.* New York: Oxford University Press, 1981a.

———. *Catholics in the Promised Land of the Saints.* Milwaukee: Marquette University Press, 1981b.

Herlihy, David. *Medieval and Renaissance Pistoia: The Social History of an Italian Town, 1200–1430.* New Haven, Conn.: Yale University Press, 1967.

Hernández Alvarez, José. *Return Migration to Puerto Rico.* Berkeley: Institute of International Studies at the University of California, 1969.

Herreshoff, David. *The Origins of American Marxism.* New York: Pathfinder Press, 1973.

Hobsawm, E. J. "The Great Gramsci." *New York Review of Books* 21 (Apr. 4, 1974): 5.

Illich, Ivan. *The Church, Change and Development.* Edited by Fred Eychaner. Chicago: Herder and Herder, 1970.

Jackson, Anthony. *A Place Called Home: A History of Low-Cost Housing in Manhattan.* Cambridge, Mass.: M.I.T. Press, 1976.

Jennings, James, and Monte Rivera, eds. *Puerto Rican Politics in Urban America.* Westport, Conn.: Greenwood Press, 1984.

Jones, Maldwyn A. *Destination America.* New York: Holt, Rinehart & Winston, 1976.

Julián de Nieves, Elisa. *The Catholic Church in Colonial Puerto Rico (1898–1964).* Río Piedras, Puerto Rico: Editorial Edil, 1982.

Lachmann, L. M. *The Legacy of Max Weber.* Berkeley: Glendessary Press, 1971.

Landy, David. *Tropical Childhood.* New York: Harper Torchbooks, 1965.

Lankevich, George J., and Howard B. Furer. *A Brief History of New York City.* Port Washington, N.Y.: Association Faculty Press, 1984.

Leroux, Penny. *Cry of the People.* New York: Penguin Books, 1988.

Levine, Daniel H. *Religion and Politics in Latin America: The Catholic Church in Venezuela and Colombia.* Princeton, N.J.: Princeton University Press, 1981.

Lewis, Gordon. *Puerto Rico: Freedom and Power in the Caribbean.* New York: Harper & Row, 1963.

Lipset, Seymour, and Martin Solari. *Elites in Latin America.* London, Oxford, and New York: Oxford University Press, 1967.

López, Alfredo. *The Puerto Rican Papers: Notes on the Re-Emergence of a Nation.* Indianapolis: Bobbs-Merrill, 1973.

McCarrick, Theodore. "Puerto Rico and the Lay Apostolate." In *Lay Apostolate in Latin America Today,* edited by Margaret Bates. Washington, D.C.: Catholic University of America Press, 1960.

McNamara, Patrick Hayes. "Bishops, Priests and Prophecy: A Study in the Sociology of Religious Protest." Ph.D. diss., University of California, 1968.

———. "Dynamics of the Catholic Church: From Pastoral to Social Concern." In *The Mexican American People,* edited by Leo Grebler, Joan Moore, and Ralph Guzmán, 449–85. New York: Free Press, 1970.

Maduro, Otto A. *Religion and Social Conflicts.* Maryknoll, N.Y.: Orbis Books, 1982.

Manrique Cabrera, Francisco. *Historia de la literatura puertorriqueña.* Río Piedras, Puerto Rico: Editorial Cultural, 1969.

Marqués, René. *La carreta.* Río Piedras, Puerto Rico: Editorial Cultural, 1963. Trans. by Charles Pilditch as *The Oxcart.* New York: Charles Scribner's Sons, 1969.

Matthew, David. *The Medieval European Community.* New York: St. Martin's Press, 1977.

Maynard, Theodore. *The Catholic Church and the American Idea.* New York: Appleton-Century-Crofts, 1953.

Martí, José. "El cisma de los católicos en Nueva York." In *Cuba, Nuestra América y Los Estados Unidos,* edited by R. Fernández Retamar, 257–67. México: Siglo XXI, 1973.

Meyer, Gerald. *Vito Marcantonio: Radical Politician, 1902–1954.* Albany: State University of New York Press, 1989.

Mills, C. Wright, Clarence Senior, and Rose Goldsen. *The Puerto Rican Journey: New York's Newest Immigrants.* New York: Harper and Brothers, 1950.

Mintz, Sidney. "An Essay in the Definition of National Culture." In *The Puerto Rican Experience,* edited by Francesco Cordasco and Eugene Bucchioni. Totowa, N.J.: Littlefield Adams, 1973.

Moore, Donald T. "Puerto Rico para Cristo." Ph.D. diss., South West Baptist Seminary, Forth Worth, Tex. Published by *Sondeos,* N. 4–3, Cuernavaca: CIDOC, 1969.

Moore, Joan, and Harry Pachón. *Hispanics in the United States.* Englewood Cliffs, N.J.: Prentice-Hall, 1985.

Mörner, Magnus. *Racial Mixture in the History of Latin America.* Boston: Little, Brown, 1967.

Morse, Richard W. "La transformación ilusoria de Puerto Rico." *Revista de ciencias sociales* 4, no. 2 (1960).

Moya Pons, Frank. *Después de Colón.* Madrid: Editorial Alianza, 1987.

Murnion, Philip. *The Catholic Priest and the Changing Structure of Pastoral Ministry, New York, 1920–1970.* New York: Arno Press, 1978.

Newman, William M., ed. *The Social Meaning of Religion.* Chicago: Rand McNally, 1974.

Niebuhr, H. Richard. *The Kingdom of God in America.* New York: Harper & Row, 1959.

Nisbet, Robert A. *The Sociological Tradition.* New York: Basic Books, 1966.

Novak, Michael. *The Rise of the Unmeltable Ethnics.* New York: Macmillan, 1971.

O'Brien, David J. *The Renewal of American Catholicism.* New York: Paulist Press, 1972.

Ocampo, Tarcisio. *Puerto Rico: Partido Acción Cristiana, 1960–1962.* Cuernavaca: CIDOC, 1967.

O'Dea, Thomas. *The American Catholic Dilemma.* New York: Sheed & Ward, 1962.

———. "Five Dilemmas in the Institutionalization of Religion." *Journal for the Scientific Study of Religion* 1 (1961): 30–39. Reprinted in William M. Newman, ed., *The Social Meaning of Religion.* Chicago: Rand McNally, 1974.

Orsi, Robert Anthony. *The Madonna of 115th Street: Faith and Community in Italian Harlem, 1880–1950.* New Haven, Conn.: Yale University Press, 1985.

Padilla, Elena. *Up from Puerto Rico.* New York: Columbia University Press, 1958.

Padilla, Félix. M. *Latino Ethnic Consciousness: The Case of Mexican Americans and Puerto Ricans in Chicago.* Notre Dame, Ind.: University of Notre Dame Press, 1985.

———. *Puerto Rican Chicago.* Notre Dame, Ind.: University of Notre Dame Press, 1987.

Pantojas, Emilio. *La iglesia protestante y la americanización de Puerto Rico.* Bayamón, Puerto Rico: PRISA, n.d.

Parsons, Talcott. *The Structure of Social Action.* New York: The Free Press, 1937.

———. "Max Weber and the Contemporary Political Crisis." *Review of Politics* 4 (1942).

Poblete, Renato, and Thomas O'Dea. "Anomie and the 'Quest for Community': The Formation of Sects among the Puerto Ricans of New York." *American Catholic Sociological Review* 21 (Spring 1960): 18–36.

Potter, George W. *To the Golden Door.* Boston: Little, Brown, 1960.

Perea, Salvador. "Historical Notes and Interpretation on Vocations and Clergy in Puerto Rico." In *Spiritual Care of Puerto Rican Migrants,* edited by Ferrée et al, 4/25–4/31. New York: Arno Press, 1980.

Picó, Fernando, S.J. *Libertad y servidumbre en el Puerto Rico del siglo xix.* Río Piedras, Puerto Rico: Ediciones Huracán, 1981a.

———. *Amargo café.* Río Piedras, Puerto Rico: Ediciones Huracán, 1981b.

———. *Los gallos peleados.* Río Piedras, Puerto Rico: Ediciones Huracán, 1988a.

———. *Historia general de Puerto Rico.* Río Piedras, Puerto Rico: Ediciones Huracán, 1988b.

Pietri, Pedro. *Puerto Rican Obituary.* New York: Monthly Review Press, 1973.

Rendón, Armando. *Chicano Manifesto.* New York: Collier Books, 1971.

Ribes Tovar, Federico. *El libro puertorriqueño de Nueva York.* 2 vols. New York: Plus Ultra, 1968.

———. *Albizu Campos: Puerto Rican Revolutionary.* New York: Plus Ultra, 1971.

Rivera, Edward. *Family Installments: Memories of Growing up Hispanic.* New York: William Morrow, 1982.

Rivera Bermúdez, Ramón. *Historia de Coamo, la villa añeja.* Coamo, Puerto Rico: Imprenta Costa, 1980.

Rivera Pagán, Luis. *Senderos teológicos: el pensamiento evangélico puertorriqueño.* Río Piedras, Puerto Rico: Editorial La Reforma, 1989.

Robertson, Roland "The Problem of the Two Kingdoms: Religion, individual, and society in the work of J. Milton Yinger." *Journal for the Scientific Study of Religion* 17, no. 3 (1978): 300–312.

Rodríguez, Clara E. *Puerto Ricans Born in the U.S.A.* Boston: Unwin Hyman, 1989.

———, Virginia Sánchez-Korrol, and José Oscar Alers, eds. *The Puerto Rican Struggle: Essays on Survival in the U.S.* New York: Puerto Rican Migration Research Consortium, 1980.

Rodríguez, José Ignacio. *Vida del presbítero don Félix Varela.* New York, n.p., 1878.

Saldigloria, Romeo. "Religious Problems of the Hispanics in the City of New York," In *Prophets Denied Honor: An Anthology on the Hispanic Church in the United States,* edited by Antonio M. Stevens-Arroyo, 166. Maryknoll, N.Y.: Orbis Books, 1980.

Saloutos, Theodore. "Exodus, U. S. A." In *Divided Society: The Ethnic Experience in America,* ed. Colin Greer, 134–60. New York: Basic Books, 1974.

Sánchez-Korrol, Virginia E. *From Colonia to Community: The History of Puerto Ricans in New York City, 1917–-1948.* Westport, Conn.: Greenwood Press, 1983.

Sandoval, Moisés, ed. *Fronteras.* San Antonio, N.M.: Mexican American Cultural Center, 1983.

———. *On the Move: A History of the Hispanic Church in the United States.* Maryknoll, N.Y.: Orbis Books, 1990.

Sassoon, Anne Showstack. *Gramsci's Politics.* New York: St. Martin's Press, 1980.

Seda Bonilla, Eduardo. *Requiem para una cultura.* Río Piedras, Puerto Rico: Ediciones Bayoán, 1980.

Sexton, Patricia Cayo. *Spanish Harlem: Anatomy of Poverty.* New York: Harper & Row, 1965.

Silva Gotay, Samuel. "La iglesia católica en el proceso político de la americanización de Puerto Rico: 1898–1930." *Cristianismo y sociedad,* 86 (1985): 7–34.

———. "El Partido Acción Cristiana: Trasfondo histórico y significado sociológico del nacimiento y muerte de un partido político católico en Puerto Rico." *Revista de historia* 7 (Jan.–Dec. 1988): 146–81.

Silvestrini, Blanca G., and María Dolores Luque de Sánchez. *Historia de Puerto Rico: Trayectoria de un pueblo.* San Juan: Cultural Puertorriqueña, 1987.

Smelser, Neil J. *Essays in Sociological Explanation.* Englewood Cliffs, N.J.: Prentice Hall, 1968.

Spalding, John Lancaster. *The Religious Mission of the Irish People and Catholic Colonization.* New York: n.p., 1880.

Stark, Werner. "The Routinization of Charisma: A Consideration of Catholicism." *Sociological Analysis* 26 (Winter 1963): 203–11.

Stern, Robert L. "The Archdiocese of New York and Hispanic Americans." *Migration Today* 5, no. 6 (June 1977): 18–23.

———. "Evolution of Hispanic Ministry in the Archdiocese of New York." Prepared for the Archdiocesan Office of Pastoral Research, June, 1982. Monsignor Robert L. Stern's Personal Files. Catholic Center, New York.

Stevens-Arroyo, Antonio. "Marxism and Hispanic Movements." *New Catholic World* 220, no. 1317 (May–June 1977): 126–28.

———, ed. *Prophets Denied Honor: An Anthology on the Hispanic Church in the United States.* Maryknoll, N.Y.: Orbis Books, 1980.

———. "The Indigenous Elements in the Popular Religion of Puerto Ricans." Ph. D. diss., Fordham University, 1981.

———. "Puerto Rican Migration to the United States." In *Fronteras,* edited by Moisés Sandoval, 269–76. San Antonio, N.M.: Mexican American Cultural Center, 1983.

———. "A Latino Critique of Post-Ethnic Catholic Church." Paper delivered at the Annual Meeting of the Society for the Scientific Study of Religion, Virginia Beach, Nov. 10, 1990.

———. "Catholic Ethos as Politics: The Puerto Rican Nationalists." In *Twentieth-Century World Religious Movements in Neo-Weberian Perspectives,* edited by William H. Swatos, Jr., 175–91. Lewiston, N.Y.: Edwin Mellen Press, 1992.

———, and Ana María Díaz-Ramírez. "The Hispano Model of Church: A People on the March." *New Catholic World,* July-August, 1980: 153–57.

———. "Puerto Ricans in the States." In *The Minority Report,* edited by Gary and Rosalind Dworkin, 2nd ed., 196–232. New York: Rinehart & Winston, 1982.

Steward, Julian, et al. *The People of Puerto Rico: A Study in Social Anthropology.* Urbana: University of Illinois Press, 1972.

Strang, William. *Business Guide for Priests.* New York: n.p., 1899.

Sutton, Constance R., and Elsa M. Chaney, eds. *Caribbean Life in New York City: Sociocultural Dimensions.* Staten Island, N.Y.: Center for Migration Studies, 1987.

Tomasi, Silvano. *Piety and Power: The Role of Italian Parishes in the New York Metropolitan Areas, 1880–1930.* New York: Center for Migration Studies, 1975.

Torres-Díaz, José. *Sínodo Diocesano de Puerto Rico, 1917.* San Juan: Archdiocese of San Juan, 1919.

Tumin, Melvin, and Arnold Feldman. "The Miracle of Sábana Grande." *Public Opinion Quarterly* 19, no. 2 (1955). Reprinted in *Portrait of a Society,* edited by Fernández Méndez, 356–69. San Juan: Editorial Universitaria, 1972.

Vallier, Ivan. "Religious Elites: Differentiations and Developments in Roman Catholicism." In *Elites in Latin America,* ed. Seymour C. Lipset and Aldo Solari, 190–232. New York: Oxford University Press, 1967.

———. *Catholicism, Social Control and Modernization in Latin America.* Englewood Cliffs, N.J.: Prentice-Hall, 1970.

Van Delft, M. *La Mission Paroissiale, Pratique et Theorie.* Translated by Fr. Van Groenendael. Paris: n.p. 1964.

Varacalli, Joseph A. *Toward the Establishment of Liberal Catholicism in America.* Washington, D.C.: University Press of America, 1983.

Vega, Bernardo. *Memorias de Bernardo Vega: Una contribución a la historia de la comunidad puertorriqueña en Nueva York.* Edited by César Andreu Iglesias. Río Piedras, Puerto Rico: Ediciones Huracán, 1980. English version published by Monthly Review Press, 1984.

Vidal, Jaime. "Popular Religion Among the Hispanics in the General Area of the Archdiocese of Newark. Part IV." In *Nueva Presencia: Knowledge for Service and Hope—A Study of Hispanics in the Archdiocese of Newark.* Newark, N.J.: Office of Research and Planning, Archdiocese of Newark, 1988.

Wagenheim, Kal. *Puerto Rico: A Profile.* New York: Praeger Publishers, 1970.

Wakefield, Dan. *Island in the Sun.* Boston: Houghton Mifflin, 1959.
Walsh, Albens. "The Work of the Catholic Bishops' Committee for the Spanish-Speaking in the United States." M.A. thesis, University of Texas, 1952.
Weber, Max. *The Theory of Social and Economic Organizations.* Edited by Talcott Parsons. New York: The Free Press, 1947.
———. *The Protestant Ethic and the Spirit of Capitalism.* Translated by Talcott Parsons. New York: Charles Scribner's Sons, 1958.
———. *The Sociology of Religion.* Translated by Ephraim Fischoff. Boston: Beacon Press, 1963.
Wells, Henry. *The Modernization of Puerto Rico.* Cambridge, Mass.: Harvard University Press, 1969.
Wills, Garry. *Bare Ruined Choirs: Doubt, Prophecy and Radical Religion.* New York: Delta, 1971.
Yinger, Milton. *Religion in the Struggle for Power: A Study in the Sociology of Religion.* Durham, N.C.: Duke University Press, 1946.
———. "Response to Professors Bouma, Robbins, Robertson and Means." *Journal for the Scientific Study of Religion* 17, no. 3 (1978): 321.
Zizola, Gregorio, and Antonio Barbero. *La riforma del Sant'Offizio a il "caso Illich".* Turin: Pietro Gribaudi Editore, 1969.

JOURNALS, PERIODICALS, NEWSPAPERS, RECORDINGS

Albizu Campos, Pedro. "Discurso Día de la Raza: 12 de octubre de 1948, Ponce, Puerto Rico." Recorded speech, edited by Ovidio Dávila and Isolina Rondón.
America 116, no. 13, (Jan. 1967); 116, no. 17 (April 1967); 163, no. 2 (July 14–21, 1990).
American Catholic 22, no. 3 (Fall 1961).
American Journal of Sociology 71, no. 4 (1966).
American Catholic Sociological Review 21 (Spring 1960).
Américas 29, no. 4 (Apr. 1977).
Catholic Historical Review 36 (Oct. 1950).
Cristianismo y sociedad 8 (1985).
Current Sociology 21, no. 2 (1973).
Daedalus: Journal of the American Academy of Arts and Sciences 110, no. 2 (Spring 1981).
Historical Records and Studies 5 (Nov. 1907).
Journal for the Scientific Study of Religion 1 (1961); 17, no. 3 (1978).
Latino Journal 1, no. 1 (Jan. 1990).
MACLAS Essays: Journal of the Middle Atlantic Council for Latin American Studies 4 (1991).

Man of La Mancha. A musical play based on Miguel Cervantes, *Don Quijote de la Mancha.* Recorded by Michael Kapp, Kapp Records Inc., Red Label Series, No. KRS—5505.

Migration Today 5, no. 6 (June 1977).

Migration World 15, no. 1 (1987).

New Catholic World 220, no. 1317 (May–June 1977) and (July–Aug. 1980).

New Yorker, Apr. 28, 1970.

New York Review of Books 21 (Apr. 1974).

New York Times, Nov. 19, 1973; May 17, 1974.

Public Opinion Quarterly 19, no. 2 (1955).

Review of Politics 4 (1942); 35 (Oct. 1973).

Revista de ciencias sociales 2, no. 3 (1958); 4, no. 2 (1960).

Revista de historia 7 (Jan.–Dec. 1988).

Revista del Instituto de Cultura Puertorriqueña 3, no. 9 (Oct.–Dec. 1960).

Social Justices 58 no. 2 (May 1965).

Social Thought 4 (Summer 1978).

Sociological Analysis 26 (Summer 1978).

INTERVIEWS

Fitzpatrick, Joseph P., S.J., Fordham University, Bronx, New York. Dec. 1981 and Jan. 1982.

Fox, Robert. St. Paul Roman Catholic Church, New York. Feb. 1983.

Kalbfleish, Edward. Archdiocese of New York Cursillo Movement, New York. Feb. 1983.

Stern, Robert L. South Bronx Pastoral Center, Bronx, New York. Jan.–Dec. 1982.

Stevens-Arroyo, Antonio M. Brooklyn College, City University of New York, Brooklyn, N.Y. Dec. 1981–Dec. 1982.

INDEX